The Four Stages
of Highly Effective
Crisis Management

How to Manage the Media
in the Digital Age

The Four Stages of Highly Effective Crisis Management

How to Manage the Media in the Digital Age

Jane Jordan-Meier

CRC Press
Taylor & Francis Group
Boca Raton   London   New York

CRC Press is an imprint of the
Taylor & Francis Group, an **informa** business

CRC Press
Taylor & Francis Group
6000 Broken Sound Parkway NW, Suite 300
Boca Raton, FL 33487-2742

© 2011 by Taylor and Francis Group, LLC
CRC Press is an imprint of Taylor & Francis Group, an Informa business

International Standard Book Number: 978-1-4398-5373-3 (Hardback)

Library of Congress Cataloging-in-Publication Data

Jordan-Meier, Jane.
   The four stages of highly effective crisis management : how to manage the media in the digital age / Jane Jordan-Meier.
      p. cm.
   Includes bibliographical references and index.
      ISBN 978-1-4398-5373-3 (hardcover : alk. paper)
      1. Mass media--Management. 2. Crisis management. 3. Online social networks. 4. Public relations. I. Title.

P96.M34.J67 2011
302.23'068--dc22   2010043717

Visit the Taylor & Francis Web site at
http://www.taylorandfrancis.com

and the CRC Press Web site at
http://www.crcpress.com

*This book is dedicated to my late parents, Joyce and Leigh Seccombe,
wonderful country parents from the bush in North West NSW, Australia.*

*Without my mother's dedication, commitment to, and
encouragement of my education, I'm not sure that this book would
have been possible. Thanks Mum for the determination!*

*My father's steadfast belief that women could achieve anything
in life was both inspirational and supportive—I took that belief
and support to heart and followed my dreams. This book is also
a by-product of those dreams and his love. Thanks Dad!*

CONTENTS

SECTION II   *Stages of a Crisis*

SECTION III   *Spokespeople—Speed Matters and Perception Is Everything*

SECTION IV Media Interviews—Rules of Engagement in a Crisis

SECTION V   *Communication—Rules and Tools*

PREFACE

Just five years ago when the idea of this book was first mooted, Twitter did not exist, Facebook was barely a year old, and YouTube was in its infancy. Most crisis communication was managed through the traditional mainstream media. Press releases, news conferences, and regular updates were the mainstay of crisis media management. Blogs were the biggest player on the social media scene.

Now? Twitter has revolutionized how crises are managed since citizen journalists armed with smartphones and Flip cameras—all tools in our pockets—break news. The microblogging service has become an invaluable fire hose of information. Facebook has over half a billion (and counting) registered users creating a virtual news channel with fans galore from every nation, race, and creed. The social media powerhouse has also cemented its influence among mainstream media. Facebook is now the number one source for journalists to research their stories. According to the "2010 Journalist Survey on Media Relations Practices,"[*] a staggering 73.4% of journalists used Facebook for such research!

YouTube? Now part of "Lord" Google's empire, YouTube is localized across 22 countries in 24 different languages. It has almost double the prime-time audience of all three major U.S. broadcast networks combined! It is simply a fact that social media can disseminate information faster than any newsroom ever could.

We have moved from the power-of-one to the power-of-many. And look at us, "we the people." We own the news. We have little, if any, loyalty to any one media outlet; and we surf, swap, and share from multiple platforms. Billions of ears and eyes watching and, in some cases, waiting like the powerful Mommy bloggers to jump to the defense of the cause.

The audience has taken control. They are the truth filters. No longer can you claim how they have (the old media) "butchered this story." Secrets are ousted—typically they always were, but now any citizen can pick up a phone, send a message, and be heard, almost instantaneously. Whistleblowing legislation enables and protects such candor, and because that

---

[*] "2010 Journalist Survey on Media Relations Practices," *Bulldog Reporter*, TEKGROUP International, October 2010.

has not always worked, there is now WikiLeaks, which constantly shares secrets posted anonymously for the world.

The challenges for the crisis media manager are immense—how does one actually cover all this territory? It seems so overwhelming. But there are pioneering brave souls, social media warriors, and many conservative organizations looking for the proverbial 100-year flood to make the big leap. They have embraced the challenges and have seen that policy and good training *really* does "drive the train." They have been generous with their stories and case studies, many of which are presented in this text.

This book is an example of much of what happens today—how much we aggregate, monitor, and share *whatever* we want, *whenever* we want, and *wherever* the spirit takes us.

In writing this book, I have been both curator and aggregator—selecting case studies, examples, and articles to present the best of the best and the worst of the worst, and pulling together principles, trends, and guidelines.

Today, there is little original reporting—typically still the domain of the traditional newspaper. Secondary sources abound. These secondary sources have been credited and sourced to the best of my ability. You will find many references in this book to articles, research papers, and white papers from Europe, the United States, and Australia, to name a few. Also, like any good newspaper reporter, I have sought out original sources. I have interviewed working journalists, professors, and consultants alike to present their views and insights regarding this brave new world, bringing crisis media management into the digital age.

I have taken the new media principles of engagement, speed, trust, and accountability and applied them to the prevailing norms of how traditional mainstream media report a crisis. While I was the managing director of the leading media training company in Australia, we developed a methodology for crisis media training and planning based on years of observation and research on the patterns of reporting in a crisis. This methodology and framework applies just as much to the new as it does to the old.

My aim is to give you some confidence that you can predict and plan, and indeed to convince you that the old principles apply and are even more important today. Yes, you do need to take responsibility and act fast: Tell it all and tell it fast. Yes, you need to be open and honest; yes, train, educate, and exercise your plans. And did I say fast?

THE BOOK

In the five sections of this book, you will learn or have validated the best practices in crisis media management and what this means in the Web 2.0 era.

In Section I, we will look at the role of the media in reporting a crisis, the trends in reportage, and how the roles of the new and the old are enmeshed. A crisis is defined and discussed. And I take an in-depth look at Twitter's role in a crisis. Media ethics are also examined.

In Section II, you will learn about the four stages that the media report in a crisis, the characteristics of each stage, and what this means for decision making in a crisis.

Section III deals with spokespeople, according to the four stages, plus the vexed question of whether and when to use the chief executive officer (CEO). I also discuss the CEO's interaction with social media and introduce you to the role of the frontline staff as well as policy guidelines.

Media interviews are discussed in detail in Section IV—everything from phone interviews to e-mail and print, and how to stage and manage a news conference, to dealing with bloggers. Media training, including who to train for which stage, is also discussed. And finally, you will find guidelines for social media policy.

Section V covers the communication aspects of crisis media management and how to get your message across. A comprehensive guide to the new media tools is presented—from Facebook, Twitter, and YouTube to Digg, Wikipedia, Flickr, and social media releases (SMRs), plus a guide on what tools to use and when.

The appendices provide some useful resources, including a checklist for briefing a spokesperson, a sample form that shows how to log a media inquiry, a sample media release, a step-by-step flowchart for creating a crisis communication plan, a sample social media release, social media policy guidelines, and a list of things to avoid sharing in SocialMediaLand.

ACKNOWLEDGMENTS

I first and foremost want to thank my husband, Norm Meier, a guru in the world of business continuity. This book could not have been written without his unwavering support, encouragement, and loving patience. He has put up with late nights, early starts, and general upheaval as the book spread from room to room! I have appreciated his valuable insights, suggestions, and edits. His extensive experience in disaster recovery and emergency and crisis management, not to mention business continuity, plus our many discussions about the all-too-frequent crises, have been invaluable in helping to shape this book.

This book would not have been possible without the 15-year support of my business partner, Susan Templeman, as we forged a solid media training business partnership. The rigor of the Media Skills' training methods, combined with the tools and techniques that we teach our clients, form the basis of this book. I am grateful too for the insights that I have gained from my many clients in many different industries and in different countries during my career in public relations and crisis media training and coaching. I thank them all for their trust and high-stakes candor as we shared many a situation together. They have been an inspiration.

Templeman and my husband have read almost every word I have written and taken the time to provide feedback and comments. I am enormously grateful. What a journey!

Acknowledgment must also go to my Media Skills colleagues—both past and present, particularly Fiona Van der Plaat and Sonia Zavesky for reading, editing, and making valuable suggestions to early drafts of Section II. Not to mention their role in the development of the crisis skills methodology. A big thank you for all that you have done over the years, not only for Media Skills but in the development of the crisis communication practice.

I appreciate and thank all the countless communications professionals who have provided information, invaluable insight, and wisdom as they shared their stories and allowed me to use their research. Their generosity is much appreciated, and I hope that I have done justice to their information.

It has been an international journey with input from Europe, the United Kingdom, Australia, and the United States. Look for Swiss Mike Schwede's excellent analysis of monitoring tools; Jonas Nielsen, of the

Danish-based Mindjumpers, for case studies; Scotland's Craig McGill for blogging tips; Australians Jeff Bullas, for many excellent tips and tools, and Robyn Sefiani, for her Queenwood case study; plus U.S. consultants Erik Deckers, Gerard Braud, and Paul Gillin among others for their wisdom, tips, and analyses. I have enjoyed and appreciated Sefiani's friendship and professional support for many years. Thank you to you all.

Thanks also to Kris Olson from Innovis for her story about using social media during the North Dakota floods, and Mediascape for research and the Victorian bushfire case study. Craig Pearce back in my home country of Australia was also very helpful with comments, contacts, and an excellent paper on social media and crisis communication. And thanks also to student Matthew Kaskavitch at the University of Wisconsin, Stout. His interview and information on Facebook dark groups was excellent.

The many journalists with whom I have worked over the years have been an inspiration with their reporting skills and insights into the patterns of reporting—so predictable in so many ways. My thanks to all of you, and in particular, to those interviewed whose views you will see in this book. Chris O'Brien, Brian Stelter, and Julio Ojeda-Zapata are but three to be mentioned. Thanks to Bernard O'Riordan, a favorite journalist in Australia, for his encouragement and support with articles and comments; and to Neil McMahon for the Macquarie Bank case study and paper on social media and crises in Australia.

There have been many academics whose time, knowledge, and insights I have valued. Thank you to Kirsten Mogensen, Associate Professor at Roskilde University in Denmark. Mogensen was an enlightening interview subject and generous with her research. Professors and lecturers at Pennsylvania State University, too; Shyam Sundar and Renae Nichols, whose early interviews provided a fundamental framework and basis. Thanks to Liz Meier-King for helping make that possible. Thanks to Dr. Fiona Martin, former journalist and now lecturer in online media at the University of Sydney, Australia, for her insightful interview and for reviewing copy. Many other fine academics are quoted and cited—thank you all for your contributions to the book.

To all my colleagues and friends in the International Association of Business Communicators (IABC), particularly the San Francisco chapter, thank you for all your support and encouragement, especially in my moments of doubt and panic! Molly Walker is a gem and has the best contacts! Margaret O'Hanlon, for your insights and reading an early draft, thank you. I am indebted to Michaela Hayes for reading the book outline and Section I. Her comments were invaluable. Thanks also to Elizabeth

Williams for taking the time to read a late section draft, and to Terry Peckham and the board, thank you for your encouragement; it has meant a lot. And to Bianca Smith, a fellow Australian and IABCer who took the time to read Section V in its raw state, I owe a big thanks. My acknowledgments to Nigel Glennie of Cisco Systems, a fellow IABC board member who provided case studies and interesting information on social media by e-mail.

To everyone who has graciously given me permission to quote them and use bits of white papers, a very big thank you. You will find them referenced throughout the book. Look also for white papers in the appendices.

IABC also provided me with incredible resources in the form of copy editing and all-around writing support and advice. A huge thank you goes to Marcus Gonzales, a San Francisco–based writer and editor, for his mammoth efforts in not only editing the final manuscript but for keeping me on track. Another big thank you to Sally Salay, whose initial edits and feedback put me on the right path of this journey. Their patience and skill were only too evident and enormously helpful for this novice author. My acknowledgments also to Adrian Granzella Larssen for helping with a few last-minute efforts.

Don Karecki from K&M Publishers is the reason that this book got off the ground. After being a keynote speaker and conducting a "Managing the Media in a Crisis" workshop at the Business Continuity Conference in New Orleans during my first year of living in the United States, when I was overwhelmed by everything and everyone, he suggested that I put the content of my workshop into a book. His patience and understanding when life took a sharp U-turn is appreciated. I hope that I have done justice to the unswerving confidence and faith that he has demonstrated toward this book. Thank you for all your support and encouragement.

To my family, in particular my daughter, Gemma, whose opinion on social media was instructional and is featured in this book; my son Nicholas for his continuous encouragement and support; and my sister, Pammie, for reading some early raw copy. Thanks also to my friends who have been encouraging with e-mails, Facebook messages, and more. Thank you for your unwavering friendship, love, and support.

And finally the team at Taylor & Francis/CRC Press, especially Mark Listewnik, for taking this book and making it all happen.

AUTHOR

A former journalist, Jane Jordan-Meier has been at the forefront of media training for 15 years, developing unique and powerful methodologies in crisis media management. From her base in the United States, she works with corporations, government departments, and nonprofit agencies in North America, Australia, and New Zealand. She is recognized as one of the world's top media and crisis management experts.

Throughout her career, Jordan-Meier has worked at the highest level of strategic planning and communication, including the Australian bicentennial celebrations and the Sydney Olympic Games. Her clients range from experienced chief executive officers (CEOs) of global corporations to those doing their first media interviews. She works with organizations in crisis as well as those wishing to raise their profile with positive media interviews. Many of her programs and training have won awards from her peers in the public relations and communication professions.

In the 1990s, recognizing the need for executives to be highly skilled in handling the media, Jordan-Meier co-established Media Skills, a media training consultancy. With former journalist Susan Templeman, she created a suite of methods for developing and delivering strategic media messages. This led to the development of a unique approach to managing crisis communication. The methodology has been licensed and used by a network of trainers around the globe.

Jordan-Meier is a frequent guest speaker on crisis communication and media management at conferences in Australia, New Zealand, and North America. A licensed and accredited media trainer and coach, she holds a master's degree in communication management. She has also taught communication, at both undergraduate and postgraduate levels in Australia's top communications schools, as well as several professional development courses in Australia, New Zealand, and North America.

Section I

Media, Crisis, and New Reporting Tools

In a crisis there is a relentless and unforgiving trend towards an ever-greater information transparency ... hundreds of millions of electronic eyes and ears are creating a capacity and new demands for accountability.[*]

—*Nik Gowing*

OVERVIEW

In this digital age, news is everywhere, 24/7—multiple platforms, multiple channels, multiple choices.

Our appetite for news has increased. We have control, and it has become an important social act.

News is personalized—we share, we swap, we surf; we comment, we link, we witness; we report, we create, and we publish our Daily Me.

No longer is news a one-way street in the hands of a few: Instead of "King" Rupert, we have "Dame" Arianna and "Lord" Google. We have journalists galore—social journalists, citizen–journalists, and yes, still an Army of professional, trained journalists. They are all armed with a dizzying array of social tools to report a crisis—and fast.

---

[*] Nik Gowing, Reuters Institute for the Study of Journalism, "'Skyful of Lies' & Black Swans," 2009, p. 1.

We have speed and scale at unprecedented levels. Aggregation is the name of the game: Indeed it's the very DNA of Web 2.0.

The Internet is at the heart of the change. It's where the action is. In a crisis—read *big news*—that's where we congregate—online. We'll swap links in e-mails; post news stories onto our Facebook pages; we'll tweet our horror, our support, our eyewitness accounts, and retweet others' stories; and we'll highlight and spread news stories that matter to us wherever and whenever we can. We'll haggle over the meaning of events in blogs, discussion groups, and forums.

No surprise then that every @tom, @dick, and @harry has an opinion today and has the means to express it anywhere, anytime. As noted Internet expert, writer, and author, Clay Shirky, who is also Adjunct Professor at New York University, says, we are experiencing "the largest increase in expressive capability in the history of the human race."[*]

It is also no surprise that you are just as likely to be interviewed on Twitter or Skype as you are by a TV reporter with a video camera or a radio reporter with a microphone in your face.

How do you—the crisis media manager—survive and help your organization survive in this digital age? Very simply, your organization's crisis plan is *incomplete* without a comprehensive digital strategy.

You *must* incorporate social media into your plans. People are getting their news in multiple formats, on multiple platforms, from a myriad of devices, so your crisis plan must adapt to this new reality. Your plan will need to accommodate this "golden age" for news consumers who can access—at will—the best (or worst) stories from around the world whenever the spirit moves them. They have that capacity at their fingertips. What capacity and capability do you have at your fingertips in a crisis?

In this section, we will examine the following:

- The habits of today's news consumer
- The trends in news consumption
- How the new media—read *social media*—are impacting news gathering, particularly in a crisis
- How the traditional mainstream media—read *old media*—are plunging into social media territory
- The role of the media in a crisis and whether it has changed
- The role of citizen journalists

---

[*] Clay Shirky, *Here Comes Everybody: The Power of Organizing without Organizations* (London: Penguin Press), 2008, p. 106.

- The rise of the hyperlocal news sites
- Some journalists' code of ethics and how that might help us get into their psyche

But first things first: I am a firm believer in context. This means we need to delve into the meaning of *crisis* so that we have a shared understanding of what it is. Then we will turn our hearts and minds to the media and find out more about the "golden age" or "Red Bull," as one consultant I interviewed characterized today's crisis media.

1

What Is a Crisis?

An issue ignored is a crisis invited.[*]

—*Dr. Henry Kissinger*

How does a company get into crisis mode in the first place? Mostly because it does something wrong, illegal, unethical, or immoral and tries to hide it. Think Enron, Toyota, and quite possibly BP, which at the time of writing was managing potentially the worst oil spill in world history, rivaling the infamous 1989 Exxon disaster. Certainly Tiger Woods, seemingly "Mr. Nice Guy" with a carefully crafted family image, fell into this category when news broke of the sordid tale of his multiple affairs.

UNFOLDING CRISIS

A crisis unfolds something like this:

- An issue has been brewing for a while, say a bad or shady deal that had been swept under the carpet some months or years before (a smoldering issue).
- A disgruntled employee leaks compromising details of said bad deal to the media—big names, big players, big dollars = *big* news story (the trigger).
- Front-page news ensues, immediately attracting attention of local and federal officials, regulators, and various law enforcement agencies = *bigger* news story.

[*] Dr. Henry Kissinger as quoted in Peter Ruff and Khalid Aziz, *Managing Communications in a Crisis* (England/United States: Gower Publishing England), 2003, p. xii.

5

Crisis Is Triggered

All crises have triggering events. Something happens that brings you to your knees; the media spotlight is pointing right at you. The court (of public opinion) has been raised out of its passive state and is voicing its opinions. Your crisis has been triggered because, to paraphrase Dr. Henry Kissinger, you have ignited a "smoldering" issue.

Noted public relations theorist James Grunig,* who completed a 15-year study of best practices in communication management for the International Association of Business Communicators (IABC) Research Foundation, strongly states that you have a crisis when you fail to engage in issues management. Indeed, 75 percent of all crises can be described as "smoldering" issues. If they had been taken care of and dealt with swiftly and appropriately in the first place, they would not have turned into full-blown crises. Often, sadly, it's the bottom line that keeps the issue hidden or unfixed.

Take Toyota or BP. As Ian I. Mitroff, professor at Alliant International University, San Francisco, and a senior investigator in the Center for Catastrophic Risk Management at University of California, Berkeley, says, "The costs of prevention pale in comparison to the full costs of a crisis."† If Toyota and BP had spent the necessary monies—a tiny fraction of the cost of the recall and cleanup, not to mention profits—then we could save lives, inflict less environmental damage to our fragile planet, and generally have less stress on already stretched government budgets.

United Airlines and Sigg, the Swiss-based makers of reusable water bottles, are two other examples that ignored smoldering issues. Both experienced very public and pointed lessons on how not to handle a crisis.

Sigg, which proudly marketed itself as eco-friendly, knew the warnings about the use of bisphenol A (BPA), a toxic chemical, in the lining of its trendy and expensive reusable water bottles. Despite the warning, Sigg waited three years before disclosing that its liner contained BPA. Their customers were outraged at what they saw as deception. After a torrent of online anger and outrage, the chief executive officer was forced into making an apology.

United Airlines had a very public outing of wanton baggage mishandling that resulted in more than 8 million views on YouTube and a newfound fame for Canadian singer–songwriter Dave Carroll, who now

---

* James Grunig, Ph.D., Professor Emeritus, University of Wisconsin.
† "Open Forum," *San Francisco Chronicle* (www.SFGate.com), May 28, 2010.

6

lectures on customer service! Carroll's song about how United smashed his $3,500 Taylor guitar* when he was flying from Nova Scotia to Nebraska became an overnight sensation. Media—new and old—had a field day: a compelling news story and negative publicity triggered by Carroll's song on YouTube.

Carroll and his band, *Sons of Maxwell*, told their woeful tale with rhythm, harmony, rhyme, not to mention some wicked humor, and their 4-minute, 37-second complaint, "United Breaks Guitars," racking up more than 8.3 million views (as of May 26, 2010) on YouTube. That's more than twice the population of New Zealand or Ireland.

CASE STUDY 1.1
The Boy and Boeing

Here is how Boeing averted a crisis, or at least some very negative publicity, with some good old-fashioned, honest, and speedy communication.

In early May 2010, eight-year-old Harry Winsor (son of John Winsor, Chief Executive Officer of the U.S. ad agency Victors and Spoils) decided to send Boeing one of his concept designs for a new plane, done in crayon. The result was a crash course in social media for the plane manufacturer. Boeing sent a standard rejection letter to Harry. Dad posted comments on his blog. Twitter fired up and blasted Boeing with a how could you (treat "a creative and engaged child like that").

For a suited-up type of company, Boeing learned their lesson well and quickly. Instead of defending their position, they acted fast with a very personal touch. A Boeing engineer sent Harry a long and personal letter, and Boeing's Communications Director also responded personally, inviting Harry to get a tour of Boeing's factory. A happy ending. How would have your company reacted?

The lessons? Act swiftly and transparently or beware the billions of electronic eyes and ears, which can and will do their best to embarrass you into action. Better still, plan, rather than react. If you have the proper crisis management plans in place before a crisis, then you have valuable time to limit the damage.

---

* Dave Carroll, Dave Carroll Music, http://www.davecarrollmusic.com/ubg/story/, July 6, 2009.

A Crisis Stops the Show

Put simply, in the words of veteran crisis communication consultant Jim Lukaszewski, a crisis stops the show.

A crisis is always a *significant disruption* to a business, social environment, or organization. It results in national news media coverage and is, inevitably, a situation where the public needs information to make better decisions.

A crisis is a *single point in time* that is a show-stopping, company-stopping, people-stopping, country-stopping event. It is a *triggering event* that stops business, alarms or threatens people, and puts your reputation at risk. The Institute for Crisis Management defines a *crisis* as "a significant business disruption which stimulates extensive news media coverage. The resulting public scrutiny will affect the organization's normal business operations and could also have a political, legal, financial, and government impact on business."*

A crisis will most certainly cause people to panic, taking them out of their "passive state" and propelling them into action, as seen in the violent aftermath of the deadly officer-involved shooting at a Bay Area Rapid Transit (BART) station in northern California in early 2009, when thousands took to the streets protesting and rioting: unintended consequences certainly for BART—but clearly smoldering racial issues for northern California and many other parts of the United States and around the world, all of which focused on BART.

Whatever the crisis, you will feel the heat of public opinion, increasingly online as well as with the traditional legacy media like CNN, the BBC, *USA Today, The Economist, The Wall Street Journal,* or the *Financial Times.* The San Francisco Zoo felt such heat when a tiger escaped her cage and attacked and killed a man on Christmas Day 2007.

By any definition, the New Year's shooting at the Oakland BART station and the tiger mauling at the San Francisco Zoo were business interruptions—true crises that will scar reputations for years to come, if not forever. Take the Exxon Valdez oil spill in 1989. The mishandling of that oil spill—considered one of the most devastating human-caused environmental disasters ever—is forever etched into our minds and into the pages of textbooks, speeches, and presentations on how not to handle a crisis. As Shel Holtz describes crises, they are "reputation killers."

I like Shel Holtz's airline example for defining a crisis. Holtz, a veteran communication consultant specializing in the use of online and social

---

* Institute of Crisis Management, "Crisis Definitions," www.crisisexperts.com.

communication, says that the crash of an airplane is not a crisis for an airline company. It is certainly an emergency. It is definitely a tragedy. But, Holtz explains, a crash, as devastating as it is, does not meet the criteria for a crisis because an airline can *anticipate* the possibility that a plane may go down and *plan* its communication. "A railroad can establish procedures for a derailment, and an oil company can expect that an accident can lead to an oil spill from a tanker."[*] How well an airline or transportation company responds to an emergency will determine how long they will be in the public spotlight and exactly how much damage will be inflicted on their reputation.

One can only wonder whether the unlikely and disturbing incident where two Northwest Airlines pilots were too distracted debating issues and busy on their laptops that they missed their Minneapolis destination by 150 miles was planned for in the crisis manual!

No wonder we have such crises. Sadly, the majority of companies fail to plan. According to Geibel Solutions Marketing, fewer than 20 percent of businesses have crisis communication plans, or if they do have a plan, they fail to effectively exercise and drill that plan.[†]

Case in Point: Virginia Tech

Much has been written about what happened at the Virginia Polytechnic Institute and State University (Virginia Tech) campus and what the school could have done differently to prevent the 2007 shooting tragedy. They had a plan and you can still find that plan on the Internet! Their biggest problem was that they did not have a step-by-step process that adequately addressed what to do. Nor did they appreciate the impact of social media on their student population.

Crisis communication expert Gerard Braud, said that Virginia Tech's lack of preparedness made him "very angry" and that a good communication plan could have saved lives.[‡]

The communication vacuum and lack of prompt action resulted in 32 lives being lost. The story was etched forever in our memories by the chilling vision and sound that was broadcast seemingly ad infinitum on CNN

---

[*] Shel Holtz and John C. Havens, "Business & Economics," *Tactical Transparency: How Leaders Can Leverage Social Media to Maximize Value and Build Their Brand* (New York: John Wiley and Sons), 2008.

[†] Jeffrey Geibel, GEIBEL Solutions Marketing, "Crisis Communication: Some Tips for When It Is Your Turn to Bat," http:www.geibelpr.com/crisis.thm/, December 10, 2010.

[‡] Gerard Braud, interview with author, July 9, 2009.

(no doubt in the absence of any other first-hand footage). Lesson: If you fail to be fast with your footage, the "bad" images will forever symbolize and taint your image and reputation.

A witness who was too close to the shooting sent CNN some video in which gunshots could distinctively be heard. CNN ran that clip every 8 to 12 minutes. With good planning and testing, that would not have happened. People would have been safe and nowhere near the area, said Braud.

As the saying goes, if you fail to plan, then you are essentially planning to fail! That has always been the case. But one could argue that social media have driven us into a new era where planning is not an option. Still, planning is a requirement in this era of increasing scrutiny, demand for transparency, and 24/7 interactivity, all of which are characterized by great expectations of speed. Indeed, it is more important than ever to adhere to the "old" models of crisis communication: Take responsibility, tell it all, and tell it fast.

2

The Role of Media in a Crisis

The public is the only opinion worth anything at all.

—*Mark Twain*

The media are the *reporters of the high court of public opinion*. That role has not changed; if anything it has been amplified in our wired, connected world, where we, the news consumers, are more and more active in the news process.

What is changing is who the reporters are—they are more likely to come from the journalist citizenry than they are to come from the trained pool of journalists in the traditional media of radio, TV, and newspapers.

What is also changing is where and how they source and report the stories of disasters, crises, and emergencies, and how the stories are aggregated and shared. And, above all, the speed of reporting has increased exponentially.

As veteran broadcaster Jim Lehrer says, all journalism is about how events impact people. It is still "Johnny and Jane chasing the ambulance." But it is where and how the Johnnies and Janes are chasing stories that have changed. Instead of paved streets and roads, the ambulance chase is more likely to take place on social networks, the Internet superhighway.

Social media, Internet talk, and particularly Facebook and Twitter, are increasingly used by the traditional mainstream media (MSM) as their first indication of events to cover. The Mumbai massacre 2008, China earthquake 2008, Indonesia bombings 2009, Iran elections 2009, the deadly Victorian bushfires 2009, the fatal shootings at Fort Hood in 2009, and of course the famous miracle landing on the Hudson of US Airways Flight 1549 are just some of the bigger events that propelled the MSM into social media.

CASE STUDY 2.1
The Victorian Bushfires of 2009

Social media came into their own in Australia with the reporting and sharing of information about the deadly bushfires in Victoria in February 2009. Within hours of the story breaking about the worst bushfire in Australia's history, individuals were commenting on Facebook, Twitter, MySpace, and Flickr with condolences and horrific firsthand accounts. Mainstream media battled to provide comprehensive coverage of the tragedy and incorporated the accounts into their reporting, just as their counterparts around the world had done during the Mumbai massacre and the Iranian elections.

Google also created a real-time map with the latest up-to-date information about the fire locations and their statuses based on data provided by Victoria's Country Fire Authority (CFA).

Australia's then Prime Minster Kevin Rudd used his Twitter account not only to give messages of hope and sympathy but to tell his 7,000-plus followers how to make cash and blood donations and how to seek emergency government assistance.

According to media analysis firm Mediascape, who evaluated the media coverage, there were more than 18 billion media impressions on the bushfires. There were more than 500 groups related to "Black Saturday," the day that the deadly fires' first hit became known, on Facebook and 400 more related to the bushfires. More than 5,000 videos were on YouTube and 18,000 pictures on Flickr.

The CFA, which is responsible for fighting the fires in that southern state, had published more than 9,000 messages on Twitter by February 9 (just two days *after* the first fires devastated the pristine Victorian bush).

The CFA also used YouTube to upload special briefing messages from Chief Officer Russell Rees and to thank all volunteers and staff during Black Saturday and the aftermath.

The Victorian government has since announced plans to use social media Web sites like Twitter and Facebook, alongside traditional warning mechanisms, to "improve the quality and timeliness of bushfire warnings."

Australia ranks in the top 10 countries with the highest number of Facebook and Twitter users. Indeed this country with nearly the physical size of the United States, and also with 22 million people, is one of the most networked of all developed countries.

Twitter's role in those crises and emergencies leaves no doubt about its power as a global, real-time, citizen–journalist style news wire service.

It also highlights its place as a platform and content generator for traditional media outlets in a crisis, where the immediacy of getting news out fast is the driving factor.

That immediacy, that imperative to be first with the news, is as much driving change as the platforms that enable the speed. Twitter (and other social media tools) has "warped" the sense of news reporting. Brian Stelter, media reporter at *The New York Times*, says that the "heartbeat" is faster online. Fiona Martin, ex-broadcaster and now lecturer in online media at the University of Sydney, says that much online news is no longer journalism but "churnalism."

In an interview for the book, Martin cited the example of the venerable ABC (Australian Broadcasting Corporation), which since 1947 has prided itself on the independence and accuracy of its news reporting. Now, she says, in order to constantly update its online and 24-hour television news services, the ABC has started publishing stories direct from AAP (Agence France Press), and other wire services. ABC radio journalists, who once provided the bulk of daily broadcast updates, "cannot produce enough news fast enough" for the Web.[*]

Speed is one thing, credibility of sources another. The lifeblood for any reporter, sources are found everywhere at almost any time but come with varying degrees of credibility—all very critical factors to consider in a crisis. What do we believe? Whom do we trust?

The news of Michael Jackson's death is one recent example and also demonstrates the dichotomy of reporting the *big* news stories in today's news-obsessed world. Brian Stelter explains how Michael Jackson was being reported as dead online but alive in the MSM. He says *The New York Times* was criticized for not reporting the death online, with Stelter himself, a voracious commentator and writer on media and pop culture, getting lots of negative comments and questions on his blog. Celebrity news Web site TMZ reported the pop icon's death a full hour *before* it was confirmed on MSM. CNN was reporting the news in the old-fashioned way—checking and verifying sources—and would not confirm the death until they had heard from official sources.

The dilemma for news reporters of verifying sources versus breaking news is the same dilemma that crisis communicators and managers face today: what to release when, who to say what, considering the greater expectations for speed, as well as transparency *and* accuracy.

---

[*] Fiona Martin, Australian Broadcasting Corporation (ABC), interview with author, August 10, 2009.

Whatever the medium, all journalists, professional or citizen, will have the same basic questions. All crisis stories have three distinct elements:

1. What happened?
2. What does it mean?
3. What should I think (analysis)?

And there will always be plenty of hypothetical *what if* questions asked in a crisis. Journalists, who always write with their audiences in mind, will also want to know *why* something happened in the first place. (Corporate America, Australia, and Great Britain, can expect that the media will almost always point the finger at them.) Blame is never far from their minds when lives have been lost or there is some hint of a corporate crime, misdemeanor, or as we have seen with Toyota and BP, very serious and dangerous practices. The media—old and new alike—will punish anyone who is perceived to be behaving badly.

As we travel farther into this book together we will look at the stages of a crisis and how the media report them. We will also look at the questions that are inevitably asked at each of those four stages and what they mean for spokespeople, messaging, and general crisis communication planning.

For now, let us settle on this: In a crisis, it is *the communication that affects the public's opinion.* Also, the news media play a crucial role in the court of public opinion. They are influential in shaping how communities act, think, and feel about an organization's reputation, its values, and its actions—they can assist you in a crisis. Think about how you can partner with the media. One thing is for sure: *How the media are managed can hurt or help you in a crisis.*

3

Social, Interactive, and Everywhere All the Time

Let's look at some trends that impact how we plan and think about managing the media in a crisis in today's digital age.

- News is social.
- News comes from multiple platforms.
- Old media are being forced to use new media.
- Hyperlocal news is on the rise.

News is social, says the "Grand Dame," Arianna Huffington, that is, of Huffington Post fame. Arguably one of the most influential people in U.S. media today, Huffington says that "we now engage with news, react to news, and share news,"* and we will become increasingly empowered. News is no longer a passive, one-way street in the hands of a few. We own it!

It is our conversations, our opinions, and our reactions that determine, to a great extent, the news today. We participate in the news, if not by contribution, by sharing and linking. The death of pop icon Michael Jackson and the indiscretions of Tiger Woods showed just how much we care and haggle over opinions. Twitter went into a meltdown when the King of Pop left this earthly plane. The big disasters will also get our attention and drive our comments. Any big brand in trouble will be dissected, as we saw with BP, United Airlines, and Dominos.

---

* From Arianna Huffington's (Huffington Post) testimony to the U.S. Senate Commerce Communications Subcommittee on the future of journalism and newspapers, May 5, 2010.

TODAY'S NEWS FROM MULTIPLE PLATFORMS

Another major trend that crisis communicators need to consider is how we access our news. It seems we have no loyalty anymore, at least in the United States, where recent research by the Pew Internet and American Life Project study, showed that a massive 92 percent of Americans *use multiple platforms* to get their news on a typical day, including national and local TV, the Internet, local and national newspapers, and radio.

According to the Pew study, Americans say that they "get news from four to six media platforms on a typical day. Just 7 percent get their news from a single media platform on a typical day."[*]

On the other side of the Pacific, the story seems much the same. Australians are using various platforms, often simultaneously. According to Nielsen's 2010 Internet and Technology Report, almost half of Internet users (49 percent) surveyed multitask television and the Internet at the same time, and 39 percent multitask radio and the Internet.[†] And despite the rise in Internet usage, the traditional media such as TV, newspapers, and radio all saw a rise in consumption.

Consumers have choices—there simply has been an explosion of channels, and everything and anything can get republished, particularly with the ease of access from one channel and platform to another. As Paul Gillin, American writer, speaker, and social media strategist says: "Many people cross-post with Facebook and Twitter. The fire jumps the tree line very quickly (in a crisis)."[‡]

OLD MEDIA PLAY A ROLE IN THE SOCIAL MEDIA REVOLUTION: SOCIAL OR LEAVE

For the old media, it has become an *imperative to be part of the social media revolution*. If they are not part of the action, they will miss out. So they follow each other voraciously—it has always been so. The media have always been competitive, but it is more evident today with the speed and acceleration of news. The old media simply cannot afford to miss that breaking news

---

[*] Pew Research Center's Internet and American Life Project Report "Understanding the Participatory News Consumer," March 1, 2010.

[†] As quoted on Mumbrella, an Australian marketing and media news Web site (mUmBRELLA), http://mumbrella.com.au/nielsen-traditional-media-consumption-rises-with-the-Internet-19346, March 1, 2010.

[‡] Paul Gillin, interview with author, June 30, 2009.

story on Twitter or BNO (Breaking News on Twitter), which has broken numerous stories.

One of the Old Guard has drawn a line in the sand and told its journalists to use social media as a primary source—or leave.

Peter Horrocks, director of BBC Global News, said it was important for editorial staff to make better use of social media and become more collaborative in producing stories. "This isn't just a kind of fad from someone who's an enthusiast of technology. I'm afraid you're not doing your job if you can't do those things. It's not discretionary,'" he is quoted as saying in *Ariel*, the BBC in-house weekly newspaper.

Citizen–journalists abound and are increasingly a major force in the news-gathering process. CNN has its "iReporters," and the majority of the major mainstream media (MSM) encourages some form of journalist citizenry or at least the sharing of their news. For example, one of Australia's leading daily newspapers, *The Sydney Morning Herald*, encourages sharing on Facebook from its online version. *The Wall Street Journal* has an active Facebook presence, as does the BBC. Nearly all MSN news Web sites are multimedia, and many have some presence on Twitter.

To illustrate just how much the new media is part of the old media is *The New York Times* interview in May 2010 with Facebook's public policy executive, Elliott Schrage, amid the privacy controversy. The Times crowdsourced the interview questions through their original blog post and their Facebook page. They collected roughly 300 questions, which they then presented to Schrage. In another interesting, if not alarming trend for crisis managers, the veritable *Wall Street Journal* (*WSJ*) now uses the frequency of readers' daily key-word searches on its Web site as one determinant for future *WSJ* coverage. As Eugene Donati, a colleague, remarked to me, it certainly is an interesting concept "dripping with peril" for crisis managers, "with journalists surrendering the role of gatekeeper in this way."[†]

That is the new reality: a hybrid melting pot of ideas, platforms, channels, and sources; technology-enabled savvy news consumers to collaborate to produce the news; the old and the new working together.

Table 3.1 outlines key differences and similarities between new and old media.

---

[*] Posted by Mercedes Bunz, "BBC Tells News Staff to Embrace Social Media," PDA: The Digital Media Blog, www.guardian.co.uk, February 10, 2010.

[†] Eugene Donati, Adjunct Professor, New York University, e-mail with author, September 6, 2010.

Table 3.1 Comparing Old and New Media

Social/New Media	Old/MSM Media
Active participants—No control, but influence. Ownership not clear, but the power belongs to the community. The reach of key influencers is phenomenal.	Passive audience—You have some control. Media perform the role of gatekeeper. They select and package the news.
Targeted communication—Target niches. You are engaging with "real" people. It matters far more what the community does with your content than what you do with your content. We are all news producers today. Two-way: Multiple conversations occur simultaneously.	Mass communication—One message fits all. Very linear, very predictable, homogenous as you switch from channel to channel. One-way: Broadcast.
Conversation—They talk. You listen. You talk. They listen! Dialogue as important if not more important than message delivery.	One-way communication—You talk. They listen (you hope!).
Earn attention and trust—They can leave anytime. You'd better add value to the conversation. They have choices; they can and do exercise their ability to choose. Demand for hypertransparency.	Buy attention—Your advertising pays for the media, so they'd better listen! The lack of choice almost forces people to listen.
Easy to use, quick, affordable, accessible.	Can be time-consuming, not easy to navigate, need time to cultivate relationships with key reporters.
Everyone's a journalist (treat them that way); fewer barriers to access, but many more journalists to consider when developing relationships. Very resourceful.	Trained, experienced reporters with areas of specialty/special interest. Barriers to access.
Available 24/7, no deadlines. Everything happens at lightning speed.	Deadline driven: Under increased pressure to get stories out quickly. Trending to "churnalism."
Very powerful medium to channel emotion, context, and experience. Potential of bias high. "Purists" tend to hang in the social media space. Potential for inaccuracy and rumor.	Provides independent, third-party view: Newspapers can provide context and offer analysis. Influential newspapers and business magazines can provide "moral" authority.
Can help you organize people based on location, business, and interests—trending to hyperlocal and/or hyperspecial interests.	Broader reach: Local newspapers reflect and highlight community concerns.

POWER TO THE PEOPLE: THE RISE OF HYPERLOCAL NEWS

> It won't tell us much about the catastrophe in Haiti, but when a store closes on Lincoln Avenue a *hyperlocal* Web site can be all over it. As far as viable new media models go, for the time being *hyperlocalism* might be the best one we've got.
>
> —*Macmillan Dictionary, Chicago Reader* (January 2010)

From Nova Scotia in Canada to Fitzroy in Melbourne, Australia, and from Bakersfield in California to Devon in the United Kingdom, you will find a thriving and growing band of *hyperlocal* news sites delivering news and content relevant to small communities or neighborhoods that have been overlooked by the traditional media.

While the business models are still evolving, most have journalists of some kind tracking the school board meetings, local government initiatives, and even neighborhood squabbles. Sports news is also big.

Some are tiny labors of love and read and look more like blogs. Others are more sophisticated with strip and banner ads on the home page. Some are linked to the traditional mainstream newspapers like Yourhub.com which is part of *The Denver Post*. The best of the online content is typically published into its regular print publication.

Patch is one of the more sophisticated examples. According to *The New York Times*, Patch was conceived and bankrolled by Tim Armstrong from AOL after he found a dearth of information online about where he lives.[*] Patch has created numerous sites for communities across the United States, including ones in New Jersey, California, and New York. Manhattan Beach Patch is one such site with plenty of sports and government news on the home page.[†]

Collaboration is the name of the game for most hyperlocal sites, and many have great names! One site I love is The People's Republic of South Devon in Great Britain. Like many of the hyperlocal sites, they encourage participation: "Anyone can join in. In fact we actively encourage it on our quest to take reporting and community reporting up to the next level (whatever that means)."[‡]

Local content and news that would not otherwise get published are the lifeblood of the hyperlocal. Their very existence is further evidence of

---

[*] Henry Blodget, "Tim Armstrong's 'Patch' To Cash In On Death Of Newspapers?" *The New York Times*, http://www.businessinsider.com/tim-armstrongs-patch-to-cash-in-on-death-of-local-news-2009-2, February 22, 2009.

[†] ManhattanBeachPatch, http://manhattanbeach.patch.com, Junuary 14, 2011.

[‡] The People's Republic of South Devon (Great Britain), www.peoplesrepublicofsouthdevon.co.uk, May 16, 2010.

the shift in the media landscape from consumers of news to participants in news. They will only grow more as we the people take back our news, and the big journalism heavy hitters like the Knight Foundation (www. kcnn.org) support citizen news networks.

Hyperlocal news sites are worth noting for crisis media management because:

- They are staffed and/or owned by professional journalists, many of whom are refugees from the MSM.
- Many are local investigative reporting projects.
- They are part of the linked economy—linking to their bigger MSM cousins or influential bloggers, including neighborhood blogs with clout and/or supplement from other sources like government.
- They care *passionately* about what is happening in their local neighborhood.

If you are a business with a large community presence, such as a community bank, then you need to be participating in the hyperlocal news scene. It is as important as the big, scary MSM when it comes to a crisis, if not more so.

MAINSTREAM MEDIA ARE STILL A FACTOR

The traditional MSM are digitized. They enable sharing and aggregating and encourage commentary. So what? Do they still have the power to swing public opinion in a crisis? The answer is yes and no, somewhat but diminishing.

As usual, the statistics tell the story. In the United States, for example, according to the 2010 Pew Internet and American Life Project studies:

- 78 percent of Americans say they get their news from a local TV station.
- 73 percent get their news from cable stations like CNN or Fox.
- 54 percent listen to radio at home or in the car.
- 50 percent say they get their news from their local newspaper. The report, issued in March 2010, also shows that *61 percent of Americans get at least some of their news online.*[*]

---

[*] "Understanding the Participatory News Consumer," Pew Research Center's Internet and American Life Project, http://www.pewinternet.org/Reports/2010/Online-News.aspx, March 1, 2010.

The problem is that circulation of newspapers in most major news markets around the world, with the possible exception of India, is in decline and newsrooms are shrinking. Some look like ghost towns.

While the statistics above seem to point to the MSM as the main source of news, the reality is that if you are relying on the traditional MSM to get your message out in a crisis, you will be missing out. I am grateful to Erik Deckers, whose analysis of the Pew 2010 Internet and American Life Project study amplifies this critical point:

> While 78% of American citizens may be getting their news from a local TV station, the local TV stations do not have the time to devote more than 1–3 minutes to any particular news story.
>
> If 50% of the people get their news from a local newspaper, *50% are not.* 54% of the people listen to the news on the radio, but we don't know if it's national or local, NPR, or conservative.[*]

The bottom line is that if you are relying on the traditional MSM to reach as many people as possible in a crisis, then you are, to quote Deckers, "missing up to half of your audience and you are not getting enough time devoted to your story." In a situation like the H1N1 virus, Decker says, "You need more than 1 to 3 minutes devoted to the issue, and all the facts that people need to know."[†] You will need more than the traditional media release and news conference to get your message out quickly to all the affected stakeholders. Simple fact: You need social media to help you reach them—and fast.

---

[*] Erik Deckers, *Crisis Communication and Social Media for Government Crisis Communicators* (E-book: http://problogservice.com/crisis_communication_ebook/Social%20Media%20 and%20Crisis%20Communication%20for%20Government%20Communicators.pdf), 2010, p. 5.
[†] Ibid.

4

Social Media's Role in Crisis

There is news, there is insight, and then there is Twitter.
It's my feed to the second by second pulse of life.[*]

Social media tools are shaping how crises are communicated, and social media tools are shaping the way the media report news. The new and accessible communication platforms and technologies, such as blogs, social networking sites, Really Simply Syndication (RSS) feeds, and other formats, have had a dramatic effect on the collection and dissemination of news, particularly in a crisis.

Professional journalists—new and old alike—are using Twitter to enhance and augment traditional reporting practices. It is another tool in their kit, and many journalists, like Australian radio producer Andrew Davies with the Australian Broadcasting Corporation, are now logged on to Twitter throughout their working day. "I try and start my day by looking at what people are saying and talking about on Twitter," he said. "I love being able to read all the fantastic links to interesting Web sites, ideas, and news that people have sent out."[†]

Davies's daily habits are echoed by many of the journalists I interviewed and researched for this book. Danny Shea, media writer with the highly influential Huffington Post, says that he gets the news faster and more

---

[*] Posted by Jemima Kiss, "What Do You Use Twitter For?" PDA: The Digital Media Blog, www.guardian.co.uk, February 23, 2009. See the following—@juliansaunders: "There is news, there is insight, there is opinion, and then there is Twitter. It's my feed to the second by second pulse of life."
[†] Posted by Julie Posetti, "How Journalists Are Using Twitter," MediaShift Blog, www.pbs.org/mediashift, May 27, 2009.

efficiently with the microblogging site Twitter. Danny checks Twitter first thing in the morning and several times a day. Brian Stelter, media reporter at *The New York Times*, checks his Twitter account every 20 to 30 minutes.

Journalists have become heavily reliant on social media tools. According to a survey in September 2009 from Middleberg Communications and the Society for New Communications Research, the use of social media tools among journalists has increased significantly.[*] In just one year their use of social media networks to assist in reporting has increased almost 30 percent, up to 70 percent from 41 percent in the previous year. And a whopping 90 percent agree that social media are enhancing journalism. They use blogs to keep up to date with their beats, they use their Twitter followers for story ideas and chasing down leads and sources, and almost 40 percent say they visit a social media site once a week for research.

Blogs are popular as is Wikipedia, and journalists' use of online videos has doubled. RSS feeds are also popular, with almost 20 percent of journalists receiving five or more feeds every week, and a further 44 percent receiving at least one regular RSS feed.

As Jeremy Porter says on the Journalistics Blog, "Journalists have no choice but to use these tools to find sources fast (an instant), crowdsource suggestions, tips, and interviews."[†] Two journalists I spoke with, saw Twitter as the new police scanner. Many newsrooms had police scanners and monitored the networks to ascertain what stories to cover—the scanner was a source for news. Now it is Twitter acting as a siren for reporters.

Twitter became big news once journalists realized its power as a tool for breaking stories during the Mumbai, India, massacre in 2008. In the aftermath of the microblogging platform hitting the headlines, there was an explosion of professional journalists in the Twittersphere. Julie Posetti, who has been studying the shift, says:

> This growth has been fueled by increasing mainstream awareness of the importance of social media to the future of a crisis-ridden industry and the elevation of Twitter as a platform for news dissemination, citizen journalism, and audience interaction.[‡]

---

[*] "2nd Annual Middleberg/SNCR Survey of Media in the Wired World," Middleberg Communications and the Society for New Communications (SCNR), http://sncr. org/2010/02/19/journalists-use-of-social-media-is-surging-according-to-2nd-annual-middlebergsncr-survey-of-media-in-the-wired-world/, February 19, 2010.

[†] Posted by Jeremy Porter, "70 Percent of Journalists Use Social Networks to Assist in Reporting," Journalistics Blog, http://blog.journalistics.com/2009/70-percent-of-journalists-use-social-networks-to-assist-in-reporting/, September 23, 2009.

[‡] Posted by Julie Posetti, "How Journalists Are Using Twitter," MediaShift Blog, www.pbs. org/mediashift, May 27, 2009.

The platform was used extensively during the deadly Australian bushfires in the State of Victoria in February 2009 when mainstream media (MSM) incorporated Twitter into their coverage. The Australian Broadcasting Corporation, where Posetti used to work, was particularly impressive in its use of Twitter. Leigh Sales, anchor of the corporation's respected nightly news program *Lateline*, told Posetti: "I'm giving Twitter a red-hot go."[*] So too are most MSM media journalists.

Posetti says that she is convinced that Twitter is now a "vital journalistic tool for both reporting events and breaking down barriers between legacy media and its audiences."[†] Journalists are using the platform to "broadcast" links to content they or their news outlets have produced in an effort to build a new audience. She comments that Twitter is also used as a live reporting platform by a few and some share images, audio, and links to "other online content they find interesting."[‡]

Many are using social media to *crowdsource*: to find sources and contacts for stories, story angles, background, and case studies. Julio Ojeda-Zapata, consumer technology reporter and columnist for the *St. Paul Pioneer Press*, says that Twitter is an "invaluable fire hose of information."[§] He values the use of hash tags for following the thread of a story, critical in a crisis. For example: #BP oil spill, #Tiger Woods, or #Red Cross.

The majority of the journalists I spoke with echoed the findings of the various research, saying that they use the company Web site or blog in a crisis. Chris O'Brien of the *San Jose Mercury News* was particularly impressed with Google's response when their Gmail site went down. They had a statement up in 15 minutes. That is evidence, he says, of the superaccelerated world we live and work in.[¶]

Brian Stelter, media reporter at *The New York Times*, was "amazed" at how quickly the story of the airplane landing on the Hudson unfolded and how quickly Mayor Bloomberg held a news conference.[**] Others, notably Martin and O'Brien, said they would automatically go to Facebook in a *big* story to see what stories were emerging and what information they could ferret out.

---

[*] Posted by Julie Posetti, "How Journalists Are Using Twitter," MediaShift Blog, www.pbs.org/mediashift, May 27, 2009.

[†] Posted by Julie Posetti, "Rules of Engagement on Twitter," MediaShift Blog, www.pbs.org/mediashift, June 19, 2009.

[‡] Ibid.

[§] Julio Ojeda-Zapata, *St. Paul Pioneer Press*, interview with author, August 28, 2009.

[¶] Chris O'Brien, *San Jose Mercury News*, interview with author, September 4, 2009.

[**] Brain Stelter, *The New York Times*, interview with author, July 17, 2009.

Blogs and bloggers were also seen as "very influential" and have had a tremendous impact on news. They can drill down much farther, they can "own" a story, and they can be obsessive. The 2010 Public Relations Industry Research Report of United Kingdom public relations consultants showed that digital media of one sort or another played a key role in igniting crises, with bloggers being the most common cause.*

Just as you would be monitoring the trending topics on Twitter, setting up Google Alerts, or having a good old-fashioned media morning with real-time reports, so are the journalists themselves. Everyone is searching and looking at each other. "While I'm looking in this mirror, I see that you are looking at me." What will they see? What will they report? Have they connected with a range of disgruntled people on Twitter? What's on Facebook; what's on LinkedIn? What will the media find on your Web site?

Face the facts: Social media are not going anywhere anytime soon. The media landscape has changed forever, so to quote "Dame" Arianna Huffington, "We're not in Kansas anymore, Toto."†

---

* Dynamic Markets Limited, "Public Relations in a Dynamic Era Independent Report," April 2010, p. 3.
† From Arianna Huffington's (Huffington Post) testimony to the U.S. Senate Commerce Communications Subcommittee on the future of journalism and newspapers, May 5, 2010.

5

Media Ethics: What Drives Traditional Media Behavior?

I am constantly asked by clients in crisis media training sessions about journalistic ethics. Most people characterize those in the profession as either cynical dirtbags or opportunists who will do almost anything to get a story, and they question whether journalists have any ethics at all.

In a crisis, people see journalists as invading personal privacy, overstepping the boundaries of decent human behavior. They see victims being exploited. Quite often the people whose stories bring us—the viewers, readers, and listeners—the human face of the crisis feel exploited, that they have had a rotten experience with the media. However, others are thankful that their stories may help put the bad boys behind bars.

So, what drives journalistic behavior? Are there norms, ethics, and codes that they work by?

Journalists have long claimed to be the watchdogs for democracy. They will be hypercritical and skeptical; they will point out flaws in order to protect society. Kirsten Mogensen, associate professor at Roskilde University, Denmark, whom I interviewed for this book, says that it would be a mistake to underestimate that role when dealing with journalists.

Mogensen, a visiting scholar at Stanford University at the time of our interview, is an ex-broadcast and print journalist and has studied the norms of journalists for many years. She strongly advocates that journalists are driven by democratic and human rights values.

As Mogensen stated, "Several studies have suggested that leading journalists across different types of news media in elective democracies have

27

similar norms and values in relation to their role as journalists."* Mogensen argues that we need good, reliable information (from journalists) as a basis for our actions (in a democratic society). We need to know we can trust that basic democratic rights and norms are being upheld. She and others strongly believe that as the American journalistic code says, "Public enlightenment is the forerunner of justice and the foundation of democracy."†

Those norms that underpin the reporting of professional journalists, as opposed to "shock jocks" (more likely to be paid personalities than trained reporters), are very similar around the world. The codes of ethics, which guide their modus operandi, are dominated by phrases like *seek truth, scrutinize power, defend free speech, protect confidential sources,* and *freedom of expression*.‡

The International Federation of Journalists, which represents 600,000 journalists in 200 countries, promotes "human rights, democracy and pluralism."§ This principle is the very underpinning of professional journalistic reporting.

Lofty ideals you might say, but what about day-to-day journalism?

Certainly journalists want to get the *best* story, the *hot* story, the story that might get them a raise, earn them an award, or garner them recognition by their peers.

Editors and executive producers want to beat their competitors; there are ratings to consider. And in a crisis, they know ratings will spike, circulation will go up. Crises and disasters are *big* news. The media are *very* motivated to get the best coverage they can.

Sometimes this means that they will pool resources and agree to certain types of coverage in the interest of protecting the ideals of democracy and human rights, as was the case with many recent disasters like 9/11, where journalists saw that they really could act in the public interest.

In an acute state of crisis, like 9/11, deadly bushfires, or devastating earthquakes, the media, says Mogensen, act like a form of "first aid" that would normally be unacceptable.

The media feel it is their duty to serve society during a crisis. But never underestimate the basic motivation of most journalists in a crisis—to get to the bottom of an issue, a crisis, and find out what *really* happened and *who* has responsibility and can be blamed. As the Canadian, Australian,

---

* Kirsten Mogensen (Associate Professor, Rodkilde University, Denmark), interview with author, May 5, 2010.
† Ibid.
‡ Society of Professional Journalists, www.spj.org/ethicscode.asp. (Retrieved January 14, 2011.)
§ International Federation of Journalists, www.ifj.org/en/pages/about-ifj. (Retrieved January 14, 2011.)

and British codes all suggest, journalists are motivated to make the world a better place, and they fiercely defend their right to adhere to this lofty principle.

So, you can expect journalists to be dogged in their search for the truth, particularly if they think there has been wrongdoing. They will work (on society's behalf) to expose and investigate abuses of power and protect the public's health and safety in as many ways as they can, and sometimes this may lead to overexposure of the horror that they have witnessed firsthand.

6

Twitter: Is It a Fad or the "8-Bazillion Pound Gorilla?"

Twitter is quickly becoming the lens into all that moves us
as individuals and also as a global society.[*]

OVERVIEW

A few weeks ago, when it was safe and sane to go for dinner in the middle of Bangkok, some colleagues and I were in the middle of dinner at a Japanese restaurant when a loud boom was heard in the distance.

All three of us reached immediately for our BlackBerries. A year ago, we might have e-mailed our editors to see what the news wires were reporting, or checked a television set for an update. But in Thailand's fast-moving and violent political crisis, there was no time to wait for those "old media" to tell us what was going on.

What we needed to know was: What were people tweeting?[†]

This account from Mark MacKinnon, which appeared in *The Globe and Mail*, really says it all. This is the new reality in crisis media management.

---

[*] Posted by Brian Solis, "I Tweet Therefore I Am," BrianSolis Blog, www.brainsolis.com, May 14, 2010.
[†] Mark MacKinnon, "Twitter's Role in Bangkok Conflict Unprecedented," Bangkok—From *Saturday's Globe and Mail* (*The Globe and Mail*), www.theglobeandmail.com/news/world, May 21, 2010.

We have seen in previous chapters how much the mainstream media are using Twitter when reporting a crisis. The microblog is a powerful, real-time reporting tool for citizen–journalists, first responders, and organizations alike. It has become the online circulatory system for news, pumping information between media organizations, consumers, and businesses throughout the world.

Twitter, like its social-networking cousins, is all-pervasive. As Brian Solis, a globally recognized digital analyst, sociologist, and futurist, says, social media is "an extension of who we are." These sites form "valuable social hubs that connect people,"[*] and we see this time and time again in a crisis: from Mumbai to Iran, Australia to Haiti, and China to Bangkok; not to mention the Icelandic volcano eruption, the disastrous oil spill in the Gulf of Mexico, Tiger Woods's dirty little scandal, and Toyota's recall woes.

Indeed, Twitter has proven to be a significant player in incident media. But Twitter has its detractors, who question its long-term feasibility. Is it a fad, as many still claim, or will it gain further strength and stability and become the mainstay for emergency and crisis communication? Will it become the motherboard on a computer, the gateway for status updates across all social media platforms, with entire teams in corporations devoted to tweeting, as some futurists and technology pundits predict? Will it grow to the size, stature, and omnipresence of an "8-bazillion pound gorilla,"[†] to coin business communicator and leading social media commentator Shel Holtz? Or will it go the way of once popular sites such as Second Life, as technology analyst firms such as Gartner have suggested?

In this chapter, we will further explore Twitter and see what we can learn from its history and, more importantly, how, when, and by whom it is being used in a crisis.

BACKGROUND

For anyone who has not yet been exposed to Twitter, we'd better not get ahead of ourselves with some enticing case studies without a proper definition.

---

[*] Posted by Brian Solis, "We Are the Champions," BrianSolis Blog, www.briansolis.com, May 27, 2010.
[†] Shel Holtz, "Communication Applications from Crisis Communication and Social Media," Webinar: Lecture Three, http://www.shelholtzwebinars.com, May 4, 2009.

Twitter's home page, at the time of this writing (2010), describes itself as follows:

Twitter is a rich source of instant information. Stay updated. Keep others updated. It's a whole thing.*

Wikipedia defines *Twitter* as follows:

A social networking and microblogging service that enables its users to send and read messages known as *tweets*. Tweets are text-based posts of up to 140 characters displayed on the author's profile page and delivered to the author's subscribers who are known as *followers*. Senders can restrict delivery to those in their circle of friends or, by default, allow open access.[†]

To me, Twitter is part library, part news service, and part gossip—a modern-day town crier. Others have called it the *Post-it note of social networks*. At the very minimum, Twitter is a barometer for fascination, education, and obsession. It is real-time, so in a crisis, raw emotion is as frequent as real news. Twitter information will always be someone's perception of what they witnessed, what they have seen, what they have experienced. It is the voice of the people.

Twitter began its life in 2006 as a result of an attempt to break a creative slump in a brainstorming session. Quite the brain wave!

According to Wikipedia,[‡] American software architect and businessman Jack Dorsey introduced the idea of an individual using a Short Message Service (SMS) to communicate with a small group. Dorsey and software engineer Biz Stone decided that SMS text suited the status message idea and built a prototype of Twitter in about two weeks. Investor and entrepreneur Evan Williams, formerly of Google, joined the creative pair, and Twitter was on its way to making history.

Its growth and overall awareness have been staggering. At the time of writing, Twitter had more than 105 million registered accounts with the average age of users hovering around 39. While Facebook has more registered users (500 million and counting at the time of writing), the

---

* Twitter Home Page, www.twitter.com, May 15, 2010.
† Wikipedia, "Twitter," http://en.wikipedia.org/wiki/Twitter, May 15, 2010.
‡ Mark Glaser, "Twitter Founders Thrive on Micro-Blogging Constraints," Public Broadcasting Service (PBS), http://www.pbs.org/mediashift/2007/05/twitter-founders-thrive-on-micro-blogging-constraints137.html, May 17, 2007. (Retrieved November 5, 2008.)

popular microblog is catching up in terms of awareness. According to the American research firm, Edison Research, Twitter's awareness exploded from 5 percent in 2008 to 26 percent in 2009 to near ubiquity at 87 percent in 2010, only 1 percentage point less than Facebook.[*]

While growth has slowed, after increases of up to 1382 percent in one year (2008–2009), Twitter's power is undeniable. It is a sign of mainstream acceptance when "Lord" Google comes a-courting, in this case with dollars. According to Brian Solis, Google paid to receive the full real-time Twitter "fire hose" in December 2009, with feeds in 40 languages and a linking feature to help users find the most relevant content shared.[†]

The numbers tell the story and show the growing trend of searching within networks (no doubt one reason why Google is taking real-time feeds from Twitter). In May 2010, Twitter was predicting that it would reach a billion searches per day!

POINTLESS BABBLE: A CRITIC'S TAKE

While Twitter has many fans, there are many who still question its feasibility for long-term use and influence. In its September 2009 cover story, *The Ragan Report* claimed that "communicators think it's a fad."[‡] Their case: Users are tired of the pointless babble, such as "I'm eating a ham sandwich," says Gerald Baron in his September 28, 2009, Crisisblogger entry, "Where Does Twitter Go from Here?"[§] Ragan and PollStream polled professional communicators and found that 54 percent of responders claim that it will plateau. Of those polled, 40 percent do not have a microblogging plan, for reasons such as "fearful managers, lack of time and staff, or simply not believing it would benefit the company."[¶]

Gerard Braud, crisis communication expert, points out three of Twitter's key shortcomings. For one, at the time of our interview in late

---

[*] Edison Research/Arbitron Internet and Multimedia Series, "Twitter Usage in America: 2010 Report," April 29, 2010.

[†] Posted by Brian Solis, "The State and Future of Twitter 2010: Part Three," BrianSolis Blog, http://www.briansolis.com/2010/04/the-state-and-future-of-twitter-2010-part-three, April 23, 2010.

[‡] Lindsey Miller, "Is Twitter Just a Fad? Corporate Communicators Say 'Yes,'" *The Ragan Report*, September 2009, pp. 17–18. (Note: This article is based on an IE Twitter poll conducted by Ragan Communications and PollStream.)

[§] Posted by Gerald Baron, "Where Does Twitter Go from Here?" Crisisblogger Blog, www.crisisblogger.com, September 28, 2009.

[¶] Lindsey Miller, "Is Twitter Just a Fad? Corporate Communicators Say 'Yes,'" *The Ragan Report*, September 2009, pp. 17–18. (Note: This article is based on an IE Twitter poll conducted by Ragan Communications and PollStream.)

2009, Braud thinks that Twitter fits the "shiny new object syndrome."* Users are excited by its novelty, but will soon push it aside for the next great thing. Next, he questions its viability as an ongoing communication tool because of the time it takes to monitor Twitter. You can only successfully monitor and update if you have the "luxury of warm bodies,"† he said. Finally, Braud is concerned about Twitter's stability. It can be easily overloaded: The flurry of tweets surrounding Michael Jackson's death brought Twitter to its knees. In such cases, using Twitter as your main communication vehicle is like relying on cell phones: convenient, yes, but when the networks are overloaded and do not work in a crisis? Frustrating and potentially disastrous.

My 20-something daughter, in addition, does not understand how Twitter can match the power of connection and growing influence of Facebook. She cites the recent Facebook fan club activity that has advocated successfully for the resurrection of *Hey Hey Saturday*, a very popular Australian TV variety show from the 1990s. Facebook's power is that people, once powerless individuals, can unite to become a force that compels an organization—in this case a TV network—to act in their best interest. Does Twitter, for all of its benefits, have this power? she questions.

SAVING LIVES, SAVING REPUTATIONS

Never before has a social media website played the kind of role in a conflict that Twitter has played in Thailand's nine-week-old anti-government uprising, keeping people informed even as it amplified the hate on both sides of the country's divide. Some say Twitter—or rather its users—may have even saved lives as fighting consumed the streets of Bangkok.‡

—*Mark MacKinnon, The Globe and Mail, May 21, 2010*

Debate about Twitter's future remains; however, one thing is certain: the absolute need to include Twitter into your monitoring and listening plan for both issues and crisis management.

Here, its influence is illustrated in the 2010 Thailand riots. The patterns of coverage were similar in the Haitian earthquake, the elections in Iran, and the deadly bushfires in Australia in February 2009. Citizen–journalists, concerned bystanders, the injured and hurt, mainstream

---

* Gerard Braud, interview with author, July 9, 2009.
† Ibid.
‡ Mark MacKinnon, "Twitter's Role in Bangkok Conflict Unprecedented," Bangkok—From *Saturday's Globe and Mail* (*The Globe and Mail*), www.theglobeandmail.com/news/world, May 21, 2010.

35

reporters, first responders, protesters, government agencies, and relief workers all tweeted, becoming, to paraphrase London-based journalist Andrew Spooner, our own news wire service, breaking stories and events instantly.*

For emergency responders and relief organizations, Twitter has become an essential tool in crisis media management. American Red Cross, for example, has used the micromessaging blog to get information out ever since the California wildfires in 2007.

Since Hurricane Katrina, the Federal Emergency Management Agency (FEMA), which had more than 12,000 followers at the time of writing, has also effectively used Twitter. The organization has held news conferences with Director David Paulison on the site with a full transcript and audio/video from the session posted online. FEMA has also been smart to realize Twitter's leveraging power. For example, during the Boulder, Colorado, wildfires in early 2009, one of the most active tweeters was a graduate student doing extensive individual research. FEMA worked with the student to engage and interact with her network of followers to amplify messages about the federal response to the fires.

Probably the best and most consistent example of how organizations effectively use Twitter in a crisis is the Los Angeles Fire Department (LAFD). Much has been written about its early adoption of Twitter, which it has used almost since inception. The department has multiple accounts but uses its main page (@LAFD) to focus on breaking news stories, alerts, and advisories. As of May 2010, @LAFD had nearly 8,000 followers and even higher spikes during emergency situations.

Like many responsible for managing emergency communication, LAFD's goal is to keep people from being cut off from information in a crisis like they were during Hurricane Katrina. Keith Humphrey, LAFD's public service officer, explains that the people housed at the Superdome during the disaster "were darn hungry. They were darn thirsty, but they were not dying from hunger or thirst. What they were dying from a little bit at a time was a lack of information. We were dying from a lack of information as well. We didn't know what was going on. It was a two-way lack of conversing."†

---

* Andrew Spooner, cited in "Twitter's Role in Bangkok Conflict Unprecedented," UpdatedNews, http://updatednews.ca/?p=20734, May 22, 2010.
† Hilton Collins (LAFD), "Emergency Managers and First Responders Use Twitter and Facebook to Update Communities," www.emergencymgmt.com/safety/, July 27, 2009.

Twitter can also help control rumors and misinformation that could, if left untouched, put your reputation at risk. Take the example of the U.S. Air Force. According to Government 2.0 Club, an American organization that leverages social media to improve government, a witness falsely reported a crash of an Air Force C-17; but moments thereafter, the story was appearing as breaking news on CNN. Within 17 minutes, the Air Force used Twitter to counter the reports, resulting in CNN's retraction of the story less than an hour later. The Air Force's ability to respond was phenomenal in that they immediately took control of the rumor at lightning speed.*

UK High Court Serves First Writ on Twitter

Twitter's legitimacy has gone beyond the corridors of power to the hallowed halls of justice. High courts have been getting in on the action, too.

In late 2009, Britain's High Court ordered its first injunction via Twitter. According to Reuters UK, the High Court did so as that "was the best way to reach an anonymous Tweeter who had been impersonating someone." Solicitors from Griffin Law sought the injunction against @blaneysblarney, arguing that it was impersonating right-wing blogger Donal Blaney. (Incidentally, when I searched for that Twitter handle, there was no one of that name in the results. The injunction obviously worked!)

As Reuters wrote, "the legal first could have widespread implications for blogosphere." Twitter has recognized the issue, however, and launched a system to verify the authenticity of tweets. For example, Bill Gates, President Obama, and the Dalai Lama all have "verified" accounts, marked by a blue tick on their home pages.†

BREAKING NEWS: TWITTER AND THE MEDIA

As seen in Chapter 3, Twitter has also transformed the media, making the traditional mainstream stations and publications virtually reliant on its users and technology. With millions of eyes and ears armed with Flip cameras, netbooks, and smartphones, tweeters can disseminate information faster with their eyewitness accounts than any newsroom has ever had the ability to do.

News outlets have responded to this trend by incorporating Twitter in their broadcasts. Fox News regularly reaches out to its viewers for instant updates during severe weather conditions. CNN cultivates, actively encourages, and regularly incorporates Twitter feeds into news stories as eyewitness accounts. Instead of reaching for the phone or sending news crews

---

* Posted by "1kthrockclose" (Lisa Throckmorton), "Twitter in Crisis Communications with the Air Force," Government 2.0 Club Blog, www.government20club.org, March 28, 2009.
† Matthew Jones, "UK High Court Serves First Writ on Twitter," Reuters, http://www.reuters.com/article/idUSTRE5904HC20091001, posted 5:29 PM EDT, October 1, 2009.

to the scene, the network receives instant news, images, and video from viewers via their mobile Twitter accounts. What a boom for mainstream media, as they struggle with dwindling audiences, to have such connections to their viewers, not to mention the leads and sources. The media can cherry-pick their way through the information, particularly if they have a large following like CNN. (At the time of writing, CNN had more than a million followers; BBC more than 400,000; and Fox News over 200,000.)

Probably the most famous breaking news story on Twitter was US Airways' miraculous Hudson River landing on January 15, 2009. Broken on TwitPic by US Airways passenger Janis Klum, the news of the incident was reported all over Twitter before any mainstream news outlet even knew about it. By the time the TwitPic server crashed from a surge of users trying to access the photo, more than 7,000 people had seen it and many had copied it on their blogs or distributed it through many other channels, including mainstream media.

As I am writing, millions of people are tweeting madly about BP and the massive oil spill in the Gulf of Mexico. Hugh Hefner (of Playboy fame) tweets, "Man can walk on the moon but can't fix an *oil spill* destroying the environment? What the f…!"* Indeed!

THE POWER OF 140 CHARACTERS

For crisis communicators, Twitter and its principle of short, instantaneous updates has tremendous strengths and depth as a tool to quickly disseminate news, messages, and information. It's hard to dismiss Twitter's flexibility and speed in a crisis. You can update frequently, you can make short announcements that link to more in-depth information, and you can answer questions and get immediate feedback. These are crucial attributes in a crisis when people want to see and hear that you are engaged and, more importantly, doing something quickly about the problem. Crisis pundits, journalists, and I all agree: there is no faster channel than Twitter to get a message to your audiences.

Twitter also offers the capacity for, and nearly requires, authenticity and transparency—both vital ingredients for a well-managed crisis. People respond well to genuine emotion, authentic tone, and immediate dialogue—and the format and tone used in Twitter-talk require all of these components. It's for this reason that many governments and state and federal organizations around the world have officially adopted Twitter into

---

* *Twitter* post by: Hugh Hefner, May 2010.

their emergency management programs. For example, the former Prime Minister Kevin Rudd used Twitter extensively during the devastating bushfires in Victoria, Australia, to express his support, to extend condolences, and to tell affected people where and how to access government assistance.

RULES OF ENGAGEMENT

We can no longer ignore or minimize the changes unfolding before us. Everything begins without fully knowing what to do, why it's important and whether or not we're doing everything the right way. But it is in the process of *engagement* that we learn and mature.[*]

—*Brian Solis, "We Are the Champions," May 27, 2010*

Hopefully, these examples will have demonstrated the compelling reasons for using Twitter in a crisis. As a communicator for your organization or brand, if you are not using Twitter, you are likely being ignored by a huge contingency of your audience. Today, consumers and mainstream media are heavily reliant on the microblog for their news and information. Nothing is hidden from Twitter. And when the online conversation is about you, not only do you want to be part of it, but you want to serve as the "official" Twitter voice of your brand.

Now, we must look at exactly how to incorporate this tool in your crisis media strategy. Remember the good old days when we used templates for our crisis media releases and stand-by statements so that they could move quickly? It is actually just the same in Twitterville. Apply that same principle to Twitter (and other social media). Not only will it save you valuable time (and you need that in today's lightning-fast age of communication), but it lets management know that you are prepared to operate in that space during a crisis.

The words that you use will be similar to what you have used in the old days—just reduced to 140 characters. For example:

Aware of incident XXX. More information as soon as possible. Follow @ XYZ for latest news and updates. (104 characters)

If you're not yet Twitter-fluent, my advice is to do whatever it takes to get up to speed with the tool, immediately. Make sure that Twitter (and

---

[*] Posted by Brian Solis, "We Are the Champions," BrianSolis Blog, www.briansolis.com, May 27, 2010.

other key social networks like Facebook) is part of your drills, exercises, and crisis media training, and explain to the executive team how it can and will all work in a crisis. Give them examples that illustrate the power of these tools, such as showing them the number of tweets there were in the first 24 hours of Domino's Pizza's online drama with its two rogue employees, the BP oil spill in the Gulf of Mexico, the Toyota recall, or the Icelandic volcano eruption (in Box 6.1 you will see just how the airlines used Twitter to get their messages out in that crisis). Whatever your industry, a variety of incidents can serve as excellent examples of Twitter's power and influence.

You must also decide far in advance of a crisis how and when the technology will be utilized, as well as who will serve as the official Twitter "voice." When an incident occurs, you have precious moments to act, and these decisions must be made ahead of time.

Twitter is a powerful news channel, sometimes a much-needed counselor and support as we saw in the deadly bushfires in the Australia, and a direct communication link between organizations and their audiences. It also empowers individuals when others want to silence those voices. We saw this power magnificently and bravely represented in the Iranian elections.

Time will tell whether Twitter does indeed become the 8-bazillion-pound gorilla of crisis communication. But I, for one, am willing to take that bet.

BOX 6.1 TWITTER EXAMPLES: THE ICELANDIC VOLCANO

Social media proved to be a boon for the airline industry—probably the only silver lining in an otherwise frightful few weeks for the travel industry. There was widespread usage on Twitter when #ashtag was created with more than 55,000 mentions in just 7 days.

BRITISH AIRWAYS

We're asking customers with bookings up to 2 May to delay travel if they can, to free up seats for stranded passengers. (http://bit.ly/cUmnwM about 10 hours ago via TweetDeck)

If you're still trying to get to your original destination & haven't rebooked/cancelled, pls provide us w/ some details. (http://bit.ly/apnDGg about 10 hours ago via TweetDeck)

We're doing all we can to help the tens of thousands of customers who've been delayed around the world by these unprecedented circumstances. (About 11 hours ago via TweetDeck)

@TomPearman you can cancel your ticket on ba.com or speak to your travel agent if you booked through them. (7:25 AM Apr 21st via TweetDeck in reply to TomPearman)

KLM

Are you stranded? Need an earlier flight? check out http://www.facebook.com/klm and click 'rebook' so we can help you! (About 5 hours ago via Web)

@arikoskinen—Please do not share your personal data or booking codes in tweets with requests for rebooking. Please send us a Direct Message! (About 7 hours ago via Web in reply to @arikoskinen)

VIRGIN ATLANTIC

@clubskii—Our lines are really busy, but working hard to answer asap. Please hold on, you are in a long queue.

@Graham_Walsh Glad you got on a flight tomorrow Graham. Have a safe flight home.

Online Check In is now OPEN, except for renumbered flights. See link for renumbered flights: http://www.tinyurl.com/vaatwash. (4:22 AM Apr 21st via Web)

Update: UK airspace is opening. We're working on a flying programme right now. More info after 11pm BST tonight. (#ashtag 1:37 PM Apr 20th via Web)

Source: Shashank Nigam, "How Social Media Helped Travelers during the Icelandic Volcano Eruption," Mashable, http://mashable.com/2010/04/22/social-media-iceland-volcano, April 2010.

SECTION I SUMMARY

We have discussed a lot in this section—everything from the definition of a crisis, media's role in affecting public opinion, and ethics in journalism to trends in news coverage, as well as Twitter's role in crisis media management.

There is no doubt that we stand on shifting sand in the evolution of news. Clearly, the new media and social journalists are playing a huge role in not only the distribution of news and in the manner in which it is written but in the future of the old legacy media. As a hybrid melting pot of views emerges, we have learned that the new and the old need each other.

The "kingdom of news" has new rulers. And it is mostly us, the news consumers, who are leading the charge, along with think tanks, activists, and partisans. We have become the new, powerful *fifth estate*.

We have multiple platforms in which to share our news. We forage, hunt, and gather so *we can get the news we want when we want it* from a variety of sources rather than have it arrive at appointed times, hearing only the news they want us to hear and from their dais. Rarely do we receive our news from only one news platform.

Whether your crisis is hyperlocal or global with impact on a grand scale, it is quite simple: Your crisis media plan and communication strategy *must* incorporate social media and value it as a key channel to help you get your message out in an unfiltered and timely manner. Remember, preparation and speed are of the essence in a crisis, and social media allow you to act swiftly. You need those carrier pigeons equipped with jet propulsion packs!

Incorporate social media as part of your plans in a proactive way. See it as a two-way street, not just for getting your message out but as a channel for hearing from your stakeholders, understanding their concerns, and addressing them. You must be prepared to act more on your feet than ever before, but the good news is that social media can be a very effective tool to averting a full-blown crisis or, at a minimum, mitigating it. The heartbeat is simply faster online—whether we like it or not. The bottom line really is this: Ignore the social media at your peril.

And finally, remember that the traditional media are, in the main, a highly principled lot driven, yes, by ratings, but as much by their need to defend and uphold "democratic" principles, that obligate them in their duty to "serve society" in a crisis.

Section II

Stages of a Crisis

The news media play a crucial role in the court of public opinion. They are influential in shaping how the community thinks and feels about an organization's reputation, its values, and its actions. Depending on how the media are managed, they can hurt or help in a crisis.[*]

STAGES OF A CRISIS

Technology may have redefined the media landscape, but the patterns of how the media report a crisis are still apparent.

If you take a close look at any crisis, you will see distinct, predictable patterns in how the media behave. I group these patterns into what I call the Four Stages—a methodology that we, at Media Skills, developed over a decade ago (Figure SII.1).

That's the good news. The bad news is that, now, the reporting of a crisis happens at a blistering speed thanks to the advent of social media.

It is also worth keeping in mind that journalists see their role as the public's "ears and eyes"—they are the watchdogs for democracy, they are the *reporters of the high court of public opinion*. As discussed in Chapter 5, it is their very ethics that drive them to seek the truth, particularly if they sniff a sordid allegation, a wrongdoing, or illegal or unethical behavior. And they are more likely to side with the victim than with big business.

---

[*] Media Skills, "The Media, A Crisis and You Workbook," 2004, p. 2.

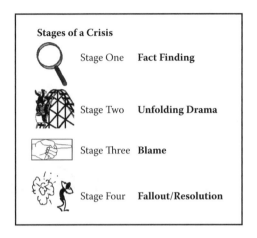

FIGURE SII.1 The media report a crisis in discernable patterns. We developed this four-stage approach at Media Skills to assist our clients in understanding how the media may react and report in a crisis. (This figure is used with the permission of Media Skills.)

The media, which operate under shared norms and values, will dig in and try to understand what has happened in a crisis, says Kirsten Mogensen, associate professor at Roskilde University in Denmark. Numerous studies have shown that "leading journalists across different types of news media in elective democracies have similar norms and values in relation to their role as journalists."[*]

PATTERNS OF REPORTING

Communication research also confirms patterns of reporting during crises.

In studying the reporting of September 11, 2001, in popular news magazines such as *Newsweek*, *Time*, and *U.S. News & World Report*, researchers with the *American Communication Journal* found that "narrative patterns all play out in predictable ways during crisis reporting …" and, importantly,

---

[*] Kirsten Mogensen and David Norfors (Stanford University), "How Silicon Valley Journalists Talk about Independence in Innovation Coverage," presented to the International Association for Media and Communication Research (IAMCR) Annual Conference, July 2010.

patterns of reporting allow for some "future predictability in how future crises may be covered."[*]

These same researchers found that news coverage of a crisis follows specific narratives; and readers, perhaps unknowingly, expect "certain narratives to appear at certain times."

The PEJ News Coverage Index (November 10, 2009) also confirmed that the pattern of reporting in an analysis of the Fort Hood coverage: "... began as a breaking news story, with the media answering the 'who, what and where' questions."[†] Not surprisingly, the spotlight quickly turned to Major Nidal Malik Hasan—his possible motives and his religious background.

Certainly it has been my experience working in and around the media for more than two decades, being in "war rooms" with clients, and being an avid student of the news that I can attest to these patterns and cycles of news coverage in a crisis.

Those predictable patterns certainly help you plan better, help you stay ahead of the game when you find yourself warding off fire from more directions than ever, because every man and his dog can have an instant, unrestricted say on any matter, thanks to Twitter, YouTube, and "Lord" Google!

And then there is the incredible speed with which crises are reported today. In the Haiti earthquake, cell phone interviews with survivors not only made it into broadcasts out of Haiti very quickly, but they were accompanied by cell phone video and Skype reports. You can predict this to happen as the media move through the cycles of coverage of a crisis. In this section, we will explore the following:

- The patterns, cycles, and stages of a crisis in more detail.
- What characterizes each stage.
- What to expect.
- What to do in each of the four stages.

While there are no absolutes, the stages of reporting a crisis will guide you in your decisions and choices for spokespeople, tools, channels, training, and policies. And you will soon see that the better you manage the first two stages, the better off you will be. Smart, savvy, and speedy communication with both the old and new media will help you mitigate the

---

[*] Christopher T. Caldiero (Fairleigh Dickinson University), "Crisis Storytelling: Fisher's Narrative Paradigm and News Reporting," *American Communication Journal*, Vol. 9, No. 1, Spring 2007.

[†] Tom Rosenstiel, "Fort Hood Shooting Tops News Agenda," *PEJ News Coverage Index*, www.journalism.org, November 10, 2009.

damage to your reputation. Take time to study these cycles and patterns in reporting, and you will soon realize that you can anticipate and plan: You can still manage (not control) the media coverage in a crisis in this adrenaline-charged age.

But before we dive in and look at each of the stages in more detail, let me help you a little by giving you a picture of how the stages work. Imagine, if you will, that each stage is symbolized by a light. That light shines intensely at times, particularly if you are perceived to be doing the wrong thing, are hiding something, or were tardy in your response. In that case, you'll be feeling the intense heat of the media spotlight.

7

Stage One—Fact-Finding Stage

> After a major event, the first news will often come through social media—particularly the platforms focused on instant distribution such as blogs and microblogs.[*]

For Stage One, the spotlight is beaming squarely on the incident.

The traditional mainstream media (MSM) are looking to confirm the basic details of that show-stopping event. "What happened?" is the key question. This is the *breaking news* stage. They want to gauge just how big this event is. Just as you are wondering what resources you are going to dedicate to this, the media are, too. Do they send out a crew? Do they stop what they are doing and assign a team of reporters to cover all the angles, and have a dedicated person monitoring all the news feeds? Do they organize a live feed? Do they engage Twitter? Do they mobilize their citizen reporters?

To find out what happened, the MSM talk to eyewitnesses, victims, anyone who is willing to speak and be heard. Frequently, they turn to Twitter during these early stages to see what is being said, to "get the scoop," find sources and/or quotes. The MSM were quoting Fort Hood eyewitness and unofficial spokesperson soldier Tearah Moore long before official word came from the Army.

Social media are very active in Stage One, breaking stories as they are on the spot, and can report their news immediately, as we saw with the

---

[*] Gerald Baron and John "Pat" Philbin (March 23, 2009), "Social Media in Crisis Communication: Start with a Drill," *Public Relations Tactics*, April 2009, p. 1.

now legendary Hudson River landing of the US Airways flight. CNN has its Army of iReporters, and the majority of the MSM encourage eyewitness reports from the journalist citizenry. Indeed they have cultivated the citizen–journalists, many of whom are now regular (unpaid) contributors to the news-gathering process.

Twitter, in particular, plays a major role in breaking news, acting much like a police scanner as observed by a number of journalists I spoke with during my research. The following tweets highlight that very notion:

- *BreakingNews*: British Airways apologizes for mistakenly telling passengers on a London–Hong Kong flight to prepare for crash landing. (http://bit.ly/bJDA9Y, posted August 27, 2010.)
- *BreakingNews*: Delta pilot arrested for carrying a concealed weapon at Atlanta's Hartsfield–Jackson International Airport—WXIA. (http://bit.ly/9LcVka, posted May 17, 2010.)
- *BreakingNews*: Two people shot at Old Navy store in Chicago; condition of victims, status of suspect unknown—NBC. (http://bit.ly/b4vkTS, posted May 7, 2010.)
- *BreakingNews*: 8 hurt in a Disney bus crash at a toll plaza at Epcot Center in Orlando, Fla. (http://bit.ly/cUKCOS, posted March 24, 2010.)
- *BreakingNews*: Oil rig explodes in Decatur, Texas; four tanks on fire; at least two burn victims reported. (http://bit.ly/cERrwu, posted March 19, 2010.)*

At this initial stage, when something has just happened, it's all about *impact* for the media. They want to know, "Is this a *big* story?" and "How far-reaching is the impact?"

The global financial collapse was a *big* story when the stock markets around the world took a nose dive in September 2008. Michael Jackson's death was also a *big* story. He was considered the "King of Pop" and had millions of fans around the world. The Fort Hood crisis was huge. Thirteen people were killed in what is considered the deadliest U.S. Army domestic incident in decades. Tiger Woods's sex scandal was big; the Toyota recall was massive, involving millions of cars around the globe, and the BP oil spill in the Gulf of Mexico, possibly the worst in human history. All *huge* stories, with a big impact.

---

* "Twitter Breaking News," www.Twitter.com/BreakingNews.

Key News Ingredients

- ☐ Impact

- ☐ Timeliness

- ☐ Currency

- ☐ Proximity

- ☐ Novelty

- ☐ Prominence

- ☐ Human Interest

- ☐ Conflict

FIGURE 7.1 This list shows the "news values," sometimes called news criteria that determine how much prominence a news story is given by a media outlet. (From the Media Skills Collection. Adapted from Australian journalist academic Murray Masterton, "Theory of News Values," 1998.)

To gauge impact, the media take the following questions into consideration:

- How many people are or were involved?
- Where exactly did it happen?
- When did it happen?
- Who is involved?
- What caused the accident?
- When do you expect everything to return to normal?
- What can be done to ensure that this never happens again?

The more the news ingredients (Figure 7.1) that are evident, the more likely the story will be front page news and, as they say in the media, "have legs." The crisis will be front and center for days. What may well be a ratings bonanza for the traditional MSM may well be your worst night-mare being played out in cyberspace and in words and vision on cable TV and computer screens across the globe.

The more the ingredients, the higher the news value, and the higher the likelihood to be a front-page, lead story for days.

Questions at Stage One are often speculative in nature as the media, acting in the interest of public safety, want to know that the community is safe (from whatever has happened), that the response has been swift, that victims have been dealt with compassionately, and that there is a reason for the calamity. These last two fit into the second and third stages, since they are often at the heart of the *how* and *why*, but today they can come up very quickly as the fire jumps the tree line and quickly jumps from Stage One to Stage Three.

The key lesson to Stage One, is to *only say what you know to be fact. Resist the temptation to speculate.*

You need to think like a reporter and think ahead. The going gets very tough in a real "show-stopping" crisis—you will be in for the long haul (ask BP). Monitor, monitor, monitor—everything, everywhere.

STAGE ONE CHARACTERISTICS

What might be happening?

- Speculation, rumor, and misinformation flourish.
- Only a minimum of facts is known.
- The phone lines are congested.
- Panic is possible.
- Vox pops (short sound bites from eyewitnesses, typically the average Joe on the street) are used as a reflection of popular opinion.
- News may break on social media with instant news distribution on Twitter.
- There may be updates on Wikipedia.
- Chatter on social media sites begins to spike.
- Citizen–journalists are breaking the news.
- You are the butt of jokes and the focus of newspaper cartoons.

Expect the media to:

- *Seek confirmation on the facts*—Who, what, when, where. Is it truth or rumor?
- *Assess impact*—How big of a deal is this? The ST factor (see Chapter 8) and *currency* (i.e., What is topical now? What is on the media agenda all the time, for example, taxes?) are key news values.
- *Gauge implications*—*So what?* What are the personal, social, environmental, and economic implications?
- *Start to speculate on cause*—Who is responsible?

What to do:

- Take responsibility, act fast, and meet deadlines.
- Demonstrate concern and empathy. Remember this is a reputation-forming (good or bad) time.
- Collect facts—Assess the situation, anticipate possible escalation, and get facts out as fast as possible.
- Dispel rumors—Only say what you know to be correct.
- Activate a crisis communication plan; *inform employees regularly*—Remember they talk often and to lots of people.
- Authorize (trained) spokespeople—Think carefully about putting your key spokesperson, particularly the chief executive officer, at the "crime" scene.
- Decide on your key message for the crisis *and stick to it* (more in Chapter 8).
- Issue standby statements. (Showing that you are activating a plan is reassuring.)
- Call in external support—Incident-specific and content experts.
- Think ahead—Who can be exploited? Where and what are the vulnerabilities? Who are the self-appointed critics? Who will grandstand? Who will be the instant experts? What favors can you pull in?
- Research similar incidents that may surface again in the context of your crisis. Learn how they were handled by the organizations or people at the center of the storm.
- Think about how the crisis will be symbolized (e.g., the Exxon Valdez and BP oil spills will forever be symbolized by birds covered in oil). Symbols and names will be remembered forever.

8

Beware the ST Factor: Remember the Context

The oil spill in the Gulf of Mexico claimed the unwelcome title of the nation's *worst* ever on Thursday ...[*]

Collapse of Scotland's *biggest* airline, Flyglobespan, strands more than 4,500 passengers ...[†]

106 bank failures—*worst* since 1992 ...[‡]

Beware of the ST factor when facing a crisis. Words that end in *st*—some have called it the superlative factor of news—are most often used to contextualize a situation, an event, or an organization. They are particularly used by journalists in a crisis—for and against you.

---

[*] *San Francisco Chronicle*, www.SFGate.com, May 28, 2010.
[†] www.Feedraider.com, Feedraider, December 17, 2009.
[‡] "Worst Bank Closures: 106 Banks Shut Down in 2009," UP Ibalon Bicol, http://pibalonbicol. blogspot.com/2009/10/worst-bank-closures-106-banks-shut-down.html, October 23, 2009.

For example:

The cascade of bank failures this year surpassed 100 on Friday, the *most* in nearly two decades.*

Here are some other examples (the majority of these appeared in the lead paragraph, emphasis added):

- "Study Backs U.S. Estimate: Confirms Oil Spill as *Worst* Ever" (Headline, *USA Today*, www.usatoday.com, posted 10:16 AM, September 24, 2010.)
- "An independent scientific study finds that the U.S. government, after several errors, was finally accurate in estimating the size of the Gulf oil spill and confirms that it is the *worst* marine oil accident ever." (*USA Today*, www.usatoday.com, posted 10:16 AM, September 24, 2010.)
- "He's been dubbed a 'genius of fraud.' Others say that the man at the centre of the *biggest* trading scandal in banking history simply 'lost his mind.'... Loss in bad bets under the noses of executives at France's second *largest* bank." (AAP Report, *Sydney Morning Herald*, http://news.theage.com.au/world/rogue-trader-racks-up-82-billion-loss-20080125-1o65.html, January 25, 2008.)
- *BreakingNews*: "Divers in Finland Find What Is Believed to Be World's *Oldest* Bottle of Drinkable Champagne." (www.Twitter.com/BreakingNews, http://bit.ly/bAk5YXv, posted 3:54 AM, July 7, 2010.)
- "Argentines have lost their title as the world's *biggest* beef eaters after the *worst* drought in 70 years ..." (Rodrigo Orihuela, *Washington Post* in the *San Francisco Chronicle*, September 24, 2010, p. A5.)
- "The unemployment rate in the Eurozone rose to 9.2% from 8.9% in March, the *highest* rate since September 1999, the Eurostat data agency said." (*BBC News Online*, http://news.bbc.co.uk/2/hi/8078655.stm, United Kingdom, posted 09:51 GMT, June 2, 2009.)
- "Gulf spill is likely *worst* environmental disaster in U.S. history; Obama point person on environmental policy tells NBC's *Meet the*

---

* Associated Press (AP), Washington, posted 12:14 AM ET, October 24, 2009.

Press." (www.Twitter.com/BreakingNews, posted 6:19 AM, May 30, 2010.)

- "Kuwaiti women broke a milestone on winning their *first* seats ever in parliamentary elections—16 female candidates were in the running." (www.Twitter.com/BreakingNews, posted 8:14 PM, May 16, 2009.)

- "A First: U.S. Judge Orders Air Force to Reinstate Lesbian Officer." (*USA Today*, OnDeadline, www.usatoday.com, posted 5:25 PM, September 24, 2010.)

- "When IVF goes wrong—The Whitneys' case is just the *latest* high-profile case of a mix-up involving *in vitro* fertilization." (Habiba Nosheen, "Fertility Clinic Loses Embyros, Couples Sue," *NPR News*, www.npr.org, October 24, 2009.)

- "For the *first* time since automatic cost-of-living adjustments (COLA) have been in effect, people in Social Security will not receive a COLA in their monthly benefit checks." (Nancy Leamond, "AARP: Cost of Living Increase a No-Brainer," *NPR News*, www.npr.org, October 21, 2009.)

I think you get the picture.

The ST factor can relate to a number of news values that will determine where the story is placed. If it is high in impact (e.g., biggest, largest, worst) and affects a lot of people, it will most likely go to the front page or lead the news, as we saw in the *San Francisco Chronicle*, when the Bay Bridge in San Francisco was closed after pieces from the Labor Day weekend repair hit three cars, including one driven by a tourist. Similarly, the BP oil spill has earned the title of the worst oil-related disaster in American history. The impact of the spill is global, putting it at the front of the news for months.

Then again, an ST may simply be the novelty factor. This is an old example but clearly demonstrates the ubiquitous nature of the ST factor—superlative at its best (or worst).

Less than a week to go before the Atlanta Olympics begin, just as our *largest* ever team is due to start its campaign for Australia's *biggest* medal tally, one of the athletics squad's *best* known names is claimed to have used drugs.

—*The Australian, July 1996*

So, plan for the ST factor when thinking about crafting your message, your response, or for what may be said about your organization.

FIGURE 8.1 This cartoon is not only an extreme example of what makes news but also shows how the ST factor is used. (From the *Daily Republic*, April 10, 2010, p. 11. By permission of Marshall Ramsey and Creators Syndicate, Inc.)

You may want to use an ST word to contextualize the incident. For example, this is the *first* time something like this has ever happened in our proud 150-year history. (See Figure 8.1.)

The ST factor will be present. You have been warned.

REMEMBER THE CONTEXT

No news happens in isolation—Every event is seen in the context of other events and happenings locally and internationally. Journalists will report your crisis in the context of the *last big thing* and the *next big thing*.

It is common practice around the world for the media to "issue link," even going back several decades. For example, in the 2005 BP plant explosion in Texas, reporters immediately linked the fatal fire to a previous accident, as far back as the 1940s. And not surprisingly, the oil spill in the Gulf of Mexico was immediately and continuously compared with the Exxon Valdez spill in 1989.

A story about Baby Einstein refunds (the Walt Disney Company offering refunds on all those videos that did not make children into geniuses) has been reported in the context of infant intellect and the educational claims, comparing them with another company, Brainy Baby.

Often the context comes from what we fear most, for example, bad boys behaving badly or safety being compromised. In this case, it was pilots being drunk at the wheel or asleep at the wheel.

In October 2009, two Northwest pilots overshot the Minneapolis runway by 150 miles. Most of the early (Stage Two) reports confirmed that the pilots had been breathalyzed (and passed), and were reporting widespread speculation that they were asleep (what we fear most). There was much speculation, in the absence of anything official, for the reasons why they did not begin their normal descent and failed to respond to air traffic controllers. The truth came out—it always does. There are no secrets anymore. The pilots were on their computers! Journalists will jump to conclusions and draw comparisons with other issues to find context to help us try and make sense of what happened. It is as predictable as the stages reporting.

The *Exxon Valdez* oil spill more often than not provides the context for how not to manage a crisis. (And the BP fiasco in the Gulf of Mexico will also provide context for the worst case study.) Conversely, Johnson & Johnson provided the context for best practice for how they handled the Tylenol tampering. Both are decades old, but they live on.

The October 2009 forced closure of the Bay Bridge in San Francisco is another classic example of how your own context can come back to bite you in a crisis. The busiest bridge in the region was closed on October 27, 2009, after three pieces of the emergency repair fell onto three cars. The area of the bridge where the pieces fell off was where, over the Labor Day weekend, crews found a crack during a planned, four-day shutdown of the span. The fatal flaw had been discovered during a routine inspection as part of the bridge's massive earthquake retrofitting project. At the time, the iconic CC Myers contractors were confident that everything went "perfect." Apparently not! Be very careful about the context that you use in a crisis. It may come back to bite you!

Johnson & Johnson (J & J) was under fire on a few fronts—Motrin Moms, the phantom "Motrin Purchase Project," recall of more than 100 million bottles of children's medicine during the writing of this book. Inevitably, there were questions about its quality control, and the reporting about J&J's handling of quality issues linked the recalls. In our profession we call this *issue linking*—when the media report the immediate crisis and immediately link it a previous incident, the last big thing that happened. Note issue linking and ST factor in paragraph two of the following:

> Congressional investigators said Wednesday that Johnson & Johnson hired a private company that bought up defective packets of pain relief in 2008 before recalling the pills months later, after prodding from federal regulators.
>
> The new questions about J&J's handling of quality issues came about during a hearing about its *latest* recall involving over 100 million bottles of children's medicine, some of which contained lead.[*]

Lesson? When you are planning your messages (on a sunny day when all is calm) or conducting mock interviews in your annual drills, think about the last big thing that happened in your industry, in your company, or to your product, and write it into your scenarios. This discipline will serve you well in an actual crisis. There is a very high probability that your crisis will be reported in that context, as the Bay Bridge contractors, BP, and Johnson & Johnson found out. You can predict and plan for the media coverage and, therefore, the messaging as you manage the media communication.

---

[*] Matthew Perrone, Associated Press, *The Boston Globe*, www.boston.com, May 28, 2010.

9

Stage Two—The Unfolding Drama

Stage Two is very important for the organization at the center of the storm, as the spotlight moves from the incident to the response and the victims, as we saw so clearly with the coverage of the Virginia Tech and Fort Hood shootings and the oil spill in the Gulf of Mexico.

This is the reputation-forming stage, the make it or break it stage; the stage where the rallying on social media sites, both negative and positive, becomes a focal point.

The spotlight, with widening and growing intensity, points at the organization and people who appear to be at the center of the storm. It will roam around and catch whomever will talk about what has just happened. Experts start to appear on CNN, victims start talking in-depth about their experiences, and the organization starts to give its side of the story.

We call this stage the *unfolding drama*, as the initial facts about the incident are now out there for debate and discussion.

This is dirt-digging time; there will be more disclosure. You cannot hide the skeletons. The truth always comes out. Just ask Tiger Woods or California State University (CSU). CSU thought they could keep quiet about the fee for Sarah Palin's speech at the CSU Stanislaus fundraiser in June 2010. Goldman Sachs similarly with its e-mails about selling its ill-begot financial products to sophisticated hedge funds. An e-mail from executive, Fabrice Tourre, urges his colleagues not to approach "sophisticated" hedge funds about selling them mortgage investments because "they know exactly how things work." Tourre also wrote in another e-mail that the market was "about to collapse." He continued: "Only potential survivor, the fabulous Fab ... standing in the middle of all these complex, highly leveraged, exotic trades he created without necessarily understanding all of the implications of those monstrosities!!!"* The truth will emerge too about what really happened to trigger the massive Gulf of Mexico oil spill.

This stage is characterized by the *how did this happen (how could this possibly happen) question*, heading to the blame game. This is especially true when there are lots of victims, lives are at risk, and there are far-reaching, harmful consequences.

Research shows that people want to know what has happened to the victims. How did people handle the tragedy and display extraordinary courage?

Think September 11, Hurricane Katrina, and the Haiti earthquake, which were of course disasters rather than crises in strict definitional terms. The media and community alike wanted to know about the victims. How did they deal with the tragedy? How did they display extraordinary courage?

There are expectations that the media will tell us what went wrong, who was responsible, and what might happen in the future. For example, in the coverage about the Indonesian jetliner that crashed in Medan, killing more than 125 people, the reporting followed the specific narrative of "How could that happen?" with news of an investigation in *The Washington Post*.

> Investigators began a probe into the cause of an Indonesian jetliner crash Monday that killed at least 147 people, including dozens on the ground who lived in the crowded residential neighborhood in the city of Medan, according to officials and new reports.... Human error and mechanical failure will be among the possibilities explored for the crash.[†]

The media stop people in the street and ask them what they think of the rescue attempts, the response, and the impact on their lives. They crowdsource on Twitter, they call for eyewitness reports. They ask the tough questions they know their audiences want to hear.

---

[*] Zachary A. Goldfarb, "Goldman Sachs Executives Face Senators Investigating Role in Financial Crisis," *The Washington Post*, www.washingtonpost.com, April 28, 2010.

[†] Ellen Nakashima, "Plane Crash in Indonesia Kills at Least 125," Washington Post Foreign Service, *The Washington Post*, www.washingtonpost.com, September 2005, p. 5.

" ... she ought to stay there." University of California Linguistics Professor Robin Lakoff said it all when describing what people would say if you stopped them in the street and asked about Paris Hilton being sent back to jail.[*]

And as we've seen in Chapter 8, the media will do their utmost to compare and link back to previous events. The media called the oil spill in the Gulf of Mexico "Obama's Katrina," and they immediately linked it to the *Exxon Valdez* spill in 1989.

The media will also scrutinize all the facts and they *dig for dirt* if they think someone is hiding something. If it is a *big* story, like the global financial collapse, the Fort Hood shootings, the death of Michael Jackson, Tiger Woods, the Toyota recall, or the BP oil spill, then questions will be asked and asked again until they get to the bottom of the story. Remember, everyone has a back story.

The spotlight will be swinging wildly from one place to another in the frenzied hunt for the truth that may put the perpetrator behind bars to make them pay for it.

Let us not forget that for the commercial mass media, many of whom are under the gun to stay afloat, it is as much about the public good as it is about ratings, viewers, and readers. As Jim Bell, executive producer of NBC's *Today Show* said in the *Los Angeles Times*, "It's a version of the high-speed chase, but on steroids ..."[†] referring to the "Balloon Boy" story. (What turned out to be a hoax to get the attention of reality TV producers, was a compelling story that both captivated and horrified us at the same time as first responders raced against time to find a six-year-old boy supposedly hiding and floating around in a hot-air balloon.) It was a ratings bonanza.

The reality is that *big* stories attract voyeurs, and everyone likes to feel a connection to some part of the story. We are also storytellers; we like to gossip. As MacIntyre reminds us, "Man is in his actions and practice, as well as in his fictions, essentially a storytelling animal".[‡] Storytelling is a common bond that we share, and the social media provide a mechanism for this, particularly in a crisis, where we all like to voice our opinion, share the gossip and the gory tales, as well as to help spread the news.

---

[*] C. W. Nervicus, "We All Wanted to See Paris Get Fabulous Comeuppance," *San Francisco Chronicle*, www.SFGate.com, June 9, 2007.

[†] Scott Collins and Nicholas Riccardi, "My Kid, the Ratings Bonanza: Beyond the 'Balloon Boy' Saga, *Los Angeles Times*, http://articles.latimes.com/2009/oct/19/entertainment/et-media-balloon-boy19/2, October 19, 2009.

[‡] As cited in Christopher T. Caldiero, "Crisis Storytelling: Fisher's Narrative Paradigm and News Reporting," *American Communication Journal*, Vol. 9, No. 1, Spring 2007.

And while the glaring lights of the mainstream media (MSM) may start to dim and you think you are out of the water, think again. That is not necessarily the case in the social media domain, as one giant pharmaceutical discovered recently.

Their product, a household name, was linked to cancer and, needless to say, attracted front-page news and chatter in the social media. When the MSM coverage dissipated, the discussion spiked online. Presumably there were a whole bunch of consumers who wished the debate to continue. There were no editorial interventions or restrictions for these commentators and would-be reporters. They were free to write what they liked, when they liked, and to share the information, accurately or not, with anyone, anywhere.

You can *expect* the social media to be a focal point in a crisis since that is where people rally.

Time and time again we have seen how Web users have rallied at social media sites after a major event like Hurricane Katrina, the Californian wildfires, the Australian bushfires, the Iranian elections, and the Haiti earthquake. And the patterns of usage are very similar.

Take the deadly bushfires that tore through Victoria, Australia, in February 2009. Twitter, Flickr, and Facebook became focal points for victims of that country's worst bushfires and for those who wanted to help them out. Here is a sample from Twitter, courtesy of the Australian Broadcasting Corporation News Online's Gary Kemble:

"One friend safe, two dead, 10 awol,'" Twitter user @strictly wrote, taking personal stock of the tragedy as the nation came to grips with the scale of the devastating natural disaster.

- @Ingenue_Em: I'm crying over the #bushfires—how can whole towns be decimated? Over 100 souls lost now, could be up to 200.
- @coljac: #bushfires Folks have nixed the stay-and-defend fire plan, but no risk atm. [Cousin] Alan+wife+son+friend burned in Gormandale.
- @tellyworth: Reminder: cash donations are by far the most helpful things right now. Goods take time and resources to move. Cash is instant.

---

* Gary Kemble, "Social Media Explodes in Wake of Deadly Bushfires," *ABC News Online*, http://www.abc.net.au/news/stories/2009/02/09/2486463.htm, posted 3:52 PM AEDT, February 9, 2009.

- @keithdon: Take a tour of what was beautiful little Marysville (Google Street View)—Now burnt completely. (http://bit.ly/1FbhnU)[*]

The Centers for Disease Control and Prevention (CDC) felt the heat of the social media spotlight earlier in 2009 when the swine flu first hit Mexico. The CDC had no choice but to intervene on Twitter when the number of people tweeting about H1N1 had reached over 10,000 per hour. (Imagine that volume of calls to a call center!) People were tweeting misinformation, saying that it was really germ warfare or that eating pork would give you the flu. The CDC corrected the misinformation, tweeting frequently with links to advisories and about the need "to cover your nose and mouth when you cough and sneeze" (April 30, 2009). (At the time of this writing, the CDC had more than 1.2 million followers.)

As the saying goes, "Where there's a will there's a way," and the technology we have today enables that "will," empowering people to express themselves like never before.

The lesson in Stage Two is to understand the power (not necessarily the wisdom) of the crowds in SocialMediaLand. Ignore them at your peril; better still, court them, find your fans, your unauthorized spokespeople, and give them a voice. Connect with your unofficial spokespeople—you will need them when the going gets tough.

The bottom line is that if you have prepared well and managed this stage well, you can jump straight to Stage Four and dodge the dreaded mudslinging in Stage Three.

STAGE TWO CHARACTERISTICS

What might be happening?

- Third parties analyze the crisis.
- The media ask hypothetical questions and seek someone to blame.
- Everyone is judging you.
- "Unofficial spokespeople" talk and comment.
- The crisis has gone viral, spreading like wildfire around the Internet via YouTube.
- Local media sites provide updates from any local resident with an Internet connection and information to share.

---

[*] Gary Kemble, "Social Media Explodes in Wake of Deadly Bushfires," *ABC News Online*, http://www.abc.net.au/news/stories/2009/02/09/2486463.htm, posted 3:52 PM AEDT, February 9, 2009.

- Rallying escalates on social media sites like Facebook and Twitter; pictures are posted on Flickr and video on YouTube.
- People everywhere vote and bookmark on sites like Digg.
- Intense personal and local stories appear on the hyperlocal news sites.
- Discussions and forums begin to appear on sites like LinkedIn.
- Hashtags (# assigned to your crisis) are appearing on Twitter.
- Comparisons to other crises, particularly if they were associated with your organization or industry (witness Exxon versus BP).

Expect the media to:

- *Look for answers* to—*How?* and *Why?*
- *Seek context*—The "big picture," and wider implications.
- *Analyze*—How you're handling the situation.
- *Seek eyewitness reports*—From citizen–journalists.
- *Compare your crisis*—With similar situations and crises in newspaper features, on talk radio, on current affairs TV, on blogs, on Twitter, and in Facebook (anti-)Fan clubs.
- *Drive current affairs interest*—On talk radio.
- *Scrutinize your response.*
- *Provide more background*—On the incident; newspapers may do special features. Focus on the "victim."
- *Fill the backstory.*
- *Call in the "experts"*—Particularly on CNN and other big cable networks.

What to do:

- Put the incident in your own context, provide the "big picture," and have a key message to address your response, policy, or procedure.
- Keep the media updated on the actions you have taken and plan to take. Make sure to inform the media about your "quick wins" (for example, what you have achieved, actions/examples).
- Debrief with those involved in Stage One.
- Assess spokespeople; have them rehearse; think about the impressions you want to create. What fits with the values of your mission statement?
- Assess messages and match them to where the major concern is—has it changed?
- Manage emotion and outrage, and forecast the questions people want answered—it is very important that you pick the panic.

- Think about media logistics and management (e.g., food, coffee, and parking) if the media conference is onsite.
- Anticipate what else (the self-appointed critics and dial-a-quotes) the media might dig up.
- Activate your ghost Web site and dark groups.
- Monitor the Internet, including key bloggers, Twitter, YouTube, and other key social media, *very closely*.
- Monitor employee feelings and attitudes, and address major concerns very quickly. Employees talk, so inform them regularly.
- Activate friends and allies. Watch reactions of foes.
- Brief and communicate regularly with partners and key influencers.
- Engage key social media.

10

Stage Three—Finger-Pointing Stage = Blame Game

Blame—The stage you want to avoid at all costs.

> In back-to-back Senate inquiries, lawmakers chastised executives of the three companies at the heart of the massive oil spill over attempts to shift the blame to each other. And they were asked to explain why better preparations had not been made to head off the accident.
> ... Liability, blame, fault—put it over here.... And despite his acknowledgment of responsibility, each company defended its own operations and raised questions about its partners in the project gone awry.[*]

The Finger-Pointing Stage—everyone has an opinion about you, your product, your organization, your industry, even your country (ask Iran)—lots of "woulda, coulda, shoulda."

Stage Three is all about blame, with the key question focused on *why*. The spotlight is more like a floodlight. Your crisis is beamed everywhere. Witness Domino's; the family, close friends, and associates of the late Michael Jackson; the Gulf of Mexico oil spill.

Research confirms this. Once the immediacy of the crisis is over, people want to know who is to blame, who has responsibility for *the mess*.

The "told-you-so" syndrome has taken over. Experts are criticizing you, and people are citing decades-old research or reports that point to

---

[*] "Blame Game: Executives Grilled on Iil Spill, 'Cascade of Failures,'" Associated Press, *Daily Republic*, May 12, 2010, p. B06.

dangers lurking in your organization, for example, the failure to report the problem or the faulty valve, or a disgruntled employee blowing the whistle on *60 Minutes* or on WikiLeaks. Influential bloggers furiously voice opinions, Twitter is out of control, and Facebook has fan clubs galore. Wikipedia has featured updates and there will be forums buzzing with your crisis on LinkedIn. Every "expert" has an opinion and the means to express it.

Your values are on display. Tiger Woods found out just how much we cared about his dirty little secrets and double life after he had so carefully crafted his pristine family image. Time will tell whether his golf game will ever be the same. His squeaky-clean image has been tarnished forever.

The sting of social media has been felt by many, including the Copenhagen Metro (the Metro), whose judgment about a film contest backfired. I am indebted to Jonas Nielsen of Mindjumpers, a Danish-based public relations and marketing agency for Case Study 10.1.

CASE STUDY 10.1[*]
Dilemma of a Danish Metro System

Each year, the Metro sponsors a short film contest to recognize the work of artists in the community. The winning film, determined by popular vote, is shown on screens in Metro stations throughout Copenhagen.

In 2009, voters chose Mette Carla T. Albrectsen's film, *XY Anatomy of a Boy*. But the Metro rejected the film because it was erotic in nature and included two men kissing. It justified its decision, saying, "You could say that we are prudes, but we want to protect a minority that would be offended. The Metro is for everybody…"

This statement sparked an online controversy. Protesters formed a Facebook group to fight the "homophobia of the Metro." Two thousand members posted pictures, discussed the issue, and wrote letters to politicians.

Three days later the Metro reversed its decision and posted this message on the Facebook group ("To Battle against the Homophobia of the Metro") page:

As a result of your passionate outcry the Metro Company is doubting whether we made the right decision to exclude the film back in March.

---

[*] Statement given by Kåre Møller from The Metro Company, MetroExpress (Copenhagen, Denmark), July 13, 2009. (Provided by Mindjumpers, www.mindjumpers.com, with permission.)

We are therefore now working on showing all ten films—including the two containing erotic undertones—on our stations. We will create a blog at www.m.dk on which the public is free to discuss whether the films are suitable for the public space. This will probably attract more outcry, but we've decided to make the discussion public. As mentioned it is still work in progress, but I thought you should be the first to know.

Best regards
Stine The Metro Company

The Facebook group members received the Metro Company's statement positively:

Well communicated by Stine Christmas Nielsen! And a good example of how a Facebook group can be used to communicate a debate directly on the same level from both sides.

We won! They will show the film! Well done and congratulations to all the people that have fought for it.

It's a fantastic piece of work you've done. It's good on all levels; for the culture and for our little country. But it's scary that Denmark is still on a Neanderthal level regarding some matters!

The mayor of Copenhagen also appreciated Metro's decision by sending them a letter of thanks.

The crisis may have ended well for Metro, but 9 times out of 10, if you stick your head out in this stage—typically 72 hours after the incident first happened (or was first reported)—God help you; you will be crucified by the media. You need to speak early and often.

The lesson in Stage Three is to manage Stage Two well—very well! Never wait until you have the right information to speak or think that your brand can withstand the public scrutiny. Reality is that it can't.

STAGE THREE CHARACTERISTICS

What might be happening?

- Fingers are pointed (from inside and outside).
- "I told you so" and "We knew it" are factors.
- Other people attach themselves to the crisis.
- There is internal blame; who is responsible?

- Hits on YouTube are in the millions.
- Antifan clubs have formed on Facebook.
- There is a frenzy of opinion on Twitter, which just may have crashed!
- Blog traffic has increased significantly.
- Search engine optimization (SEO) has increased the visibility of the crisis.
- Obscure reports surface.
- Experts come out of the woodwork.
- Victims tell their story on *60 Minutes*.
- Voting is high on Digg.
- Millions of hits on YouTube.
- Multiple #'s on Twitter
- Visitors galore view your Web site.
- You are global news.
- Forum discussions abound on LinkedIn.
- Every @dick, @tom, and @harry is commenting.
- Updates are posted on Wikipedia.
- Leaks and whistle-blowing.
- You are the gossip in the supermarket, around the water cooler, at dinner parties.
- You are the butt of jokes and the focus of newspaper cartoons (Figure 10.1).

Expect the media to:

- *Seek*—Third-party comments from the "experts."
- *Look*—For scapegoats.
- *Pit parties*—Against each other.
- *Compare*—Similar situations and crises (in-depth).
- *Expect answers.*
- *Ask questions*—About compensation.
- *Reference columns*—From analysts, academics, and social and political commentators.
- *Write op-eds and blogs.*
- *Contribute*—To the social media frenzy.
- *Increase visibility*—Of the crisis through SEO.
- *Cast your organization*—As a villain capable of vast shocking and shameful acts.
- *Ridicule*—You in cartoons.

FIGURE 10.1   This cartoon is typical of Stage Three, or when the crisis has become widespread. (From the *Daily Republic*, October 28, 2009, p. 13. Reprinted with permission of the artist, Gary Markstein.)

What to do:

- Keep your dirty laundry private, and avoid blame and mudslinging matches. (BP, Transocean, and Halliburton could have taken this advice to heart.)
- Highlight "quick wins," for example, what have you achieved?
- Show you're talking to critics, if it is appropriate and relevant to your incident.
- Remain available to the media and other stakeholders, and comment appropriately, often, and consistently.
- Reassess spokespeople, for example, is it time to roll out the big guns?
- Be careful to avoid others' disorder—only join if it is strategically important or appropriate.
- Continue to monitor the media aggressively, but avoid letting the media and other commentators drive your strategy.
- Respond appropriately to talk of threats and legal action.
- Monitor and engage social media as needed.

- Keep your Web site active, engaged, and up-to-date.
- Broadcast your side of the story on YouTube—short statements by key spokespeople.

CASE STUDY 10.2
"Danish Mother Seeking": Marketing Innovation
Turned Communication Catastrophe

An online viral marketing campaign can become a global phenomenon. It can also become a communication nightmare—at the speed of a mouse click. This case illustrates the disastrous consequences that can occur if marketing tactics are not matched with a sound issues-management strategy, and what to do when a "creative" campaign goes wrong.

On September 11, 2009, a homemade video titled "Danish Mother Seeking" aired on YouTube. Holding her baby, a young Danish woman named Karen tells the story of having a one-night stand with a foreign tourist, which led to the birth of her child nine months later. Unable to remember the man's name or nationality, Karen was spreading her story online in hopes of finding her son's father.

Immediately, Karen became viral wildfire. Viewers sympathized with her and shared her story across the Web. But within hours, people began to question the video's legitimacy. Led by social media agency Mindjumpers, the blogosphere burst with debate and spoofs of the video. Bloggers predicted that backlash would occur once viewers realized that the story was a stunt. "Looking at the amount of views ... the campaign has been a huge success. It has created a lot of awareness. But the awareness has been created under false pretenses ... and it will probably end up pushing people away from whichever brand or product is behind it," said Mindjumpers Managing Partner Jonas Klit Nielsen on a September 13, 2009, blog entry.

Traditional media also began swarming with speculation. "Karen" was soon identified as little-known actress Ditte Arnth. On the evening of September 13, Danish television station TV2 reported that the video was in fact illegitimate: It was a viral campaign planned by the government-run tourist agency VisitDenmark.

The video and its creators, advertising agency Grey Copenhagen, were chastised. Danish tabloid *Ekstra Bladet* called the campaign "grotesque" and a "waste of taxpayers' money." VisitDenmark and Grey stood behind the campaign at first, extolling it as both well intentioned and successful. Amazingly, VisitDenmark Chief Executive Officer Dorte Kiilerich told TV2, "This is a good, sweet, and really harmless story, and it is not unusual to sell false stories when you communicate.'" But after continued criticism, VisitDenmark pulled the video and issued an apology statement, and Kiilerich resigned. No wonder!

The case illustrates five key lessons to remember when planning viral campaigns:

Anticipate fallout—Today's social media consumers are cynical. And smart. The video, while creative, was bound for controversy, questioning, and eventually being ousted. Before launching a campaign, take a step back and anticipate what might go wrong and have a Plan B! There are typically unintended consequences for most big events.

Consistently monitor—With traditional media, marketers must often wait weeks to assess public response. But using Web 2.0, this process is reduced to hours—if not minutes—and you must be alert from the moment an online campaign is launched. It is unclear when VisitDenmark began monitoring, but if they had done so early on, it could have caught the backlash before its full-blown stage.

Be prepared … 24/7—The Web doesn't close when the office does. Much of the media coverage surrounding "Danish Mother Seeking" occurred on a Saturday. Particularly in the digital world, your crisis plan and team need to be prepared—and on standby—24/7.

Choose your advisors carefully—When the video's creators were revealed, Grey advised VisitDenmark to stand behind its campaign. Why? Because as its creators, they had far too much to lose by denouncing it. Your advertising agency will protect its work, *not* your reputation. It is vital to bring advisors to the table who are savvy in both crisis communication and social media. At the same time, you must stay true to the values of your own organization, not those of another agency.

Acknowledge wrongdoing—The biggest lesson of all encompasses digital and traditional crises alike. Do not be afraid to address the situation and apologize to your audiences—immediately. Online, trust and transparency are even more requisite than in traditional communication.

(I am grateful to Jonas Klit Nielsen, Managing Partner, Mindjumpers, for this case study, www.mindjumpers.com.)

---

* Dorte Kiilerich, *TV2 News*, www.news.tv2.dk, September 13, 2009 (as cited on YouTube, "Hunt for Father a Fake," *The Copenhagen Post Online*, posted September 14, 2009).

11

Stage Four—Resolution and Fallout

What happens in Vegas stays on Google. (Every action counts.)*

Stage Four: The spotlight now dims, but can easily be turned to full glare again if you slip up or something similar happens in your industry. Your crisis is perpetually in print, on Google, in Wikipedia—searchable and discoverable. Your sin will be for everyone to see forever—you cannot take it back.

Hurricane Katrina will forever be, well, until something bigger or worse happens, the standard against which we judge government responses, poor planning, and Category 4 hurricanes.

Typically, this stage marks the end of the crisis; there is some resolution. There might be a funeral, an inquest, a government inquiry, or a senate hearing. Your product goes back on the shelf, workers go back to the plant, victims return to their homes.

There is also a need to mark the end of a crisis, and today that could be a short tweet, a thank you to all who helped, or a posting on the Web site.

A decade ago, Arnott's, a food maker in Australia and subsidiary of Campbell Soup Company, was subject to an extortion attempt. The extortionist claimed that packets of Arnott's Monte Carlo biscuits had been

---

* Scott Monty, Head of Social Media for the Ford Motor Company, "The Microphone Is Always On," The Social Media Marketing Blog, www.scottmonty.com, June 12, 1009. (Note: First quoted in a presentation to Brand Camp University, October 2009.)

75

poisoned. Arnott's withdrew its entire product from sale, costing them millions. When the product finally went back on the shelf, they launched a nationwide TV advertising campaign. It was produced in the style of a news story featuring former *60 Minutes* reporter Ian Leslie announcing, with a strong call to action: "We're back; please support us."

Arnott's "resolution" story was groundbreaking in Australia and became the standard procedure for such product recalls. Several Australian companies copied the tactic, such as Herons, Nudie, and the manufacturers of Panadol, an over-the-counter pain relief medication.

The other critical component in this stage is fallout. The Enron verdict in May 2006 is a good example. Needless to say, there was extensive coverage on the Enron verdict, and it all featured some discussion on corporate ethics, the "cooking of the books," and the "blame-game" testimony of former Chairman and Founder Ken Lay and former Chief Executive Officer Jeffrey Skilling. All the coverage was reported in the context of what first happened—the swindling of billions. The Enron collapse became immortalized with the release of a play on Broadway in April 2010. There are also extensive references in what has become our social encyclopedia, Wikipedia.

Fallout and resolution coverage are always reported in the context of what first happened, so be prepared to have your name splashed across the pages on Twitter, in that YouTube video, which will be viewed again and again, and in bloggerville.

The key question in Stage Four is: *What are you going to do to ensure that this will never happen again?*

BP announced in May 2010 that "[It] will never again try to produce oil through a blown-out well that's been gushing into the Gulf of Mexico for nearly a month."[*]

That is one hell of a lesson learned!

The opportunity is to highlight what you have learned and what you have done or are doing to fix the problem. Also, make sure your own story is told in places where you reach your priority audiences directly, as Domino's Pizza did with President Patrick Doyle posting a message on YouTube.

Domino's was criticized for taking too long to respond after two rogue employees posted YouTube videos of themselves engaging in some vile public health violations. The videos went viral and were seen by millions. The pranksters were identified by YouTube viewers, who alerted Domino's officials, and the two pranksters were promptly arrested.

---

[*] Associated Press, *WKRG News*, www.WKRG.com, posted 2:50 PM, May 17, 2009.

But they did respond with a video featuring Doyle saying the store where the videos were shot had been closed and sanitized, and that the company will be conducting a review of hiring practices "to make sure that people like this don't make it into our stores."* (It was later revealed that one of the pranksters was a registered sex offender.)

The fallout from the Gulf of Mexico oil spill will probably be felt and certainly remembered for years. Several states were talking about bans (at the time of writing, California had taken all offshore oil drilling off the books), and more importantly, the U.S. government had declared a moratorium on deepwater offshore oil drilling. Federal oversight of offshore drilling will most certainly be revamped. At the time of writing, U.S. President Barack Obama banned new drilling in deep coastal waters, blocked drilling in Arctic waters, and canceled the long-planned sale of leases.

And inevitably heads will fall; there will be resignations (two at the time of writing).

> The federal official overseeing offshore drilling announced his departure Monday (May 17, 2010) in fallout from the Gulf oil spill and criticism that federal regulators have been too cozy with industry.... Chris Oynes ... has come under criticism for being too close to the industry.[†]

The resolution stage may also be marked by a government inquiry of some kind—as we saw with the Gulf oil spill when Obama announced an independent presidential commission to investigate it. The president slammed the three oil companies linked to the wrecked BP-leased, Deepwater Horizon rig—BP, Transocean, and Halliburton—for seeking to pass the blame, denouncing what he called a "ridiculous spectacle"[‡] by their top officials during congressional hearings.

AFP reported:

> A visibly angry President on Friday hit out at oil companies for trying to avoid blame over a massive slick, and vowed an all-out effort to stop the leak pouring into the Gulf of Mexico.

---

* YouTube, cited on Huffington Post, http://www.huffingtonpost.com/2009/04/16/dominos-disgusting-youtube_n_187650.html), posted 9:26 AM, April 16, 2010. (Note: This video has since been removed from YouTube.)

† Associated Press, Washington DC, *USA Today*, www.usatoday.com, posted 7:50 PM, May 17, 2010.

‡ Bloomberg, *Business Week*, www.businessweek.com, posted May 15, 2010.

'I will not tolerate more finger-pointing or irresponsibility. The people of the Gulf Coast need our help,' Mr. Obama said, as he also unveiled a review of the environmental safeguards to be put in place for oil and gas exploration.*

This is not the government input one wants in a crisis.

STAGE FOUR CHARACTERISTICS

What might be happening?

- Concluding events such as inquiries, inquests, reports, funerals, police investigations, new appointments, similar incidents, and anniversaries take place.
- The community relives emotions and memories are revived.
- Social media continue the chatter and debate on your crisis.

Expect the media to:

- *Look*—For inconsistencies between what was said during the crisis and after the crisis.
- *Expect answers*—On compensation.
- *Highlight*—Case studies on how lives were affected.
- *Expect*—Solutions and resolutions.
- *Find*—The person who will accept responsibility and provide assurances on how this will not be allowed to happen again.
- *Look*—For what has changed since the crisis began.
- *Seek*—Evidence that it is over.

What to do:

- Maintain consistent messages.
- Demonstrate solutions and resolutions.
- Work on rebuilding relationships, particularly with social networks where you have made connections and critics. *Building an understanding of social media dynamics is critical,* so that when disaster does strike again, you are in a position to make the most of the possibilities.
- Manage any residual emotion and continue to demonstrate appropriate empathy and concern toward the victims.

---

* AFP, *Sydney Morning Herald*, www.smh.com.au, posted May 18, 2010.

- Provide as many facts and information about what you learned and achieved as possible.
- Review the crisis.
- Keep monitoring the media and keep a *very close eye on the Internet.*
- Mark closure with a ceremony, celebration, or thank-you gesture.

SECTION II SUMMARY

Throughout all the stages, remember that *trust is the new black*. You are operating in an environment of low credibility, particularly if you are in the financial services sector. We have simply lost our trust in big business, in government—there have simply been too many scandals.

Corporate communication is not necessarily seen as a credible source either.

As Euan Semple, a freelance Web consultant, says, "People will invariably turn to the sources of information that they trust the most (in a crisis) and increasingly this may not be the official sources of information."*

The onus is on any communicator to be perceived as trustworthy. It is no good being upset that people do not believe you after the fact; you have to do whatever it takes to make it more likely that they will believe you when it matters.

It is also important for anyone dealing with disasters or planning for the next crisis to understand the media report in distinct, predictable phases. Proper planning will consider these stages and will call for education and training so that the relevant teams understand their roles and responsibilities in a crisis. Proper planning will also see that the teams are well prepared through annual drills and exercises. The stage approach also helps you predict what resources will be needed when and what messages will be required when. In short, these four stages will help you plan and mitigate better.

---

* "Why Crisis Planning Is Now Incomplete without Social Media," Internal Communications Hub Blog, www.internalcommshub.com, November 2009.

Section III

Spokespeople—Speed Matters and Perception Is Everything

People are much quicker at spotting inconsistencies when times are tough. CEOs should never underestimate that every twitch of their facial expression is interpreted. When people are looking at leaders, they are constantly trying to interpret them in ways that are often subliminal.[*]

— *Martin Newman*

OVERVIEW

The choice of spokespeople in a crisis is critical. How they communicate can be a break-it-or-make-it moment—for them, for the organization, for the brand.

The 2010 Edelman Trust Barometer, admittedly a survey of well-informed and educated people, showed that transparency and trust are all important. Although up from the previous year, the chief executive officer (CEO) ranking was still low. The credibility factor for CEOs was

---

[*] Martin Newman, "Not Shaken But Stirred," Report for The Company Agency, London, November 2008.

40 percent, with government officials ranking even lower, at 35 percent. Nongovernmental organizations interestingly were the most trusted institutions. Media dropped again in its credibility stakes—over the last three years, trust in media has fallen from 48 to 45 percent.

These informed stakeholders value guidance from credentialed experts over a "person like me," which, according to the Barometer, lost considerable ground as a credible voice of information for a company. To paraphrase the Edelman report, this finding begs the question of real trust in social media.*

Academics and experts, and financial or industry analysts, are the most trusted spokespeople for a company, according to the survey—definitely food for thought as you consider your choice of spokespeople. Remember the four stages, too.

Credibility is an important factor, but so is speed of response when choosing spokespeople. The expectations are very high that we will get convincing answers and get them quickly; anecdotal evidence suggests about 15 minutes. Wisdom tells us that releasing a statement in the first hour of something *big* happening is good practice. Common sense tells us to act quickly.

Senior executives and CEOs in particular often assume they will be judged solely by what they *do* in a crisis. What they say, and especially how they say it, is presumed to carry less weight. *Wrong!* As researchers at the Human Dynamics Group, Massachusetts Institute of Technology's Tech Media Lab, and Xerox and Intel research centers have shown, and as executive coach Aileen Pincus (President of The Pincus Group) so rightly says, "That's an assumption that's as widespread as it is inaccurate."†

Impressions do matter, and you have only nanoseconds to get that all important buy-in. Research shows that it takes just a staggering 115 milliseconds for us to make a judgment based on body language. "Phony expressions usually do not fool us," says Professor Beatrice de Gelder, a cognitive neuroscientist at Tilburg University in The Netherlands and Harvard Medical School.‡

---

* Edelman Trust Barometer, 2010.

† Aileen Pincus, "Presentation Skill and the CEO: Why the Chief Explanations Officer Has to Get It Right," The Pincus Group, http://www.thepincusgroup.com/art28.html. (Retrieved October 2009.)

‡ Hanneke K. M. Meeren, Corné C. R. J. van Heijnsbergen, and Beatrice de Gelder, "Rapid Perceptual Integration of Facial Expression and Emotional Body Language," *Proceedings of the National Academy of Sciences of the United States of America (PNAS)*, Vol. 102, No. 45, November 8, 2005, pp. 16518–16523.

Thanks to another professor, Albert Mehrabian, currently professor emeritus of psychology at University of California, Los Angeles (UCLA), we have known for years the impact body language has on how a message is received in a face-to-face situation. A whopping 93 percent is based on how you look and sound, leaving only 7 percent for words.

Carol Kinsey Goman, author of *The Nonverbal Advantage: Secrets and Science of Body Language at Work*, concurs. She says: "When a spokesperson is engaged in face-to-face encounters the audience is processing a continual cascade of nonverbal cues that they use as the basis for evaluating trust and credibility."[*]

Listeners and viewers of TV interviews, live breaking-news media conferences on CNN, and YouTube videos may not be able to verbalize why they react in a certain way based on what one does or does not do with his or her body. However, the instantaneous response works like a silent alarm system and affects how you and your organization are perceived.

The implication is clear—impressions do matter. As the saying goes, perception really is reality.

Now, combine these sobering statistics with the social media revolution and the universal lack of trust in corporations and their leaders among the public. The need for authenticity and transparency has never been so important.

No wonder why choosing a spokesperson is so perplexing for many organizations. Who, when, and why? Many assume that it must be the top dog, the CEO, the chairman, or the president. Not always so.

What is clear, however, is that powerful communication by powerful communicators and leaders is incredibly important in a crisis. As crisis communication expert Gerard Braud says: "Powerful communication before a crisis and *rapid communication* during a crisis have the ability to move people out of harm's way, save lives and protect reputations."[†] It is the precrisis communication that lays the foundation for that trust during a crisis.

---

[*] Carol Kinsey Goman, "What You Don't Say: The Power of Nonverbal Communication," *CW Bulletin* (International Association of Business Communicators [IABC]), http://www.iabc.com/cwb/archive/2009/1109/KinseyGoman.htm, November 2009.

[†] Gerard Braud, "What Spokespeople Should Say and Do in a Crisis," Spokesperson Training, International Association of Business Communicators (IABC), *CW Bulletin*, Vol. 7, No. 11, (http://www.iabc.com/cwb/archive/2009/1109/Braud.htmwww.iabc.com), November 2009.

In this section, we will explore:

- The spokesperson conundrum.
- How to prepare for the "new normal" of speed and community engagement.
- Who should speak, and when.
- The role of the frontline.
- Whether the CEO speaks and how.
- The principles of engaging the head and the heart.
- Developing your communication style.
- Policy guidelines for social media.

12

Who?

To help you decide whom to choose as the most appropriate spokesperson, let the stages guide you. Base your decision on the following:

- What stage of the crisis you are in?
- The seriousness of the incident.
- The values your organization espouses.
- The status of your organization's reputation in the affected market, community, state, and/or country.

Oh, and did I say how very important it is to choose a spokesperson who is the most believable, the most genuine, and the most knowledgeable, particularly in this age of transparency and authenticity?

If you're in Stage One or early Stage Two, then it is most likely going to be an operational spokesperson. And, most likely that initial response is going to be online, within minutes of something happening. That may be a tweet to your followers, a text message to your key media contacts, or a quick post to the company blog. Remember that this notification will be interpreted and quoted coming from an official company spokesperson, so think carefully about just who is the official online spokesperson for Stage One and beyond.

The time expectation is phenomenal. *San Jose Mercury* business columnist Chris O'Brien, whom I interviewed for this book, was watching closely when Google's Gmail crashed in August 2009. He noticed that the online community was impatient, expecting, even demanding, that Google say something about what they were doing to fix the problem. The time frame of expectation, O'Brien says, was within *10 to 15 minutes* of the e-mail system going down. Fast is the new normal.

My advice is that you develop a spokesperson policy that dictates who should be the spokesperson or the spokespeople for different types of crises, and not only for each stage of a crisis, but who will have authority in SocialMediaLand. It may seem like common sense, but you would be surprised by the lack of such basics in crisis media communication preparation and planning.

For example, a local manager handles what is identified as the "incident," a senior manager jumps in and manages early Stage Two, supported by operations and the CEO/chairman, depending on the seriousness and scale of the crisis. It could be that the chairman is only rolled out for the tricky Stage Three interviews. You may also decide that you will always involve the most senior person in the company after Stage One and that they will be available no matter where the crisis is. Skype and cell video are acceptable to many of the mainstream media today.

You will need to apply some common sense in selecting your spokesperson, but as a guide, you will need to match the situation and message to the spokesperson. For example, the CEO will want to be seen as taking responsibility to make things right, apologize, express empathy for the victims, and praise heroes. Then it can be handed over to an expert or someone from operations to explain *how* and *what* they are doing to fix the problem.

Social media are appropriate for all the stages. Your official tweeter should tweet and the CEO should blog throughout the entire crisis. Make sure that a relevant Facebook page is up and running within hours, continuing long after the crisis is resolved.

Whatever you do, make it fast—lives and reputations could be at stake. You simply cannot afford to wait until you know everything. Crisis communication expert Gerard Braud says that it is a fatal flaw to delay: "Executives should be advised that saying a little is better than saying nothing, because saying nothing makes you look incompetent and oblivious to the severity of the situation, or like you are hiding something."[*]

---

[*] Gerard Braud, "What Spokespeople Should Say and Do in a Crisis," Spokesperson Training, International Association of Business Communicators (IABC), *CW Bulletin*, Vol. 7, No. 11, (http://www.iabc.com/cwb/archive/2009/1109/Braud.htmwww.iabc.com), November 2009.

GOLDEN RULES

1. Credibility is king.
2. There is a need for honest and frequent communication.
3. There is no point engaging with online communities unless you are candid and transparent about your actions.
4. You must be true to your values as an organization.
5. You must demonstrate compassion for those affected by your crisis.

Those are the guiding principles in training, coaching, and prepping your spokespeople to manage a crisis. Can you tick off the following boxes for your designated spokespeople? If not, then think again.

- ☐ Authentic and convincing in what they say.
- ☐ Keep emotions under control.
- ☐ Speak persuasively.
- ☐ Think fast and formulate clear, succinct answers.
- ☐ Work under intense pressure.
- ☐ Handle the anxiety of standing before cameras.
- ☐ Command a high level of respect.
- ☐ Talk in simple, everyday, jargon-free language.
- ☐ Use positive, active language rather than default to negative, toxic language.
- ☐ Know their stuff and exude confidence.
- ☐ Understand the needs of the media and are media-trained.
- ☐ Are prepared to rehearse and speak to a "script."
- ☐ Are truth tellers.

COMMUNICATION STYLE

In a crisis, your communication style is important, too. You need to work with your key spokespeople to develop the kind of communication style that reflects the image you want to project and the values you want to protect in a crisis.

For example, if you are a "suited" kind of business, you need to adhere to that image in a crisis. To suddenly assume a goofy image in a crisis would raise more questions and attention. It was appropriate, for example, when Amazon CEO Jeff Bezos posted his views about Amazon's takeover of Zappos on YouTube. While not a crisis, it seems logical that Bezos went online with the announcement. After all, Amazon is the master of online product distribution and that strategy was in line with their image.

Zappos CEO Tony Hsieh sent a detailed e-mail regarding the $800 million deal to employees, outlining key points and proactively addressing anticipated questions. He subsequently posted the contents of the e-mail on the company's internal blog.

While opinion was strongly divided in the communication community over the approaches taken by the CEOs to announce the acquisition, both appeared true to their individual company's culture. As one reader of *Ragan's Daily Headlines* pointed out, "… Tony and Zappos are very unique, if you have ever heard him give a presentation before, you'd know that this type of over-communication is part of their culture and how they like it."[*]

As both Bezos and Hsieh demonstrated, leaders with an in-depth history and knowledge can effectively share that confidence through anecdotes and personal experiences, more effectively than graphs could ever do. Even with controversy concerning their approaches, they had conviction that the deal was a good one. Such confidence, together with compassion, is critical in a crisis.

Then you have the WTF, in-your-face style of Yahoo! CEO Carol Bartz, who doesn't mince her words—says everything from "Google needs to grow a new Yahoo! every year" to dropping the F-bomb in interviews.

In May 2010, she caused quite a stir while on stage at TechCrunch's Disrupt Conference, when she told Michael Arrington from TechCrunch to "F-off" in an interview.[†] The expletive—not one that I would ever encourage my clients to use—came shortly after Arrington challenged Bartz's accomplishments at Yahoo! by comparing them to Steve Jobs at Apple.

> And it probably takes a long time to even convince yourself what the hell to do. I don't want to hear any crap … about something magical that the fine people of Yahoo! are supposed to do in this short time so fuck off.... That one I meant.[‡]

---

[*] Dan Kolbet comments on: Lindsay Allen, *Ragan's Daily Headlines*, www.ragan.com/SocialMedia/Articles/Communicators_dissect_Amazon_Zappos_CEOs_on_style_36687.aspx, July 28, 2009.

[†] Carol Bartz (CEO, Yahoo!) during an on-stage interview at the TechCrunch Disrupt Conference, New York City, May 2010.

[‡] Ibid.

Much guffaws from the audience. And much support online. One tweet summed it up: "Words cannot express how much I love watching Carol Bartz speak. Her sass is refreshing and lovely."*

Bartz is known for being outspoken, blunt, and often R-rated with her language. That is her style. And she's not the only one to make headlines for unabashed cursing. Some major players like Microsoft CEO Steve Ballmer, Facebook's Mark Zuckerberg, and even the vice president of the United States are all guilty of spouting off this most unholy of swear words in public places.

Refreshing? Not the expletive, but the lack of spin, corporate and marketing speak—yes! Authentic and transparent, you bet. Empathetic and compassionate in a crisis—that remains to be seen.

So, style does matter as much as substance. Make sure in a crisis that you have thoroughly inoculated your spokespeople and you can predict what they may or may not do or say. The reputation and share price are on the line, maybe a job or two, or bigger still, lives and the license to operate.

---

* *Twitter* post by: Brooke Hammerling, May 2010.

13

To CEO or Not?

An oft asked question is whether the chief executive officer (CEO) should be the spokesperson. That depends! Are they the weak link in the communication? How well do they fare in that 115-millisecond test? Are they trained and drilled? Have they been put to the test? Do they have the answers to those tricky questions? Do they need to be at "the scene of the crime?"

Frequently, the CEO knows less about the details, but his or her physical presence sends two powerful messages: *I care and I am accountable.*

If your crisis is truly a *show-stopping* event and the company's reputation is clearly on the line (e.g., there have been multiple deaths, the scale of the crisis is huge—think *Exxon Valdez*, 9/11, the oil spill in the iconic Sydney Harbor, the shootings at Fort Hood (see Box 13.1), and the monumental BP oil spill in the Gulf of Mexico), then it is imperative that the head of the organization is at the scene, getting his hands dirty.

Can we imagine President Bush not speaking after the horrific attacks on America on September 11, 2001? Remember the absence of the Exxon CEO when oil spilled in Alaska in 1989, and thousands of animals died?

In contrast, BP had its most senior spokespeople on the scene after the March 2005 deadly explosion that killed 15 workers and injured more than 100. Both BP Chairman, Lord John Browne, who immediately flew to Texas from London; and the U.S. head were present. Both spoke. Men had died. While BP has been heavily criticized for their role in the disastrous Gulf oil spill, they were, nonetheless, swift in getting key spokespeople on the ground. What would their silence have said?

BOX 13.1   FORT HOOD: SENIOR LEADERS TAKE CHARGE

As we would expect from the U.S. military, they acted immediately, taking command of their crisis communication on November 5, 2009, when an Army psychiatrist opened fire on fellow soldiers, killing 12 people and wounding at least 31. The Army's reputation was on the line after the "deadliest" mass shootings at a U.S. military base in history. Supposedly, Army personnel were safe on their own base, especially from someone working in mental health. Who could be trusted?

The U.S. military designated several high-ranking personnel to be spokespeople. They all spoke appropriately for their roles and responsibilities, as well as the stages; for example, the most senior people on the base, Fort Hood Commander Lt. Gen. Robert Cone and Deputy Commander Col. John Rossi, had clear roles at different stages. Lt. Gen. Cone held the first press conference—early Stage Two, which was appropriate as he was the most senior person on the ground and of a high ranking. Col. Rossi took on the spokesperson role, after the heavy brass spoke, with updates on what they were doing operationally—again appropriate to role and stage. They were strong communicators who were clearly well trained, well drilled, and well prepared.

But, as you would expect with the scale and impact of that crisis, there were many other strong, influential voices of authority ranging from President Obama, to the governor of Texas, to Texas Senator Kay Bailey Hutchison. Army Chief of Staff Gen. George Casey, Jr., and Army Secretary John McHugh also traveled to Fort Hood and provided statements at news conferences.

Clearly, Stages Two and Three call for senior, well-trained, and well-rehearsed spokespeople who can speak not only with authority but also with a great deal of empathy as we clearly saw demonstrated by President of the International Olympic Committee (IOC) Jacques Rogge, speaking after the tragic death of Georgian luge athlete Nodar Kumaritashvili during the final training session for the 2010 Winter Olympics. Visibly and genuinely upset, Rogge took off his glasses and rubbed his eyes before speaking to the media, saying, "Sorry, it's a bit difficult to remain composed." He was then widely quoted saying:

This is indeed a sad day. I have no words to say how we feel. We are in deep mourning. The whole Olympic family is struck by this tragedy, which clearly casts a shadow over these games.[*]

There is much on the line when you are at Stage Two and particularly at Stage Three, the finger-pointing and blame stage, so choose well, and have that spokesperson well trained and well drilled.

TO CEO OR NOT?

If you can answer with great confidence the following, then you've chosen the appropriate spokesperson:

- Given the situation, what is the overall impression we want to create?
- Is our spokesperson appropriate to the scenario?
- Does our choice of spokesperson match our organizational values?
- What will be the reaction of our target audience when they hear from our designated spokesperson?
- What will our target audience think, feel, do, and say?

CASE STUDY 13.1
Toyota versus Tylenol

Inevitably, the massive recall of Toyotas around the globe has brought many comparisons with Tylenol, whose recall in 1982 is considered to be the gold standard of crisis media management. Toyota, on the other hand, has drawn much criticism. A headline in the *Los Angeles Times* in early February 2010 screamed, "Toyota, What's So Hard about Doing the Right Thing?"[†]

The Toyota story and choice of spokespeople is a good reminder of just what is at stake: values—yes, the CEO *must* be in sync with those—and also performance. (Those nanoseconds count.)

As Andrew Gilman, who counseled Johnson & Johnson during the Tylenol crisis in 1982, said in an article for *PR News Online,*

---

[*] Jeff Lee, "Jacques Rogge Confirms Luge Athlete Death," Canwest News Service, http://www2.canada.com/topics/sports/story.html?id=2557778, February 12, 2010.

[†] "Toyota, What's So Hard about Doing the Right Thing?" Business Section, *Los Angeles Times* Online, http://articles.latimes.com/2010/feb/11/business/la-fi-lazarus11-2010feb11, February 11, 2010.

Johnson & Johnson CEO James Burke "came across with three big C's: calm, compassionate and credible."[*] On the other hand, Toyota U.S. company president Jim Lentz says Gilman was "serviceable but no Burke." Toyota's Akio Toyoda, he said, did not "play well in North America."[†]

CEOs are important but not sufficient voices for their companies, as engagement is created by midlevel employees with serious knowledge of products and less perceived bias to exaggeration. Repetition of a story and cocreation help to establish credibility of content. People have to hear, see, or read a story five times before believing it—the average person has up to six sources of news daily.

These are important considerations. Ultimately, it will depend on the severity of the crisis and what stage you engage. Decide who will work best with your audience given the situation. It is a very important strategic decision. (See Box 13.2.)

BOX 13.2   10 COMMANDMENTS FOR LEADERS IN TOUGH TIMES

1. Be honest with yourself
2. Be visible
3. Tell it like it is
4. Be clear
5. Stick to Plan A wherever possible (*but know what Plan B is or will be, JJM*)
6. Be tough
7. Use confidence to create confidence
8. Balance enthusiasm and experience
9. Seize the opportunities
10. Learn to cultivate peripheral vision

Source: Martin Newman, "Not Shaken But Stirred," The Company Agency, London, November 2008.

---

[*] Andrew Gilman, "Why Toyota Is Not Tylenol: Victim, Villain or Vindicator?" *PR News Online*, www.prnewsonline.com/prinsiders/Why-Toyota-is-Not-Tylenol-Victim-Villain-or-Vindicator_13705.html#, February 11, 2010.

[†] Ibid.

These "10 Commandments" are wise indeed. My advice—show them to the CEO and use them as checklist when training and testing plans.

CEOS AND SOCIAL MEDIA

To be successful in the social media realm you need to have an authentic, human voice—as opposed to applying corporate speak. Never has this been more evident than in a crisis. As Craig Pearce said in his excellent summary of the 2009 Frocomm Crisis Communication and Social Media Summit in Australia, "The social media will not tolerate a faceless, mechanical approach."[*]

So, the question is *can* the CEO provide that all important authenticity in a crisis?

Bill George, Harvard Business School professor, former Medtronic CEO, and best-selling author, thinks so. He is a strong advocate of CEOs using the social media and says that they should plan to utilize social media as they navigate a crisis. He is a fan of Twitter and Facebook, advocating that CEOs "hop on Twitter for an hour a day and connect."[†] And in the words of Craig Pearce, "the more human and less air brushed the better."[‡]

The CEO blogging? Only if they are comfortable doing it, and do it themselves. But, I hear your trepidation.

Now the key principle, whether or not the CEO blogs or participates in discussions online during a crisis, is this: You need an established presence online *before* the crisis hits.

Take the example of 76-year-old Bill Marriott, CEO of the giant Marriott hotel chain. (While he may not write the actual blog, it is in his own words. He dictates what he wants to say and then has an assistant handle the technical aspects.)

---

[*] Craig Pearce, "Frocomm Crisis Communication and Social Media Summit," 2nd Annual Crisis Communication and Social Media Summit 2009, Sydney, Australia, http://craigpearce.info/wp-content/uploads/2009/11/Crisis-Comm-and-Social-Media-09_Conference-Report_FINAL4.pdf, October 30, 2010. (Retrieved December 15, 2010.)

[†] Bill George, "How a CEO Can Use Social Media to Navigate a Crisis," www.billgeorge.org/page/how-a-ceo-can-use-social-media-to-navigate-a-crisis, posted on Bill George's *Facebook* page: 11:00 AM, October 13, 2009.

[‡] Craig Pearce, "Frocomm Crisis Communication and Social Media Summit," 2nd Annual Crisis Communication and Social Media Summit 2009, Sydney, Australia, http://craigpearce.info/wp-content/uploads/2009/11/Crisis-Comm-and-Social-Media-09_Conference-Report_FINAL4.pdf, October 30, 2010. (Retrieved December 15, 2010.)

He has been blogging since January 2007, and very successfully. According to the Hotel Chatter travel blog, Marriott's blogs account for more than $4 million in bookings. Should he blog in a crisis? With that credibility, you bet he should!

And blog he did when the Marriott and the Ritz Carlton were victims of a terrorist bombing at their luxury hotels in Jakarta in July 2009. His first statement is in Box 13.2. Marriott continued to blog throughout that crisis.

BOX 13.2   STATEMENT RELATED TO JAKARTA EXPLOSION

Our deepest sympathies go out to the victims of the tragic bombings that took place earlier today in Jakarta, Indonesia. Immediately following the incident, police and hotel security responded and sealed off the area. Our guests at both properties were evacuated and moved to other nearby hotels. Injured guests and hotel employees were taken to the hospital for treatment. Both hotels sustained damage, but it does not appear to be structural. At the time of the incident, extensive security procedures were in place at the Ritz-Carlton and the JW Marriott. We continue to work closely with the authorities and hope to reopen the hotels soon. As always, the safety and security of our guests and associates is our top priority.*

For guest information, please contact the Marriott Family Assistance Hotline at 866/211-4610 or 402/390-3265.

---

* Posted by Bill Marriott, "Statement Related to Jakarta Explosion," Marriott on the Move Blog, www.blogs.marriott.com, posted 11:18 PM, July 16, 2009.

SPOKESPEOPLE AND SOCIAL MEDIA

During the Fort Hood crisis, the White House established a blog. It included important statements and commentary from the very top spokespeople in America.

Citizen–journalists, eyewitnesses, and concerned stakeholders also blogged about the crisis on numerous other blogs. Here is a small sample:

- The Texas Tech University (http://today.ttu.edu/2009/11/statement-from-president-bailey-on-fort-hood-tragedy/)
- Glass City Jungle, which included a statement from Congressman Bob Latta (http://glasscityjungle.com/wordpress/?p=10564)

With the Fort Hood crisis, the Army was quick to deploy social media, using Twitter and Facebook, as well as their official Web site (www.army.mil) plus the Fort Hood Web site (www.hood.army.mil) for updates. Both Web sites included multiple links to their social networking sites.

Keep in mind, social media has enabled everyone to be a spokesperson—either for you or against you. Empowered consumers and public audiences alike are joining the conversation and voicing their opinions on Facebook, Twitter, and any of the myriad of blogs that exist today. If you start forming a relationship with them before a crisis hits, you can minimize the damage a crisis evokes on your spokespeople and organization. As Rohit Bhargava, Senior Vice President of Ogilvy 360 Digital Influence, said in a presentation to the Public Interest Social Media and Crisis Forum in Sydney in September 2009, "Unlock the passion of your accidental spokespeople."

The engagement is what it is all about. Do it now; do not wait for a crisis to test the waters of social media. If you wait, you will probably drown.

14

Head and Heart

I like to get to the heart of the matter, To shake your closet and see what rattles. I like to get to the heart of the matter, Anything else would deceive to flatter. Straight to the point, get to the crux, I'll start in the middle into which everything looks.[*]

—Andrew Cottam

Communicating in a crisis is not for the faint hearted. As Dr. Timothy Pascoe, business strategist and former McKinsey consultant, says, "In a crisis, you need speed, decisiveness, authority—and often significant courage."[†]

It does take courage to step out of the "safe" business mode and step into the public arena. Not only do you need to demonstrate compassion for the "victims," but you need to convey strong conviction for the actions you are taking.

We know that you have a millisecond to prove your authenticity and that words are actually not at the heart of the matter at all. The ideal spokesperson is one who can bring both the heart and the head together. They must be totally believable when they are expressing concern.

So many times the spokesperson will have been told to say something—that is the *head* part—yet their body language and the tone of their voice (*the heart*) does not match their words. Cognitive dissonance

---

[*] Andrew Cottam (Wakefield, England), "Heart of the Matter," Visitor's Poem according to the Web site—Great Inspirational Quotes, http://www.great-inspirational-quotes.com/heart-of-the-matter-visitors-poem.html, n.d.
[†] Timothy Pascoe, "Leadership—Neither Born Nor Bred," Pascoe's Potshots Blog, www.vectorleadership.com/potshots, April 6, 2009.

occurs, the audience will not believe them, and credibility immediately disappears. As Dr. Robert Chandler advises, "Never underestimate their [stakeholders'] general need to know and be reassured that the organization is acting ethically and with professionalism."*

It is *very* important that the head and the heart come together and that the body language matches the words, particularly in a TV interview or on your YouTube and Web site video.

Let's compare two recent examples, JetBlue and Domino's.

JetBlue CEO David Neeleman was widely praised for his candor. Domino's CEO Patrick Doyle was heavily criticized. The words were there—Doyle said the right words—but the overall impression, according to crisis communication expert, Gerard Braud, was anything but right. In an interview with Braud, Doyle said it was "more of an angry rant" at employees, that Doyle was demonstrating "psychological anger at being caught out."† I suggest you check out his performance on YouTube.

"Trying to suppress real emotions requires a great deal of conscious effort and is rarely successful,"‡ says Carol Kinsey Goman, Ph.D., author of *The Nonverbal Advantage: Secrets and Science of Body Language at Work.*

Goman goes on to say, "Candor is the brain's default response. Our neural wiring transmits every minor mood in our facial expressions and physical movements, making our feelings instantly visible. This display of genuine emotion is automatic and unconscious."§

By contrast, JetBlue's Neeleman was widely praised for his communication after a weather-caused snafu that kept seven flights on the John F. Kennedy International Airport tarmac on Valentine's Day 2007 for times that ranged from six-and-a-half to nearly ten-and-a-half hours. Needless to say, when food, water, and working toilets ran out, so did the patience of the JetBlue passengers.

A very contrite Neeleman issued profuse public apologies on network television, on YouTube, on newspaper front pages, and on the JetBlue Web

---

* Robert Chandler, *Disaster Recovery Journal*, Nicholson School of Communication, University of Florida (Gainesville), September 3, 2009.

† Gerard Braud, interview with author, July 9, 2009.

‡ Carol Kinsey Goman, "What You Don't Say: The Power of Nonverbal Communication, Spokesperson Training, International Association of Business Communicators (IABC), *CW Bulletin*, Vol. 7, No. 11, (www.iabc.com), November 2009.

§ Ibid.

site. Most importantly, Neeleman looked and sounded sincere in all his public appearances.

Nonverbal communication is all important in a crisis, when every piece of communication, nonverbal and otherwise, is highly scrutinized—a good point to remember when choosing your spokespeople and when you are conducting drills.

Under scrutiny, will your spokesperson pass that crucial "grace-under-fire" test?

15

Role of the Frontline

CEOs are important but not sufficient voices for their companies, as engagement is created by mid-level employees with serious knowledge of products and less perceived bias to exaggeration.[*]

—*Richard Edelman*

In a crisis, the media, who are telling the story on behalf of their readers, listeners, and viewers, want to hear from someone who is close to, if not in charge of, the frontline operations. And often it is the frontline, the public faces or voices of the organization, that are most vulnerable, as they are often without any training or guidelines at all. Think of the receptionists, call centers, maintenance people, and security guards who may encounter the media pack for the first time. (It was the night watchman who initially encountered the media pack when Shell had a massive oil spill on the Sydney Harbor back in 1999—one year before the Olympics. He knew what to say! He had been trained.)

The media want to speak to the driver of the bus or train, the pilot, and the project manager for a firsthand report. That operational spokesperson, as long as he or she is media savvy and reasonably articulate, is going to be more believable than the chief executive officer (CEO), who is typically a long way away from the action and the local community.

The U.S. Coast Guard understands this imperative. They train and authorize their operational people at the frontline to speak to the media during an incident.

---

[*] Richard Edelman, "The CEO's Dilemma; A Year after Lehman's Demise," 6 A.M. Blog (Edelman Blog), www.edelman.com/speak_up/blog/archives/2009/09/the_ceos_dilemm. html, posted 10:40 AM, September 9, 2009.

British retailer Asda also showed its savvy when they encountered an online "attack" on their values in September 2009. With all the hallmarks of the Domino's episode, an ex-Asda employee captured a series of his unpleasant exploits and posted the video to YouTube. Instead of having the CEO respond to that brewing crisis, the staff at the affected store did the communicating, as shown in Case Study 15.1. This case study highlights not only the need for speed in response but how important it is to step back and ask the key questions:

- What impression do I want to create?
- Who is best to create that impression for us?

Then think about the method and the message and, as Edelman advises, engage the appropriate midlevel employees who have the necessary, firsthand, authentic experience.

Be nimble, be dynamic, and be savvy. Good, honest strategy will always triumph.

CASE STUDY 15.1
Asda Averts Crisis

Swift action averts a full-blown crisis for a United Kingdom retailer: right choice of spokespeople, right strategy.

British retailer Asda showed their savvy when they encountered an online "attack" on their values. Jonathan Hemus, founder of Insignia Communications, a consultancy specializing in crisis communications and reputation management, wrote in his blog post "Insignia Talks" that an ex-Asda Walmart employee (Asda is now part of the Walmart family) captured a series of his unpleasant exploits—licking raw chickens, egg-throwing competitions, and slashing staff chairs—on video, an incident that had all the hallmarks of the disgusting food episode with a rogue employee that plagued Domino's earlier in 2009. There was a crisis in the making for Asda.

Let's assume that Asda asked themselves the key questions.

What impression do we want to create? No doubt they wanted to demonstrate that the behavior of the ex-employee was abhorred at Asda and that such contemptuous acts were extremely rare, not part of a widespread culture. Who better to create such an impression than the employees at the store in question?

Early Stage Two for Asda: The spotlight was turning away from the incident to Asda's response.

How smart of Asda to have store employees offer their personal reaction to the behavior of their former workmate? Four workers from the shop floor at the Fulmore store, including the store manager and security, were filmed giving their personal reactions. "Shocked, outraged, confused" were their genuine, unscripted responses which were posted to YouTube (http://www.youtube.com/watch?v=A5zs5fUhspE).

As Hemus said in his blog posting, the approach worked because it matched Asda's values. Asda is "known as a down to earth, straightforward, and approachable company. Its crisis response personified these qualities."[*]

I wholeheartedly agree with Hemus when he points out that "being true to your brand in a crisis" is "essential."[†] During a crisis your organization and its values are scrutinized under the microscope not only by the media but by customers and competitors, friends and foes alike. It is imperative when a crisis hits that you act true to what you stand for. So, if you are a suited-up sort of company, then act in a suited-up way, but if you are a laid-back type then act that way.

Asda's smart, swift action and choice of spokespeople focused the response and online conversations to admiration for the colleagues featured in the video rather than the incident itself. The choice matched their values. Well done, Asda!

GUIDELINES PLEASE!

What is certain in this age, when everyone can be and often is a spokesperson, if not a journalist, is that you must give clear guidelines. Forasmuch as the Army did well and continues to do well in the social media space, they could not prevent a key employee from playing citizen–journalist when Major Nidal Malik Hasan began his killing spree in November 2009.

The commanders at Fort Hood immediately put the base into lockdown in line with military procedure, and all movement, including the information flow, was severely restricted. That did not stop Tearah Moore, a soldier on the base who had recently returned from duty, from tweeting the news.

Her news and analysis was the first to come out of the base. Needless to say, mainstream media and bloggers alike quickly picked up her coverage, something that she actively encouraged, according to TechCrunch's Paul Carr. Carr says that Moore tweeted to her friends that "they should

---

[*] Jonathan Hemus, "Shopfloor Spokespeople Help Asda Avert Potential Crisis," Insignia Talks Blog, September 21, 2009.

[†] Ibid.

105

pass her phone number on to the press so she could tell them the truth, rather than the speculative BS that was hitting the wires."*

Not only that, but she took a picture from her cell phone of a wounded soldier arriving at the hospital and uploaded that to Twitpic!

And as is the case at Stage One, much of what she tweeted was inaccurate and misleading, and no doubt painful for many.

Moore became the prime (mis)information source from the locked-down base, until she was forced to lock her Twitter account down.

Not surprisingly, she gained hundreds of followers that one fateful day and sent a note out to her followers to "stop following" her. She said her "Tweets are for (her) friends."† Apparently, Moore had no idea the whole world could see what she was saying!

The answer is *not* censorship, but guidelines. It is imperative today that an organization has a shared and understood social media policy, or at the very least some bullet points and advice on the intranet. Your employees need to know what is expected of them (see Chapter 16 for guidelines).

TRAINING PLEASE!

Suffice it to say that the frontline needs, at a minimum, awareness training of what to do when the media call or arrive. It needs to know what to do, what to say, and what not to say.

Certainly they need guidelines for social media, but it is folly to think that you can gag your employees. Better still, make them true ambassadors of the brand. They can help you in a crisis, not hinder you. If issues have been brewing and they are well known inside the company, and the culture is one of mistrust or even fear, then you are open to covert and overt sabotage. WikiLeaks and other whistle-blowing avenues are available, and anyone can set up a Facebook page or Twitter account. Better to embrace the new media world that we live and work in and have a solid understanding of the rules of the game *before* a crisis hits.

Justin Goldsborough, social media director at Sprint, is a strong advocate of employees actively engaging in social media. They are your subject matter experts. As Goldsborough said, "Employees who are armed

---

* Paul Carr, "After Fort Hood, Another Example of How 'Citizen Journalists Can't Handle the Truth," TechCrunch Blog, www.techcrunch.com, November 7, 2009.
† *Twitter* post by: Tearah Moore, November 5, 2009.

with the best information about a brand tell the best story."* The other important point is that you can keep the gripes internal if you give the employees the right tools and training.

Sprint set up an internal blog, among other measures designed to increase participation and engagement. The internal blog helped identify problems during the launch of the Palm Pre. According to Sarah Cometa (*Ragan's Daily Headlines*), Sprint set up a war room for a specialized team comprising workers from an array of departments so that problems could be solved quickly.†

Candid feedback is welcome; as Goldsborough says, "It is the sign of an open culture."‡ I would bet that Sprint would have minimal employee distractions and a major focus on getting the right story out there.

Good thinking and good planning, Sprint. (See Chapter 23 for more discussion on training.)

SUMMARY

In this environment of low trust and maximum authenticity, the choice of spokesperson is more important than ever.

One way of building trust is having real people represent the organization in real ways. Allow your spokespeople to have a personality that also expresses the company's values and culture as well as empathy and compassion. Take a leaf out of the JetBlue and Asda playbook.

In the social media be careful not to preach; be more informal and conversational than the more formal corporate-speak. And remember that your audience will make a decision about you in less time than it takes you to blink your eyes two times.

---

* Justin Goldsborough, "Employees Who Are Armed with the Best Information about a Brand Tell the Best Story," Case Study: Trust and the Sprint Space Community, *Communication World*, published on Entrepreneur.com, http://www.entrepreneur.com/tradejournals/article/202919832.html, July/August 2009.

† Sarah M. Cometa, "Sprint Employees' Blogs Share Expertise, Keep Gripes Internal," *Today's Headlines—Ragan's Daily Headlines*. RSS Feed received by author: RaganNewsstand.12@reply.ms00.net, posted 8:07 AM, November 6, 2009.

‡ Justin Goldsborough, "Employees Who Are Armed with the Best Information about a Brand Tell the Best Story," Case Study: Trust and the Sprint Space Community, *Communication World*, published on Entrepreneur.com, http://www.entrepreneur.com/tradejournals/article/202919832.html, July/August 2009.

When in doubt, stick to the classic spokesperson approach:

1. The more senior, the better.
2. The more he/she recognizes the concerns, the better.
3. The more human, less airbrushed, the better.
4. The more prepared and trained (to speak with both the new and old media), the better.

And finally, let the stages guide you. Play the devil's advocate and ask, who is the truth teller going to be in our organization? Who is best suited to this role? Who will withstand the pressure and have grace under fire? Choose wisely.

16

Policy Guidelines for Social Media

> ... if you think these guidelines don't apply to you, then you are probably already on the endangered species list.[*]
>
> —*Joshua-Michéle Ross*

CAN YOU FACEBOOK AT WORK? POLICY FIRST DEFENSE AGAINST RISK

Media policies or at least guidelines are a company's first line of defense against risk. The other key is education and training. It's one thing to have a beautifully crafted policy; it's another thing entirely to have it understood, accepted, and become routine for an organization's employees.

Many organizations, certainly the ones that I have worked with, have, at a minimum, a policy that says no one can speak with the media unless:

- They have been media trained.
- They have been authorized.
- All media relations are handled (read *controlled*) by corporate communication.

Most also have a rule, written or otherwise, that *all* media contact and inquiries must be logged with the media team. I concur.

---

[*] Joshua-Michéle Ross, "A Corporate Guide for Social Media," www.Forbes.com, June 30, 2009.

Today, it is increasingly important to have a formal social media policy. The social media and certainly social networking, despite the controversy with Facebook privacy, isn't going anywhere anytime soon. And it is a very different animal from the traditional technology, not to mention the traditional mainstream media. Your existing information technology (IT) policy will not suffice.

The ubiquitous use of social media by employees has given more than heartburn to many corporations. Domino's Pizza and their rogue employees' vile acts with food, captured on video and distributed on YouTube, would be one high-profile case.

Yet few companies have implemented a social media policy. Research conducted in the United States in 2009 by Russell Herder and Ethos Business Law showed that although more than 8 in 10 executives said they had concerns about social media and its implications for corporate security and reputation management, *only 1 in 3 said they had guidelines.* Worse still, *only 10 percent of those surveyed said that they had undertaken related employee training.*[*] A crisis in the making for sure.

Jason Falls, a social media educator, strategist, and public relations professional, says that a social media policy is a misnomer. Jason, who has advised an eclectic array of brands including Jim Beam and NASCAR driver Robby Gordon, says that a company should have social media policies. "It's not just making rules for who can blog and say they work for you. It's more than just telling employees what they can and cannot do on company computers."[†]

His list is *long* but worth listing (see Box 16.1) as it gives a comprehensive overview of what to think about, cover in training, or have as a bullet point in the social media policy or manual.

**BOX 16.1   JASON FALLS'S SOCIAL
MEDIA POLICY GUIDELINES**

- Employee Code of Conduct for Online Communications
- Employee Code of Conduct for Company Representation in Online Communications

---

[*] Russell Herder and Ethos Business Law School, "Social Media Embracing the Opportunities, Averting the Risks," White Paper, http://www.russellherder.com/SocialMediaResearch/TCHRA_Resources/RHP_089_WhitePaper.pdf, August 2009.

[†] Jason Falls, "What Every Company Should Know about Social Media Policy," Social Media Explorer Blog, http://www.socialmediaexplorer.com/social-media-marketing/what-every-company-should-know-about-social-media-policy/, February 3, 2010.

- Employee Blogging Disclosure Policy
- Employee Facebook Usage Policy
- Employee Personal Blog Policy
- Employee Personal Social Network Policy
- Employee Personal Twitter Policy
- Employee LinkedIn Policy
- Corporate Blogging Policy
- Corporate Blog Use Policy
- Corporate Blog-Post Approval Process
- Corporate Blog Commenting Policy
- Corporate Facebook Brand Page Usage Policy
- Corporate Facebook Public Comment/Messaging Policy
- Corporate Twitter Account Policy
- Corporate YouTube Policy
- Corporate YouTube Public Comment Policy
- Company Password Policy
- Corporate Data Backup Policy

Source: Jason Falls, "What Every Company Should Know about Social Media Policy," Social Media Explorer Blog, http://www.socialmediaexplorer.com/, February 3, 2010.

Clearly, the policy that you adopt or adapt from the many excellent resources and examples that are out there and available for free (see appendices) needs to fit with your company's culture, philosophy, and values. The following is an overview from some organizations that have made their policies available, plus tips gathered from an array of sources for this book.

GUIDE—DON'T STOP—SOCIAL MEDIA USE

The key with a social media policy is to keep everyone *not muzzled but directed and informed.* I particularly like Ford social media guru Monty Scott's analogy as he likens muzzling of employees on social networking to companies in the 1930s waging war against the telephone. It was a similar situation with e-mail just a few years ago. Blocking access could and will be counterproductive.

Ford's advice is this: "Don't share secret information. Don't trade insider information. And remember, what happens in Vegas stays on Google."[*]

Some of the best policies out there belong to more conservative organizations like the U.S. Army. Underpinning their policies and guidelines is trust. They have taken the approach that they can trust their employees' common sense. In an interview with Lindsey Miller of *Ragan's Daily Headlines*, Lt. Col. Kevin Arata, director of the Online and Social Media Division, says that they are "trusting soldiers to do the right thing, and we're educating commanders on what they should or should not do, and should or should not say."[†]

The Army's online slogan has become "don't over-regulate, educate." Good advice for any organization looking toward implementing a social media policy.

Others have also let their values guide them. The University of Texas MD Anderson Cancer Center, which has two policies, one for its internal blog and a second for its external blog, says that their employees are very tied to their organization's core values and that they are "generally not out to ruin the institution or our cancer hospital."[‡]

MD Anderson felt that it couldn't stop their employees from commenting and that "helping and supporting them would be the best way." They monitor posts, not so much to see what the employees are saying, but to protect the brand. They check comments before they are posted with Cancerwise, the hospital's external blog. Confidentiality is key, and there are a lot of guidelines about how and what to post.

For the law firm of Baker & Daniels, it has been a balancing act. Based on the ethics law in Indiana, where the firm has four locations, it would have been easier for them to resist social media altogether. However, in an interview with Lindsey Miller; Melanie Green, director of business development and marketing at Baker & Daniels, says that members of the firm have been given a lot of training, coaching, and support on things they can talk about. "We have even encouraged their lawyers to tweet as a tool to build relationships."[§] Their training has included examples of what's OK to say. So far so good.

---

[*] Monty Scott (Ford), "Facebook, Twitter, YouTube Come to Work: Employers Look for Ways to Use Social Media Sites," SPORTStechy Blog, http://sports.tmcnet.com, May 17, 2010.

[†] Lindsey Miller, "What's in Your Social Media Policy? *Ragan's Daily Headlines,* www.ragan.com, October 28, 2009.

[‡] Ibid.

[§] Ibid.

So, let's look at some of the principles that guide a good social media policy.

1. *Overall philosophy*—As Russell Herder and Ethos Business Law point out in their comprehensive but somewhat legal white paper, an effective social media policy should define the company's overall philosophy on social media and be *consistent with its culture.*[*] For example, is social networking sanctioned by the company? Are there restrictions about which outlets are approved, for example, is YouTube posting approved but not Facebook? If employees are engaged officially, are the overall corporate goals clearly articulated?

2. *Transparency*—Very important to be clear about who they are and what/who they represent. Employees should not hide behind pseudonyms on social networks. Indeed, the Federal Trade Commission (FTC) rules stipulate that any employees who post about the company products, services, or competitors *must* state for whom they work. It is also a good idea to have official company networkers read and acknowledge the FTC rules with some kind of signature, even if an e-signature.

3. *Accountability*—Employees need to know that they are responsible for what they say on social networks, and the company needs to be clear about what their expectations are of employees during nonwork hours. Diana Kelley, partner at an IT security consultancy computer security firm, Security Curve, says that it's important to keep in mind that the rules about corporate transparency are still in effect off-hours.[†]

   Employees need clear guidelines on the usage of personal identities online. For example, is it acceptable for an employee to have his or her work e-mail on a personal blog that discusses controversial issues?

   Your policy must address the question that every employee will want to know: "Will I get fired for posting something on social media?" This is similar to knowing if they could get fired for speaking to the media without authority. For some government clients I have worked with, it was indeed a sackable offense.

---

[*] Russell Herder and Ethos Business Law School, "Social Media Embracing the Opportunities, Averting the Risks," White Paper, http://www.russellherder.com/SocialMediaResearch/TCHRA_Resources/RHP_089_WhitePaper.pdf, August 2009.

[†] Diana Kelley (Security Curve), "How to Set Social Networking Policies for Employees," eSecurity Plant, http://www.esecurityplanet.com/article.php/3877481/How-To-Set-Social-Networking-Policies-for-Employees.htm, April 20, 2010.

The policy needs to define acceptable limits for its employees so that it can avoid potential conflicts of interest. If nothing else, employees need to be reminded that what goes on the Internet stays on the Internet!

4. *Monitoring*—The policy should state how and to what extent employees' usage of social media will be monitored and what the disciplinary measures might be. This needs to be very transparent.

5. *Productivity*—The policy needs to enhance productivity, not detract from it! Many managers equate social media activity to wasting time. It's similar to allowing employees to make personal phone calls at work or not. However, as Russell Herder and Ethos Business Law point out in their excellent white paper, "the new work force does not live in a nine-to-five world."* The policy needs to be on job performance instead of company time.

6. *Respect copyrights and fair use*—This should be a no-brainer, but just in case: Always give people proper credit for their work, and make sure you have the right to use something with attribution before you publish.

7. *Confidentiality and proprietary information*—Being transparent does not mean you give away trade secrets—the secret recipe for the new Apple gizmo code. While this may seem self-explanatory, it's sensible to remind employees that they have an obligation to protect proprietary or confidential information or methodologies. You may need to check the laws governing trade secrets in your country or state. In the United States, every state has such laws.

Will employees risk losing their jobs if they share the company (proprietary) secrets?

The bottom line is this: *Rules must be clear*; the clearer the policy, the better for all. It would be a good idea to have some sort of process where employees acknowledge the rules. Training is a good place to cover this aspect.

Let common sense prevail when forming your social media policy, involve your employees in the process, and run some scenario-based workshops to educate them on the finer points so that expectations are

---

* Russell Herder and Ethos Business Law School, "Social Media Embracing the Opportunities, Averting the Risks," White Paper, http://www.russellherder.com/SocialMediaResearch/TCHRA_Resources/RHP_089_WhitePaper.pdf, August 2009.

clearly understood. Better still, you will avoid people making assumptions, something to be avoided at all costs, particularly in a crisis.

It is all about accepting and mitigating risk. In the social media world there is risk but there are great downsides for a company that puts its head in the sand and forbids its employees from using social media. I will leave it to the Air Force for the final say. "Policy drives the train," says Joseph Fordham, Chief, Air Force Public Web.* Amen to that!

---

* Joseph Fordham, (Chief, Air Force Public Web), interview with author, May 31, 2009.

SECTION III SUMMARY

We have looked at the many types of spokespersons, when they are most useful to keep the message going, as well as the power of training supported by good guidelines.

We have also looked at trust and how important that element is. Recognize that overall trust is low and that there is a need for maximum authenticity. This means that your choice of spokesperson is more important than ever.

One way of building trust is having real people represent the organization in real ways. Allow your spokespeople to have a personality that also expresses the company's values and culture as well as empathy and compassion. Take a leaf out of the JetBlue and Asda playbook, maybe even Yahoo!

In the social media be careful not to preach; be more informal and conversational than the more formal corporate-speak. And remember that your audience will make a decision about you in less time than it takes you to blink your eyes two times.

When in doubt, stick to the classic spokesperson approach:

1. The more senior, the better.
2. The more he/she recognizes the concerns, the better.
3. The more human, less airbrushed, the better.
4. The more prepared and trained (to speak with both the new and old media), the better.

Remember too, the role of the frontline and their role in a crisis. You need them to be your ambassadors in a crisis, not your foe.

And finally, let the stages guide you. Play devil's advocate and ask, Who is the truth teller going to be in our organization? Who is best suited to this role? Who will withstand the pressure and have grace under fire? Choose wisely. Your reputation is on the line, as we saw amply demonstrated by the Gulf oil spill.

Section IV

Media Interviews—Rules of Engagement in a Crisis

Wooing the press is an exercise roughly akin to picnicking with a tiger.
You might enjoy the meal, but the tiger always eats last.[*]
—*Maureen Dowd (Pulitzer Prize–Winning New York Columnist)*

OVERVIEW

Your worst nightmare, the crisis you always dreaded has happened and the media spotlight has turned on you. Your reputation is under fire. You have to face them—the media pack—to defend your reputation and provide some perspective for what took place and what you are doing to fix it.

Today's journalists want to know what happened and why. They will test your ability to deliver credible information; they will focus on your overall responsiveness and what that means for their audiences. They will dig and dig if they think you are being evasive or have done something illegal or unethical.

Despite the rise in social media, the traditional TV media will still report on a crisis—they want and need that compelling story—that

---

[*] Maureen Dowd, www.BrainyQuote.com, (Xplore Inc.), http://www.brainyquote.com/quotes/quotes/m/maureendow391343.html. (Retrieved February 18, 2010.)

dramatic vision—think of the oil spill in the Gulf of Mexico; they want to eyeball the spokespeople and hear firsthand what is going on. They also want to hear what the victims have to say. They need the back story.

Whether the interviews are on Skype or CCN, or recorded through citizen–journalists' Flip cameras and smart phones, you need to be prepared. You have to perform. You have to be credible, at all levels. You are communicating in an environment of mistrust.

As I say to the many chief executive officers and senior managers whom I have trained and coached in times of crisis, you have to remember that a media interview is a performance. The spokesperson is like an actor—and like an actor, you are paid to perform. Remember, like an actor you will also be critically judged by your audience. Every tiny piece of your performance will be thoroughly scrutinized, analyzed, and dissected by pundits and critics alike. A very experienced colleague of mine likens a media conference to theater. You need to treat it that way. You need to think about how you look and the way you speak, and the trust persona that you portray.

Be sure to prep and test your messages; learn your lines, and practice, practice, practice.

And just like any Academy Award–winning actor, your performance must be believable. But you, unlike most Hollywood actors, are in charge of a business that has potentially hurt something or someone, so you had better show your compassion and be very genuine about it, too—remember, the head and the heart must come together. (See Chapter 14 for more information.)

The good news is that there is a pattern to the questions, depending on the stage of the crisis. The journalists' questions are predictable, perhaps not the exact words, although the opening questions most likely are, but the general approach is all but guaranteed (see Section II: "Stages of a Crisis").

We know what to expect from a journalist; we know what it takes to get our message across—no toxic language, authenticity, and plain eighth-grade words please. So, now what? What are the key skills that a spokesperson needs to effectively manage a crisis interview, be it face-to-face, over the phone, on Twitter, on Skype, or in a news conference with the traditional mainstream TV, radio, and print publications?

In this section we will look at the crisis media interview and, in particular, the many techniques that one can adopt in a crisis. You have a choice, and my aim is to illustrate that for you through practical examples. Among other points, you can expect to read about the following:

- Techniques, tips, pitfalls
- Different types of interview techniques
- Difficult questions
- What to do when you do not know the answer
- How to stage and manage a media conference step by step
- TV, radio, and print interviews
- How to avoid the poison in journalists' questions and to see the gifts
- How the new media is changing the rules for media interviews
- Media training

17

Understanding Journalists' Questions

Understanding the motives behind the difficult questions journalists ask in a crisis not only helps you prepare more thoroughly for an interview, but also helps you meet their needs without compromising your own performance or the reputation of your organization, product, or indeed your own family.

Journalists do not necessarily ask *questions from hell* simply because they are out to get you. It pays to remember that a journalist's job is to be skeptical, and when a crisis happens they are there to get the answers—to get to the bottom of what happened and to make sure that it does not happen again. If they always believed everything they were told and took everything at face value, most of the best news would never break, criminals would roam free, and bad behavior would go unpunished, or worse, unnoticed or detected.

A journalist becomes our conscience, a watchdog, a person who can ask questions that others are thinking but afraid or not in the position to ask.

Also, the questions you think are tough are often the *obvious* questions to the journalist. Many would be surprised to know they have put you on the spot because they do not necessarily appreciate the sensitivity and politics of the information they are seeking. (See Box 17.1 for a list of reasons why journalists ask the tough questions that they do. This list will be helpful in anticipating questions in a crisis.)

121

BOX 17.1   WHAT IS WITH THE TOUGH QUESTIONS?

Why do journalists ask difficult questions?

- To test the validity of your claims.
- To sort out the reality from the rhetoric.
- To probe for facts as the crisis unfolds.
- To get the other side of the story—*balance*.
- To see if ulterior motives are at play.
- To find the holes in things that seem too good to be true.
- To lever out information they think should be made public.
- To find someone to blame.
- To pit the good against the bad.
- To substantiate off-the-record or unsourced information.
- To elicit a response to another party's claims.
- To make sense out of a *jigsaw* of information.
- To resolve conflicting claims and information—who is telling the truth?
- To get to the bottom of *why* something happened and *what* is being done to ensure that it does not happen again.
- To flex their muscles.
- And, yes, sometimes to *get you* (when they feel you have lied, cheated, or simply deserve it).

So now, let's look at the rules of engagement for a media interview.

Remember that whatever you say is likely to be balanced against opinions that are different from yours. That has always been the case in live television—which, like the theater and movies, thrives on drama. It is a rule of the theater, movies, and television that you cannot have drama without conflict in some form or another. On the one side will be the baddie, the villain, and on the other side, the good guys.

One clue how to handle questions or to help you understand whether you will get more than your fair share of difficult questions is to anticipate how you will be framed—as the good guy or the bad guy.

In his book *How to Make the Most of Every Media Appearance*, George Merlis, former executive producer of *Good Morning America*, the CBS

Morning News, and *Entertainment Tonight,* refers to typical good and bad guys (Box 17.2).

BOX 17.2   GOOD GUYS VERSUS BAD GUYS

Good Guys

- Environmentalists who do not commit acts of sabotage
- Firefighters who are not arsonists
- Poor people who are not criminals
- One-person law firms whose one lawyer dresses in Walmart suits

Bad Guys

- Polluters or anyone who can be construed as a polluter
- Rich people, unless they got rich by being actors, singers, comedians, or novelists
- Partners in large law firms who wear $2,500 suits

Source: George Merlis, *How to Make the Most of Every Media Appearance: Getting Your Message across on the AIR, in PRINT, or ONLINE* (New York: McGraw-Hill), 2004, p. 101. (Reprinted with permission.)

Populist current affairs TV shows such as *60 Minutes* and others often portray their stories as shocking and shameful or warm and wonderful. Think Captain Sully Sullenberger versus Bernie Madoff.

In the unfiltered, unedited social media world, the bad are often corporate fat cats, politicians, and big brands perceived to be behaving badly—think Nestlé and Proctor & Gamble. Governments will also be heavily criticized in this low trust environment. We are quick to judge people we perceive to be acting unethically or who are not responding quickly enough. The good comes into play when we are surprised by a corporation or government's *speed* of response and how *genuine* they are in their efforts to fix problems.

Paul Gillin,[*] American writer, speaker, and social media strategist, whom I interviewed for this book, says that "purists" hang out in the social media space so you are likely to attract more criticism in SocialMediaLand.

---

[*] Paul Gillin, interview with author, June 30, 2009.

And then there is the downright cool, who have millions of followers and hefty Facebook fan pages like Ashton Kutcher, Ellen DeGeneres, Zappos Shoes, President Obama (when he was campaigning,) Ford's Scott Monty, and most recently Bill Gates and the Dalai Lama. (For the record, purpose-built Facebook pages created more than *5.3 billion* fans in January 2010, and these will be both good and bad!)

In a crisis, where the stakes are very high, it pays to stop and think about how you and your crisis might be framed so that you can prepare appropriately. Dig deep and know what and where the skeletons are likely to be *before* you do any interview. And remember that once you put "it" on the Internet, "it" remains there forever.

18

Techniques to Get Your Message Across

Now, here is a conundrum—questions are gifts! Journalists' questions are simply a strategic opportunity for you to communicate a vitally important message to your key audiences. Sure, you have to listen attentively to hear the right word or phrase that presents the opportunity to grab the gift and respond appropriately. But it is possible, even in the most hostile of situations, to get your message across.

First, let's think about the media interview and how it is structured. The interview is designed to be a question-and-answer format. The journalist asks you a question and you respond with an answer. They ask another question, you respond, and so it goes.

BOX 18.1   Q = A

(Question = Answer)

Box 18.1 shows the basic formula of how we converse. This means the questioner is doing all the leading. The journalist is in control as you politely follow his or her line of questioning. What if you changed that basic formula and used the journalist's question as a springboard, a bridge to your prepared, rehearsed, and learned lines? (You are the actor on the stage, after all.)

The skills needed to transition from the journalist's questions to your responses do require practice and more practice. Many of their questions are *counterintuitive*, often the exact opposite of, for example, what an attorney may advise in a deposition or in court, or what your parents and teachers may have taught you when you were growing up. The media interview technique is the *exact opposite* of "Just answer the question" in most instances.

The biggest mistake you can make is to think that an interview is like a conversation. It is anything but a conversation (and beware the journalist who says, "Talk to me as if we are having a conversation"). It is anything but a friendly chat! Remember, it is the journalist's job to get you to relax and give them a good, newsworthy story. They will often start an interview with broad, general questions to warm you up, or they will appear friendly and chatty before the interview begins—all designed to get the necessary facts and background of a hot issue. You need to be in active listening mode and need your wits about you at all times!

BRIDGING TECHNIQUE

So, let's look at some alternatives to the Q & A routine. To get your message across in a media interview you need to do what we call *bridging*, which leads to a formula like this:

$$Q = A + 1$$

For many of you who have had professional media training, bridging should sound familiar. If not, get some training fast!

BOX 18.2

Q is the question.
A is your brief answer.
+ is a bridging word or phrase: *however, but.*
1 is your key message.

Your response, represented in Box 18.2, *must* be delivered in 30 seconds or less! In fact, in today's Twitter age of instantaneous news, your response is most likely to be edited down to just 120 characters or three short sentences or less, and aggregated, out of context in a quote or sound bite of just six or seven seconds! Yes, media interview skills are to be taken very seriously if you want to succeed and be an effective and trusted company spokesperson.

The principle behind this formula is to avoid taking the question at face value. If you simply answer the question, you will spend most of your interview on the journalist's bridge, which in a crisis will be tough, rigorous, and downright uncomfortable.

You need to find ways to get to your own bridge, where it is safe or safer ground.

No, it is not about avoiding the question—never, ever. You must always respond to the essence of the question.

Let's look at some examples. The interviewer asks you to respond to a criticism or comment on someone else's opinion:

Q: We have heard that the mayor is furious that you have rejected his attempts to negotiate with the unions on your behalf?

A: We have heard that too, *but* (bridge) our priority right now is to get the vital equipment out to the hospitals so that lives can be saved (key message).

Here is a real-life example: Australian TV's "unmissable" premiere current affairs program, *Lateline*, featured an interview with Mark Regev, Israeli Foreign Ministry spokesperson, about the apparent deliberate targeting by the Israeli Defense Forces of an observer post with the United Nations Interim Force in Lebanon. Four unarmed international observers were killed during the conflict with Hezbollah. *Lateline* coanchor Tony Jones conducted the interview.

Jones: How does an Israeli jet using laser-guided bombs manage to wipe out a UN post of which the coordinates were well known to the Israeli military?

Regev: I think that's an excellent question and I wish I had a good answer for you, but I'll be honest, I don't.[*]

Now, Regev bridges (silently) to his key message:

The Prime Minister has ordered the military to conduct a comprehensive investigation. He has promised Kofi Annan that we will share the results of that investigation with the UN and with the relevant countries that lost their servicepeople ...[†]

---

[*] Tony Jones interview with Mark Regev, *Lateline*, ABC Channel 2, Australian Broadcasting Corporation, http://www.abc.net.au/lateline/content/2006/s1697956.htm, 10:46 PM, July 26, 2006.

[†] Ibid.

This is an excellent example of not taking the question at face value but dealing with the question honestly and, most importantly, *briefly*, and then bridging to his key message. (See Box 18.3.)

BOX 18.3   KEY BRIDGING PHRASES

These phrases will help you deal with a question without biting into the poison or repeating a negative.

That is an interesting perspective …
That is a great question …
On the contrary …
I've heard that too …
There is a bigger picture …
There is more at stake or more to it than your question suggests …
There is more to the situation than you are asking …
What you are really asking me is …
Before I get to the heart of the question, let me give you some background that will be useful in understanding what is really going on …
You are asking me a legal question and you'll need to speak to a lawyer about that, but what I can tell you is …
As much as I'd like to help you, that would be breaking client confidentiality but on a broader level this is what we do in the process at that stage … (give a generic example)

WHEN YOU DO NOT KNOW THE ANSWER

I am constantly asked by clients, "What if I don't know the answer? Is it OK to say 'I don't know'?"

Yes, it is, as long as you immediately follow up and bridge to a key message that will help your credibility or help your key audience understand your motives. You will never have all the answers, and in this era of low trust, it will help your credibility if you demonstrate that while you do not have all the answers right now, this is what we do know and what we are doing, or this is what we have learned so far. Open, honest, and

128

transparent communication, please, *not* spin. Take a lead from the Israeli Defense Ministry spokesperson.

The "I don't know" response is useful when you just cannot answer the question, whether it is because you are not allowed to (for policy or legal reasons) or you simply do not know. Often in a crisis you will be asked questions that are more appropriate for more suitably qualified people, say, a lawyer or a doctor. Or, you may not have the exact, precise, or relevant information on hand. So, what can you do?

Let's take another look at how Mark Regev handled another pointed question.

Jones: We understand it was a bombing from the air. Do you know whether in fact that it was a laser-guided bomb?

Regev: No, I do not have that information and I apologize for that (but) there is nothing to hide here …*

He then goes back to his point about "a full and open investigation."

This strategy is particularly useful when you are asked to speculate or predict something.

GETTING BEHIND THE QUESTION

Often, you need to interpret the question and respond to what is behind the journalist's question. This technique, which addresses the underlying issue of the question, is a sophisticated response; but it is powerful and one to master.

For example, you may be asked a very broad question (a macro issue) but you may only be able to answer from a micro position. Or the question might be very specific, a micro question, and your role is to talk about the broader issues. The following is an example taken from an interview on an Australian current affairs program with a suburban mayor in Melbourne:

Q: How can you justify seizing 12 trucks apparently conducting legal business?

---

* Tony Jones interview with Mark Regev, *Lateline*, ABC Channel 2, Australian Broadcasting Corporation, http://www.abc.net.au/lateline/content/2006/s1697956.htm, 10:46 PM, July 26, 2006.

A: Well, we're normally considered to be a friendly sort of council, so that action is out of character, but ...* (He then bridges to his key message.)

The interviewee, an Australian mayor, responded to the underlying issue of the question—the (illegal) behavior—and addressed that behavior in his response. He responded very effectively without any hint of toxic language. If he had taken the question at face value he may have answered, "We were perfectly justified in seizing the trucks because ..."

While taking the question at face value is clearly a choice, it is the least effective interview technique. The vast majority (at least 90%) of the time, you will end up spiraling down a deep, dark well that is extremely difficult if not impossible to climb out of, and if you do, you will be damaged by the encounter.

QUESTION THE QUESTIONER

Sometimes you will be asked a vague question that is clearly open to interpretation, or worse still, one that puts (the interviewee) on the back foot making assumptions about a certain point in the question. Make sure that you always deal with or question the assumption.

For example, you may be asked about a certain report or survey in very general terms: "We have seen reports that 8 out of every 10 people being interviewed lie."

Your response could be: "What report are you specifically referring to?"

Or, if the question is unclear, you could say: "I'm not sure that I understand the question. Could you please ask that again?"

It is OK to question the questioner, but not for every question. As I say, you need your wits about you, and you need to be in active-listening mode when you are being interviewed.

GIVE-AND-TAKE IN AN INTERVIEW

Clearly, it is important to have "give and take" in an interview and to realize that you are human and not a robot, and that you will flounder from time to time. As the saying goes, "To err is human." The key is, how do

---

* Kerry O'Brien interview with Mike Hill (former Mayor, Mooreland City Council), *7:30 Report*, Australian Broadcasting Corporation (ABC), 1997.

you recover from a blunder when you are in the middle of an interview? What do you do and say?

Unlike the former Miss California (2009), you do not take off your microphone and pretend not to hear the question, have a conversation with your publicist that you think cannot be seen or heard, refuse to answer any more questions, and then walk off the set.[*]

---

[*] Larry King interview with Carrie Prejean (former Miss California, 2009), *Larry King Live*, CNN, http://larrykinglive.blogs.cnn.com/2009/11/12/carrie-prejean-threatens-to-leave-larry-king-live/, November 11, 2009.

19

Dealing with Difficult Questions

Questions come in a variety of forms. The *degree of difficulty* usually depends on the content of the question, the severity of the crisis, whether you are perceived to have acted slowly or quickly to the situation, and if you have waited to respond toward the end of Stage Two or Stage Three. It is not good to be late in a crisis. Remember that speed is of the essence in a crisis, particularly in this lightning-fast digital age.

In a high-stakes crisis interview, you will be asked to speculate, confirm, deny. You will be asked a range of questions—hypothetical questions, questions full of opinions, leading questions. How do you handle them?

Below is a list of possible questions with some suggested responses that we, at Media Skills, have collected over the years.

Q = HYPOTHETICAL

These are the questions that ask *what if?* You are required to *speculate* on possible scenarios. Hypothetical questions are highly dangerous. Before you know it, you are being held to what you said, even though it was only speculation. Hypothetical questions may also seek *guarantees* from you. And, as we all know, "the only guarantees in life are death and taxes."

Examples of hypothetical questions:

- What happens if this does not work?
- What will you do if something unexpected happens?
- If this fails, will you step down?

A good way to handle hypothetical questions is to first *identify* the question for what it is: "You're asking me to see into the future." Then move back to the safety of what already is, rather than what might be.

Q = LOADED

A *loaded* question contains an *assumption* that may well be *incorrect* or *misleading*. If you simply answer the question and ignore the incorrect part, you may seem to be agreeing or *endorsing the negative ideas*.

Examples of loaded questions:

- When did you stop beating your wife? (Assumes you were beating your wife in the first place.)
- Given your poor record, this could be seen as another failure, couldn't it? (Assumes a poor record.)

An effective way to deal with loaded questions is to tackle the underlying assumption. "Actually, our record is second to none." Then respond with your message.

> **CASE STUDY 19.1**
> **Timothy Geithner Responds to a Loaded Question**
>
> U.S. Treasury Secretary Timothy Geithner demonstrated how to handle a loaded question during an interview on June 18, 2009, about reactions to the financial rescue plan as a result of the economic meltdown in October of the previous year, with the veteran broadcaster Jim Lehrer on *PBS NewsHour*. Lehrer asked this question:
>
> Joe Nocera, financial writer for *The New York Times*, had a piece today, and he said that your plan is, quote, the Obama–Geithner plan, let's call it, is, quote, "little more than an attempt to stick some new regulatory fingers into a very leaky dam rather than rebuild the dam itself."
>
> Geithner responded:
>
> Well, as you say, we're going to get it from both sides. Some people will think we're being unfair, doing way too much, and overdoing it. And some people are going to say we're not doing enough. But let me say that the most important things we are doing, we're going to put in place stronger protections for consumers; that's a basic obligation of governments, and our systems failed to do that. We're going to make sure that the system has much stronger shock absorbers, cushions to absorb the

stress of future recessions. And we're going to make sure that govern-ment has better tools for managing future crises. Those three things are very important. They're the most important things for us to do, and we've put a set of very strong proposals to achieve that outcome.*

Do you see how Geithner responded to the essence of the question *rather than take it at face value,* and then bridged to his key message and wisely resisted the temptation to criticize or comment directly on *The New York Times* piece or admonish the journalist?

Q = LEADING

Leading questions often come as a *series,* using *closed* yes and no questions to *lead* you to a particular conclusion. Journalists use this technique to either lead you toward an *admission* or a *promise,* or merely as an attempt to *simplify* or *summarize* a complex issue.

Examples of leading questions:

- You've said you would support such an initiative and criticized the government for moving too slowly. So, that means we can expect to see this being introduced as soon as you are elected?
- So, what you're telling us from all of that is to watch out for this company?

By avoiding a simple yes or no answer, you will slow the pace and make it more difficult for a journalist to lead you.

Q = EITHER/OR

These questions are looking for *either* the black *or* white of an issue, leav-ing no room for the gray. Such questions can trap you into definitive responses you would rather avoid.

Examples of either/or questions:

- Are you going to resign or not?
- Is this investment safe, or should we be pulling our money out?

* Jim Lehrer interview with Timothy Geithner, *PBS NewsHour,* Public Broadcasting Station (PBS), http://www.pbs.org/newshour/bb/business/jan-june09/geithner_06-18.html, June 18, 2009.

- Your chairman has said this is the case. Do you agree or not?
- Is this a recession or the worst market collapse ever?

Responding to the heart of the question often works. "If it's a scapegoat you're looking for, it's a little more complicated than that. The real issue is what we do to improve the economy."

An *I don't know* type of response can also be effective. "Without having heard the government's exact words, it's a bit hard for me to say one way or the other." Then bridge to your key message or important point.

Q = CLOSED

Any type of difficult question can come in a *closed* form, demanding *a simple yes or no answer.*

For example, "Will you be paying compensation to the victims?" Using the principle that you must *respond* as opposed to *answer*, I recommend taking a word or phrase from the question and using that to frame your response. A response could be: "The best thing we can do right now for the victims is to concentrate on what went wrong and how we can all prevent this from happening again, so that's why we are doing ... (state actions that you are taking)." Or, "We have taken responsibility for what has happened, and we will be looking at all aspects of the accident to see what the best solution is for everyone, so that's why we are ... (state actions that you are taking/have taken)."

You should always avoid answering these questions definitively because not only will you miss the opportunity to reinforce your message, but there could be some doubt as to whether you are either agreeing or disagreeing with the issue.

Q = MULTIPLE

Some questions seem to have three or four different parts to them, all of which you feel obliged to answer. Treat them as *multiple choice*. Choose the question you are happiest to answer. If the journalist wants to deal with the other parts of the question, they will be asked later.

Many journalists, particularly print journalists, frame their questions as they proceed with the interview, so listen for the opportunity to see the *gift*, and choose that part to respond to.

For example:

Q: Many people are frustrated at the slow response to the accident and the length of time it is taking to clean up the mess. You have stated you are working around the clock to fix the problem and that does seem to be working. And both the Coast Guard and the EPA are now talking about the exhaustion of the crews and their concern for their safety and well-being. The environment is also a major concern. What is your reaction to this?

A: I understand and share that frustration. This is a really difficult situation. Please understand that we are putting all of our resources on this most challenging situation. As for the safety of our crews—that is uppermost on my mind, and we are flying in extra resources to solve all of the issues that are confronting us at this time. And we will continue to work around the clock until this is solved.

Q = GUARANTEE

Often a stumbling block, the guarantee question is predictable in many situations. Avoid guaranteeing anything, other than what is already the case.

Q: Can you guarantee this will work?

A: I know people would love for me to be able to give a guarantee, but it's never that black and white. What I can say is that we have taken the right steps, in the right order, at the right time, to give us the best set of conditions possible.

Or some alternative responses are as follows:

A: All I can guarantee is that I will work day and night until we have found the solution to this problem.

A: I can guarantee that we will take the results of the investigation very seriously.

In your frustration, you may be tempted to be sarcastic and say something like, "Can you guarantee that every word of my interview will be aired/printed?" That will most likely cause a confrontation with the journalist and, if live, will leave the audience wondering why you lost your cool. *Impressions do matter.*

Better to practice a response like the example given and say it with feeling!

Q = QUESTION FROM HELL

It may be a question that you are expecting, but struggle to answer without getting yourself into trouble. Or, it may be a question from out of left field that catches you by *surprise*.

The impulse will be to avoid the question from hell. But be warned: A "no comment" will only suggest that you have something to hide—even when you don't. A good control technique, thinking through the possible hot spots before the interview, will help you here.

HANDLING SILENCE

Say what you want to say, and stop. *Resist the temptation to fill the silence.* Once you have said what you want to say—zip the lip! And wait. It is the job of the journalist to fill the silence and ask another question. Your job is to respond—always—within two to three seconds. If you hesitate or take too long to respond, you will look compliant or guilty.

HANDLING INTERRUPTIONS

In fast-moving situations like crises, you will also face the challenge of interruptions. They may occur during a hostile, aggressive, tough interview, or when you are on live radio or TV and there is breaking news.

- *On live radio*—A breaking story happens and time simply runs out. An interruption could also happen if the quality of your phone line deteriorates.
- *On TV*—If being interviewed via satellite, a breaking story could happen and satellite time could run out. If you are in a panel discussion with multiple spokespeople, there are constant interruptions because people talk over each other.

You are also likely to be interrupted on live radio or TV if:

- You are taking too long to get the point.
- You fail to make a concrete point after a few questions.
- You have avoided the question.

- You are using spin, corporate speak, jargon.
- You are perceived to be lying.
- You are perceived to be the bad guy.

During my coaching sessions with chief executive officers and major spokespeople during a crisis, I often remind them that that they have choices with interruptions. These include:

- Ignore and continue with your point.
- Wait until the interviewer has asked his or her question and then go back to your response.
- Respond to the interruption and wait for another opportunity to make your point.

The best approach is to pause, allow the interruption, and then quickly make your point. At that point, you can choose to respond to the (interrupted) question. You may have heard politicians say, "if you would just let me finish." That is a phrase you could use, but be aware of how you say it. Impressions are key in a crisis. You will be judged in a nanosecond, as we discussed in Section III.

As we can see, media interviews are anything but normal conversations in which we always speculate, hypothesize, and offer opinions. Be very careful of what you say, and avoid thinking that just because a reporter is asking you questions, your opinions are worth more than the messages that you are supposed to be delivering. And, above all, be prepared.

20

Never Repeat the Poison: Avoid Negative Language

We have talked a lot in this book about toxic, negative language and the importance of using positive, active language. In a crisis, a high probability of questions from the media will lead a spokesperson to deny or confirm a statement that ends up as a negative headline, quote, or tweet.

Let's take Sarah Palin, the former Alaska governor and vice presidential candidate, as an example. Her much maligned, exclusive interview with *CBS Evening News* anchor Katie Couric is a perfect example of *what not to do.*

The interview took place during the 2008 presidential campaign at the start of the economic downturn in the United States. Couric asked a question in relation to the proposed $700 billion government bailout.

Couric: If this doesn't pass, do you think there's a risk of another Great Depression?

Palin: Unfortunately, that is the road that America may find itself on. Not necessarily this, as it's been proposed, has to pass or we're gonna find ourselves in another Great Depression. But there has to be action taken, bipartisan effort—Congress not pointing fingers ...*

---

* Katie Couric interview with Sarah Palin, *CBS Evening News*, CBS Broadcasting, Inc., September 24, 2008.

141

Palin clearly swallowed the poison words *Great Depression* and repeated it in her response. Not surprisingly, the front-page headlines the next day were all about a *Great Depression*:

- *Boston Globe*—Palin Warns Depression May Be Looming (September 25, 2008)
- *Chicago Tribune*—Sarah Palin: Depression Fears (September 25, 2008)
- *Dallas Morning News*—Palin Says U.S. May Be Headed toward Another Great Depression.[*]

President Obama, as skillful and articulate as he is, has made some mistakes, too, when the stakes were high. Similar to Palin, he repeated a negative phrase. It was toxic!

During the contentious health care debate in 2009, President Obama spent a lot of time clarifying that there were no parts of the potential health bill that would "pull the plug on grandma."[†] That expression quickly turned into "kill grandma," generating T-shirts and a multitude of "kill Grandma" blogs, headlines, and even jokes on late-night TV. Not surprisingly, "kill Grandma" were the only words that the masses heard. What Obama said as a tongue-in-cheek comment was repeated time and time again on protest signs and in media interviews.

President Obama would have been well advised to stay clear of "kill grandma." Instead of saying, "pull the plug on grandma because we've decided that we don't..."[‡] the president should have said, "It is none of our business how grandma wants to enjoy her life. We just want for her to be able to talk to her doctor in private without paying for it as an out-of-pocket expense."

The rule is to clarify without repeating a negative. Remember, the catchy, short, cutthroat phrases will always be repeated, tweeted, and aggregated.

As a coach, I advise my clients to *beware of the poison*. Yes, questions are gifts, but not all are attractive. And they need to be grasped with both hands—in this case, with one's mouth!

Buying into the negative always muddles your message. Avoid it at all costs.

---

[*] *Dallas Morning News* (Front-page headline), http://www.dallasnews.com/sharedcontent/dws/news/politics/national/stories/092508dnpolpalin.ab0a84ca.html, posted 4:52 PM CDT, September 24, 2008.

[†] Barack Obama, "Health Care Address to a Joint Session of Congress," Washington, DC, September 7, 2009.

[‡] "Obama's Health Care Town Hall in Portsmouth," *The New York Times*, http://www.nytimes.com/2009/08/12/us/politics/12obama.text.html?pagewanted=all, August 11, 2009.

21

How the New Media Are Changing the Rules for Interviews

As we have seen, the media landscape has changed dramatically. There are new players, new rules. While the principles remain the same, there are some shifts in how the media interview game is played today, by both the journalist and the interviewee (the subject, the source, the talent).

The social media have given the traditional mainstream journalists many options for interviews. They crowdsource for contacts, sources, stories. Speed is another factor. The era of *publish now, correct later* is here. "Churnalism" instead of journalism. Few original sources. The reporting of Michael Jackson's death, for example, was mostly through secondary sources.

Let's look more specifically at some of the trends.

CROWDSOURCING

One journalist I interviewed for this book told me that if he sees 10 individuals saying the same thing on Twitter, he will report that as fact. He has 10 "eye"-witnesses. For example, if there were 10 tweets saying that New York Yankees baseball player Alex Rodriquez had admitted to taking steroids in an interview with ESPN, and that fact had been "reported" by 10 different sources on Twitter, he would report that by saying "sources" had said ...

Sources are freely available today. Many journalists have Twitter accounts and have followers. They pose questions to their fans and friends, check story lines, engage in conversation with fellow reporters, and collaborate to get the best angle, the best quote, the best story.

They check their feeds constantly, they blog, and they use their read comments to source more stories. In a crisis, they monitor closely the key rounds and the influential columnists to see what they are saying, whom they are quoting, whom they appear to be following. You do the same.

LIMITING DIRECT ACCESS TO MAINSTREAM MEDIA

All the journalists I interviewed for this book said they would prefer an original voice, to talk to the company spokesperson directly. This is not always possible, particularly in a crisis.

According to Associate Professor at Roskilde University (Denmark), Kirsten Mogensen, who has done extensive research with leading journalists in Silicon Valley (the heart of innovation and technology in the United States), some companies have reduced or even denied direct access to traditional mainstream media. Even Google has limited access to the mainstream media. It is all about networks and who knows whom, says Mogensen.

Mogensen says that the network economy of Silicon Valley at least is hindering original reporting, good journalism. Her research reveals, "There is no direct, front-door access for journalists into the major companies in the Valley. Not even Markoff from *The New York Times*, representing one of the most prestigious newspapers in the world, can call Google's headquarters and expect to get to talk to the CEO."

"To control the news coverage, larger companies in Silicon Valley insist that the rules of personal networks be followed. If journalists want access they must be introduced by people who are already known,"* writes Mogensen in a paper published with co-researcher David Nodfors, Senior Research Scholar and Program Leader, Innovation Journalism, Stanford University.

Google and others are active in the social media—of course. We are talking about "Lord" Google after all! They are going direct.

---

* Kirsten Mogensen and David Nordfors, "How Silicon Valley Journalists Talk about Independence in Innovation Coverage," presented at the *International Association for Media and Communication Annual Conference*, Vol. 7, No. 6, November 2010.

E-MAIL AND BLOGS

Others are using e-mail and blogs to get their message across. For example, Mark Cuban, American entrepreneur and owner of the Dallas Mavericks, among other things, apparently only does media interviews by e-mail so that he has a complete record of them. According to Steve Rubel, Senior Vice President and Director of Insights for Edelman Digital, AdAge and Forbes columnist, and avid sports fan, Cuban uses e-mail so that he can correct misgivings on his blog.

Another high-profile source also changing the rules of the game is Dave Winer, an American software developer, entrepreneur, and writer. Winer takes a more subtle approach. According to Rubel, Winer answers questions on his blog without saying who the reporter is and exactly what questions were asked. He "creates a public record, something that can be useful for everyone."*

Both Cuban and Winer have adopted this approach because they wish to avoid being misquoted and/or taken out of context. They have taken control back. It's our news!

Their approach can be useful in a crisis, where you can be the broadcaster, the reporter. You can give your perspective, your view; you can wrest control back, but the audience will judge you on your actions as much as they will on your words. How credible your information is will be determined by the prevailing context, the perception held about your industry, your product, your spokespeople. How much do we trust you?

The Cuban/Winer approach, the advent of the crowdsourcing journalist, as well as the media conferences on Twitter where all the questions and answers are seen, are yet another indication of just how much the media landscape has changed.

There is room and indeed there are many options for reporter and source alike to demonstrate transparency, openness, and collaboration.

---

* Posted by Steve Rubel, "Reinventing the Media Interview," Micro Persuasion Blog, http://www.micropersuasion.com/2006/08/reinventing_the.html, August 11, 2006.

22

Lights, Camera, Action—The Interview

In this chapter we will look at the rules of engagement for interviews—what to do before, during, and after. We will look at TV interviews, what to wear and what to avoid, and finally what the rules are for a news conference, or *presser* as it is often called in MediaLand.

BEFORE THE INTERVIEW

Before you embark on any media interviews, there are a few simple things to be done:

1. Know your audience.
2. Know your key message.
3. Practice your message.
4. Know your media.
5. Know your dress.

Know Your Audience

Good planning is essential for any effective media interview, but in a crisis it is doubly so; the stakes are much higher.

When coaching clients, particularly for a major interview or any high-stakes communication, I advocate that they use a simple three-step process that starts with the question of what is the overall impression that

147

you want to create given the situation. That is your starting point, *not* what you are going to say. It is a mistake to start at messaging when you have not stopped to ask yourself the key question, which is, Why am I doing this interview? What do I hope to achieve? Hopefully, the answer is more than, "Because Mary (head of media) said I had to!"

Step 1:   What is my overall aim—what do I want people to think, do, or say; or how do I want them to act differently as a result of this interview? Be very specific. For example, an aim might be to reassure the residents that you are doing all you can with the resources that you have to get the job done. Indeed, the strategic reason for the interview might be to call on your neighbors, the affected community, to pitch in and help.

Step 2:   Who am I aiming my message at? Be specific. Who *really, really* matters given the situation and your strategic aim? For example, it may be the head of the local community emergency response team, relevant regulators, or an organization service.

You must know about your audience, and typically there are only one or two key groups or indeed people who you are really aiming to influence through the media. Be ruthless, disciplined, and creative when you are going through this step. Get this right and it will be much easier to come up with a key message.

Step 3:   What do I say that will motivate my audience to my aim? What do they really *want* to hear from me? What do they really *need* to hear from me? Hopefully, the want and the need will be the same!

Put yourself in their shoes, in the victims' shoes. Who is most affected by what has happened? You can bet your bottom dollar that that is the side the media will be on when they interview you. In a crisis, you *must* address the *most* affected first with a high degree of empathy—it must be authentic.

With this simple plan, you can get to an important strategic message. You will have the basis for your statements. And, if nothing else, you will have somewhere to bridge to when the going gets tough.

Know Your Key Message

Once you have worked out your key message, write down your key points and supporting messages, arrange them in order of importance, and, like an actor, learn your lines. Your messages will sound best if they are internalized. Also know your corporate values as well as your personal values when you are preparing your messages. That is what will determine the impressions that the audience will remember long after the interview is finished.

Practice Your Message

Practice delivering your statement in front of a mirror or your crisis management team. Encourage feedback and have them act as victims or key affected stakeholders. It is *very* important to read your statement and key examples aloud. It is amazing how the eye can gracefully glide over sentences until they are read aloud. Better still, learn your lines and resist reading your statement. Remember the head and the heart principle.

Know Your Media

Know the style of the reporter and the show that will be interviewing you. If it is a high-stakes one, like *60 Minutes* or a prominent current affairs TV or radio show, research other similar crises they have covered so you know what the likely questions might be. Close to the interview, watch the show and listen to the news to check if there is anything that might be related to your situation. Remember, the media issue-link. They will immediately connect your issue or crisis to something that is already on the news agenda.

Know Your Dress

If you are doing anything visual—TV interviews, recording a video for YouTube or a Web site, streaming live on the Internet—you need to think about what you will be wearing. See the "Television Interviews" section in this chapter for more information on TV interviews and what to wear. Does what you are wearing help, hinder, or support your message? Your corporate values?

DURING THE INTERVIEW

1. *Start with a strong, compelling statement* (see Section V for more details)—We mentioned *counterintuitive* earlier. Here is an example of what I mean. As I say to my clients in media training sessions,

in MediaLand everything is upside down; the punch line of the joke comes first, and then you give the background!

Let's think about how the media speak to us. They start with a conclusion, always a strong compelling statement that hooks us in to listen or read more. That is how we need to speak to them.

Start with a strong, bold statement that shows compassion—the punch line:

We are shocked and deeply saddened by what's happened here today. None of us expected that we would ever witness a tragedy of this magnitude.

Then support that opening statement with some compelling reasons or actions that demonstrate your compassion:

We rushed our trauma and rescue teams to the site as soon as we received the tragic news. We immediately called in our investigators and auditors, who will be working side-by-side with the regulators, so that we can get some fast answers as to the possible cause, and I'm meeting with all the injured late today.

Next, sum up what you have said:

We've acted quickly to get some sense of order back into our community—we needed to.

Any of this could be tweeted, shared, and swapped, and the quotes could end up on multiple platforms and seen by just about anyone, anywhere. If your crisis has global implications, it will be. Guaranteed.

2. *Be short and keep it simple*—The longer the response, the more likely you will be edited or the listener will tune out. Get to the point quickly, and do it using language that an eighth grader will understand. Follow the Robert Chandler rule of "no more than 30 words, 3 sentences, and 30 seconds."[*] (See Box 22.1.)

3. *No jargon*—This is important in any interview but particularly in a crisis when clarity is critical. Avoid abbreviations and acronyms, too.

4. *Listen, please*—Listen carefully to the question that is being asked and *think* about your response. You have a full two seconds before

---

[*] Dr. Robert Chandler (Director, Nicholson School of Communication, University of Central Florida, Orlando), "Message Maps: Blueprints for Pandemic Preparedness," 3n White Paper, http://www.continuitycentral.com/messagemaps.pdf, 2006, p. 4.

you need to respond. Take a word or a phrase from the journalist's question and use that to frame your response.

5. *Never speculate*—In a crisis, you will be asked to speculate as to the cause and who was to blame for the incident. Avoid this temptation at all costs. Say what you know to be fact. If you do not know the answers to a question, say that and then bridge to what you do know. It is also a good idea to have a compelling reason for why you cannot discuss a certain subject.

6. *Resist the urge to show off*—A crisis is never the time to display an impressive vocabulary or to present the full extent of your intellect and knowledge. Talk as you might to a neighbor, your grandmother, or a 10 year old who is probably scared. Think of the victims and what they need and want to hear from you.

7. *Be yourself*—Only you can win a gold medal of being you, so be true to yourself and your convictions. If you are confused by a question, say so. If you say something that is wrong or mistake the facts, admit your error and apologize. In a crisis, it is critical to be genuine, authentic, and human—to be seen as "one of us"—so be forthcoming to the extent that you have planned and rehearsed beforehand.

8. *Never argue with a journalist*—You will come off second best, and if it is prerecorded, that segment will most certainly air. Never embarrass a journalist either. The journalist will always have the last say, the last word on a subject—always! Best to always remember what impressions you want or need to create. Be guided by your corporate values.

9. *Avoid expressing personal opinions*—In a crisis, you will be pushed to give your personal opinion—beware. Express your compassion and commitment without making it personal. If you feel compelled to violate this rule, make certain you are very clear in distinguishing opinions from official positions and policies.

10. *Sum up at the end*—At the end of an interview or a media conference, make sure you sum up your key points succinctly and quickly. Many savvy, veteran journalists will often ask, "Is there anything else I should know/anything to add?" Often, this is when the media get their best quote or sound bite as the spokesperson has relaxed and so often spills the beans. That question is your cue to carefully sum up your key points.

11. *No such thing as no comment*—"No comment" is like a red flag to a bull. It is better to attempt an answer than to say no comment. The

phrase suggests a lack of candor, conveys a sense of secrecy, and suggests you are hiding something that you are not willing or allowed to share with the affected public, leading to skepticism and mistrust.

However, being yourself can backfire if not carefully thought through, as evidenced by the reaction to former BP Chief Executive Officer Tony Hayward with his now infamous "I'd like my life back'"* quote.

12. *Never raise issues*—You may feel tempted to raise issues aligned to your crisis—a bad idea. Try to avoid raising ideas that you'd rather not see in a story—new media or not. Stick to the script or agreed approach.

13. *Zip the lip*—As soon as you have made your point and given compelling reasons to back that up in 30 seconds or less, literally shut up! It is up to the interviewer to fill the space and ask another question. It is our job to get important messages across strategically according to the stage of the crisis.

14. *Assume that bloggers (covering your industry) will take information from your interview*—A year-long study by the Pew Research Center's Project for Excellence in Journalism, showed that bloggers "rely heavily on the traditional mainstream media for their information."[†]

And finally, *always* assume that the microphones and recording equipment *are turned on*. Never ever say something off the cuff or joke. That ill-used word or phrase may well end up on the front page of *The Wall Street Journal*, the London *Guardian*, or the *Australian Financial Review*. It will most certainly be tweeted, swapped, and shared. This was clearly demonstrated during the 2010 British elections when Gordon Brown, then Prime Minister of Great Britain, obviously forgot this golden rule during the 2010 election campaign. He was heard telling an aide that the arranged meeting with a 75-year-old constituent was "a disaster" because "she was just this bigoted woman."[‡] The rebuke was swift, forcing Brown to apologize.

---

* Tony Hayward, Chief Executive Officer, British Petroleum (BP). As reported by various media outlets (May 31, 2010).
† Pew Research Center Project for Excellence in Journalism, "New Media, Old Media: How Blogs and Social Media Agendas Relate and Differ from the Traditional Press," May 24, 2010. (From an e-mail newsletter, RSS feed received by the author.)
‡ Polly Curtis (Whitehall correspondent), General Election 2010 Live Blog, *The Guardian*, www.guardian.co.uk, posted 12:39 PM, April 28, 2010.

BOX 22.1   TIPS TO KEEP INTERVIEWS SHORT

1. Respond to a question with a sentence and a half.

Q: How is the weather today?

A: The weather is exceedingly hot (statement—has answered the main question), and (the bridge) I'd advise anyone who feels the heat to stay indoors near the newly installed (insert suitable adjective) air-conditioning unit (plus one, the half).

2. Adjectives add "color." Think of how to make this statement colorful: *The cat sat on the mat.* The (gray Persian) cat sat (sleepily) on the (black and white striped, New Zealand wool) mat.

3. Responses should be no longer than three short sentences, no more than 30 words, and no more than 30 seconds (Dr. Robert Chandler).*

4. Every statement needs a short statement to *sum it up.*

5. Metaphors are the key to keeping a message simple. For example, "China is like a giant elephant riding a bicycle—it has to maintain a fast speed so it won't crash." It is very important for the interviewee to make the point of the metaphor rather than allowing the journalist to do that! Note the point (or the *so what* factor) in this example. One needs to be very careful with a metaphor in a crisis. It needs to be *very carefully* chosen (and tested, if at all possible) because it can backfire on you. But metaphors are a very powerful way of "getting" an important message and can help a spokesperson explain something that would otherwise be very technical.

---

* Dr. Robert Chandler (Director, Nicholson School of Communication, University of Central Florida, Orlando), "Message Maps: Blueprints for Pandemic Preparedness," 3n White Paper, http://www.continuitycentral.com/messagemaps.pdf, 2006, p. 4.

AFTER THE INTERVIEW

After your interview, review your tape—if you have taped your own interview. This review will be helpful if you think you have made a mistake, particularly if it involved facts and figures. However, avoid the temptation to say, "Oh, I didn't mean to say …" That will only flag more questions. If you blundered, you will have to live with that.

If someone from your team had been sitting in on or watching/listening to the interview, then do a quick debrief. What worked, where did the interview become animated or aggressive? Were there any surprise questions? What do you need you do differently next time? If you really think that there will be an issue when the story is aired or is in print, then get ready to put something on your blog and/or the company Web site.

Once the story is published, you have some more options. For example, if the story is inaccurate, say, the figures were incorrect, you could call the journalist and point that out, but first thank them for the story and then say something like, "I thought you'd like to know that the statistic that was published is wrong. If that were true, we'd all be millionaires; I'd be rich." They will appreciate the more assertive, friendly approach rather than the aggressive approach, unless you wish not to have a relationship with that journalist ever again.

A simple thank you goes a long way.

TELEVISION INTERVIEWS

Television is all about pictures, pictures, pictures, so what you do—your body language—is *more* important than anything else. The nonverbal communication is worth 93 percent; only 7 percent is the words! What you wear and how you perform are very, very important, particularly in a crisis when the prevailing trust levels may be low. You have a nanosecond to convince the audience that you are trustworthy, so make that time count!

In a crisis, TV, and to a great extent the social media, is all about the emotion and drama and how it is conveyed in pictures, be that via CNN, ABC, and the BBC; or Facebook, TwitPic, Flickr, or any of the other social networking sites. You must be ever vigilant about how your crisis will be portrayed, how it will be remembered for years to come, by the symbols that have been created through the pictures.

Dress for the Part

In crisis media training and coaching sessions, clients often ask us what to wear—almost as frequently as they ask what to say!

It is very important to dress for the part. Dress according to the situation and the impression you want to create. For example, if you want to give the impression that you are in the middle of the crisis fixing the problem, caring for your customers and employees, then show that by having your sleeves rolled up, or at least do not wear a coat and tie. If you wear a safety helmet or other safety gear when working at an emergency site, wear that at a TV interview, as long as we can see your face and "the whites of your eyes."

For example, the Australian Nine Network's *60 Minutes* coverage of an Australian mining company at the center of the major cyanide spill in Eastern Europe highlights the dangers of appearing on the media unprepared and without having thought about impressions. The chief executive officer (CEO) was definitely wearing the wrong clothes and was in the wrong place.

This is what the viewers saw:

- Huge fish belly-up in the river being pulled out by locals with pitchforks.
- CEO being interviewed in a five-star hotel room dressed immaculately in a suit and tie.

Even if you did not hear what he was saying, the visual message was one of being aloof, uncaring, and remote. They missed a golden opportunity to do the interview on location at the site of the spill, sleeves rolled up, giving the impression of doing something about the situation and being in control. In fact, the image only reinforced typical community perceptions of mining industry executives reaping huge profits while the work conditions are dirty, dangerous, and environmentally unsound.

The disastrous Gulf of Mexico oil spill may forever be defined by the live video feed showing gushing oil and mud, seemingly forever out of control. In a crisis, *always* be thinking about the images and symbols that are portrayed.

Generally speaking, here are the rules (these rules apply to anything on the Internet, too):

- Avoid wearing pronounced stripes, checks, or small patterns, and anything shiny.
- Gray, brown, blue, or mixed-colored suits and dresses are best.
- Gray, light-blue, off-white, or pastel shirts or blouses are best.

- Women should wear neat jewelry or none at all, depending on the circumstances.
- Take your keys, phone, and pen out of your pockets.
- Avoid having a haircut right before the interview.
- If makeup is offered, use it, particularly if your interview is in a studio.

FACE-TO-FACE INTERVIEWS

If you are doing an interview face-to-face, look at the interviewer, *not* the camera. Maintain the eye-line, which is somewhere between the forehead and chin, during the entire interview. If your eyes flicker around during a TV interview, you look uncomfortable, and possibly a bit shifty. If you keep your eye-line focused on the interviewer, you will come across as being in command of your subject. Just try and relax and take your time. And remember to convey the right emotion—if people have died, smiling will be inappropriate.

Not all TV interviews will be in a studio. Most likely you will be doing interviews at the scene (of the "crime"), so be careful where you hold the news conference. The TV news producer or cameraman will want you to stand in front of the most devastating vision he or she can find—not necessarily to your advantage.

Images are everything, and often it is the pictures that define a crisis. You can negotiate where to do the interview, but make sure that the backdrop enhances, not hinders, your message. For example, the boardroom is the most inappropriate place to do your interview. What does that say about your values—locked away behind closed doors?

Think about the overall impression you want to create and have your TV interview in a venue that conveys the impression you wish to create—presumably that you care and that you are doing all you can to fix the problem. A vision of the CEO with his sleeves rolled up or at least in a shirt working at the scene or talking to victims will be better than a stiff upper lip shot in a boardroom. Witness U.S. President Barack Obama visiting the oil-ravaged coast of Louisiana in his shirtsleeves.

Animation and Gestures

Stand still! You would be amazed how much people will walk around when they are being interviewed for TV news. If you always "talk" with your hands, as I do, that's OK, just don't overdo it. It is a problem if your hands cover your face! Also be aware of knocking your microphone and other sounds that may interfere. Also, be aware of exaggerated movements or unconscious movements such as flicking your hair or tapping your fingers.

For TV news, stand comfortably with the majority of weight on one foot; imagine that it is rooted in cement. That should keep you still.

Your body language is important, so make sure that your words match your actions. You need to be slightly more animated and larger than life. Pep up your delivery so that it is energetic, rather than dull and low-key. TV is entertainment, after all, and broadcasting is a performance! The more engaging you appear, and the more you can express the emotions others are feeling, the more interested and involved the audience will feel.

Please, no bobbing heads!

Sound Good

Always take time to warm up your voice. You will come across as more articulate and authoritative. It will help prevent a "frog in the throat" during the interview. Sip room-temperature water before and during the interview. Never drink anything too hot or cold or anything with milk in it. Otherwise you will be constantly clearing your throat. A colleague of mine used to sound out the letters of the alphabet in an exaggerated form before he went on air.

Speak in Stand-Alone, Whole Sentences

For a clean sound bite for TV and radio news and a clear, concise quote for print, it is best to speak in complete, whole sentences. This will also increase the chances of your being accurately quoted. For example, if the question was how the weather is today, you would respond with:

> The weather is raw, the wind is biting and chilling to the bone, and the skies are very gray, dull, and overcast. I would advise everyone to stay inside (30 words). (You could add, "particularly as it's flu season.")

PHONE INTERVIEWS

A lot of traditional media interviews take place over the phone. Radio is mostly done by phone, and the vast majority of print interviews will be by phone. In a phone interview, just like the listener of a radio program, you have no visual clues to the interviewer's expression, general demeanor, or attitude. It gives the interviewer great flexibility and offers you, the spokesperson, some advantages, too. There are some disadvantages as well.

Let's think about the downside, particularly in a crisis. You will drop your guard, weaken the performance, and without the eye contact you may become more open, more confidential, and more revealing. As George Merlis says in his book *How to Make the Most of Every Media Appearance*, "The telephonic openness to which most of us have become accustomed is a pitfall for phone interviews … the phone has a way of lulling us into a state of self-revelation, and may lead us astray from our agenda."[*]

So, how do you keep focused and still in performance mode? For starters, stand up and gesture wildly. Your energy will flow better, and you will sound more animated and more present. And, if you can, conduct the interview in another space, away from your desk, away from your busy workday.

Put your messages in bullet form on a large piece of paper in front of you so you can see them easily. For some people, it also helps to have some reminders in front of them, like *slow down, be specific, remember to sum up, give examples, remember the victims.*

Some clients also find that having a smiley face in front of them or a picture of the damage or another important visual clue helps them stay focused.

Remember, tone is very important in a media interview. Make sure that you adopt the right tenor and calibrate your responses according to the stage and the panic your target audiences are feeling.

Impressions matter as much over the phone as they do in person.

One final piece of advice—once you have made your point, remember to zip the lip and wait for the next question. For a print interview it may take a while for a journalist to ask follow-up questions as he or she is busy typing your responses into the computer. Be patient and resist the temptation to fill the silence. Typically, reporters will tell you they are using their computers to take notes or to write stories as they go. In most countries, reporters are also obligated to tell you if they are taping you. Not so with citizen–journalists.

You may also want to tape the interview. Some journalists may object, but you could make it a condition of the interview, particularly if you are

---

[*] George Merlis, *How to Make the Most of Every Media Appearance: Getting Your Message across on the AIR, in PRINT, or ONLINE* (New York: McGraw-Hill), 2004, p. 153.

expecting a tough or hostile line of questioning. Like the reporter, you need to tell them you are recording the interview. Make this known at the beginning of the interview.

The stakes are very high when you are in crisis mode. You need to be as prepared in a phone interview as you would for an "all-in" media conference. *Write* down your key messages and be prepared to read them, but *read them with feeling, read them as if your life depended on it—it just well may.*

RADIO INTERVIEWS

Remember, radio is all about the voice. When you are interviewed in a crisis, your tone of voice will be critical and will convey as much if not more about the crisis as your words.

The other key factor with radio is that there are no pictures. You need to use words and phrases that help conjure the appropriate, relevant pictures for the listeners. This will take some careful planning when you are in a crisis.

You need to use short, succinct words, and you need to speak slowly and deliberately. And by *slowly* I don't mean listless, without energy. Passion, energy, and emotion are key to a successful radio interview, particularly if it is talk-back. Strange as it may seem, you can hear a smile, so smile if it is appropriate (it may not be in a crisis). Sadness, determination, compassion can all be heard or missed if that is what the audience is expecting. People will quickly tune into evasiveness and be quick to judge. Openness, accountability, transparency—they are the mantra for crisis radio interviews. *Your tone is everything.*

If you are the spokesperson, you will need to know whether you are live—nearly all radio talk-back is live—or taped for radio news.

For radio news, the journalist will be looking for two or three short, snappy, clean sound bites—around 15 seconds in length. By *clean* I mean no extraneous noise, no *um*s and *er*s; a complete, whole sentence that can stand alone. Remember that the journalist's question is rarely heard and that you will be edited out of context, so you will need to repeat your message at least three times to increase the likelihood of your key message being a sound bite. But that key message needs to be colorful, have meaning, and be jargon-free. Repetition simply means saying the same thing in three different ways.

If you are on talk-back radio and you are faced with contentious issues from angry or upset callers, then acknowledge their point of view—briefly— and then bridge to your key message. You can never avoid a question, and sometimes callers ring a show simply to vent and may never have a real question. It is up to you and the host to determine beforehand how you wish to handle this situation. If you agree, then agree with them. But still remember to bridge to a key point.

Once you have made your point, remember to zip the lip and resist the temptation to circle back to the interviewer's and caller's question. Better to leave the audience with your thought in their mind than the contentious one that was raised.

Remember, questions are gifts! And please, one thought at a time, one thought to a sentence. Practice this discipline.

PRINT INTERVIEWS

Print was the first mass media and today still holds an influential place in affecting public opinion. While readership may be declining and journalists from newsrooms around the globe are being let go, newspapers are the source of original reporting, and they still set the agenda for many TV and radio programs.

As Chris O'Brien of the *San Jose Mercury News* said in an interview for this book, "Newspapers are the place of record."[*] They can do the backstory, they analyze. And many, such as *The Wall Street Journal*, have a powerful online presence.

And we know from the 2010 Edelman Trust Barometer, articles in business magazines are highly credible. Independent sources such as analysts and academics are trusted sources, and they are who the media tend to gravitate to in a crisis, particularly in Stage Two. That is the modus operandi for the cable TV shows. How would CNN exist without its "experts?"

So, the print interview needs to be taken seriously. Your quotes are likely to be copied and pasted, tweeted, swapped, and shared around the world. To quote Merlis: "While the commodity of the broadcast media is time, the equivalent commodity in print journalism is space (albeit dwindling)."[†]

Here are some basic rules when doing a face-to-face interview with a print journalist:

- On meeting the journalist, give him/her your business card and treat him/her like a valued client. The business card will demonstrate two things:

---

[*] Chris O'Brien, *San Jose Mercury News*, interview with author, September 4, 2009.
[†] George Merlis, *How to Make the Most of Every Media Appearance: Getting Your Message across on the AIR, in PRINT, or ONLINE* (New York: McGraw-Hill), 2004, p. 153.

- That you are a potential source and available for follow-up questions.
- It gives the journalist a very quick overview of how far he/she can go with his/her questions based on your title (e.g., if your card says Manager/President, he/she will expect that you know a lot about the company and can speak to almost anything!).
- Speak in complete, whole sentences; use good grammar. If you fail to do this, you may be paraphrased and not directly quoted— this could lead to your being quoted out of context. So, say "The weather is fine" as opposed to "fine."
- Avoid *its, that, them*—Be specific, otherwise the journalist is highly likely to make an assumption about what you mean, and it is also highly probable that he/she will not make the same meaning as you!
- Listen carefully to the reporter's questions and use them to construct a quote, or at least a response.
- Plan at least one good analogy *before* your interview that sums up your point of view. Use that analogy to anchor your key message. Please, please, please test that analogy before the interview, too!
- Maintain good eye contact—Otherwise you may come across as shifty—not a good look in a crisis.
- Avoid negatives—These will lead to denial headlines and/or quotes, which will hinder your efforts and overall intent in a crisis. As we have seen, negative language is toxic.
- Avoid jargon—Even if you think that the business term you are using is understood, the journalist may attach a different meaning to that phrase than you do. If you do use jargon, immediately follow up with, "That's our jargon for … "
- Remember that you know more about your company or issue than the reporter—This is a good and a bad thing in a crisis. While we want openness and transparency, there are some things that only you and the board or the boss need to know. It might be the name of a victim, and you know it, but the family has yet to be informed. Say *only* what you know to be fact.
- Be passionate—Take some enthusiasm and appropriate emotion to the interview given that you are in crisis mode. If you are saddened by the event, then say so and mean it. Remember the head and the heart principle. As I say to my clients in coaching sessions, unless you are prepared to be human and give of yourself, send a postcard. If you are the storyteller, then *love* your story.

- Think of two to three main points you would like to make about your subject. Gather facts, figures, and anecdotes to support your points. Anticipate questions the reporter might ask and have responses ready. Stories are the lifeblood for print reporters. In a crisis, particularly in Stage Two, be prepared to tell a story about the "heroes" and commend them. Remember that Stage Two is all about the victims and your response. Stories *will* help you get your message across.
- Have printed materials to support your information whenever possible in order to help the reporter minimize errors. If time allows, offer to e-mail the reporter printed information in advance of the interview. This might be a map or a chart that shows the way you are fixing the problem.
- Remember your body language—In a crisis it is critical that all your actions match your words. The meta-messaging that a skilled journalist picks up on could well determine how he/she frames the story. Adjectives like *bold, blunt, angry, bewildered, exhausted* are all based on your body language—how you look and sound.

E-MAIL AND TWITTER INTERVIEWS

Given today's lightning-fast age, you are just as likely to be e-mailed and/or tweeted a list of questions and be interviewed that way. Easy, you say; I will write my responses and they will be reproduced as I wrote them. Not necessarily. Your response may be shared with other reporters in the newsroom or on their list of followers to check out the story idea.

So, set the rules of engagement up front. I learned the hard way—humbling for someone in my profession. Some years ago, I received an e-mail from a trusted journalist—or so I thought. My clients and I had been a source for many of her stories in her influential column in the "Technology Section" of the *Sydney Morning Herald*. She was asking what if I had heard about a criticism of media training. I quickly sent a response only to find it taken verbatim in her column the next day! She never divulged her intent and I never asked! The quote was OK, but it would have been so much better if I had taken a little time to think about my response and asked her a series of questions before I wrote anything! All's well that ends well, as we then had an extended interview—again only by e-mail—and she wrote a feature story for her newspaper.

Lessons learned:

1. Assume that you are being "interviewed" if you get an e-mail from a journalist. Anything that you commit in writing can and will be used.
2. Always behave as if everything and anything you say can appear on the front page of the major newspaper in the land, for example, *The Wall Street Journal.*
3. Ask the reason for the question before you commit to anything.
4. Take a few minutes to plan, as words and phrases can be taken out of context and used anywhere in an overall story.
5. Ask what the purpose of the interview is, where and how the information will be used, and if the journalist intends to speak with anyone else on this issue. In a crisis you can assume that they will.

You need to plan like you would for a print interview—good grammar; compelling language; complete, whole sentences. Be short and succinct, and make your quotes stand out.

For tweets, the journalists need a series of headlines. See if you can contain yourself to 120 characters, as the journalists may want to link your comment, and you may also want to put in a link to your Web site and/ or blog.

And remember, what is on the Internet stays on the Internet. As Renae Nichols, communications lecturer at Pennsylvania State University, stated, "You cannot take sin back."[*] The damage is done, so take care and time with your response as much as you would for any interview, particularly in a crisis situation.

DEALING WITH BLOGGERS

First, treat bloggers like mainstream journalists with a special round or as an influential columnist. You would treat that journalist a little differently from a daily news reporter. Apply that same principle when dealing with bloggers. The big difference is that they have no editors—there is no editorial chain of command other than their loyal followers and readers.

---

[*] Renae Nichols (Senior Lecturer, Communications, Pennsylvania State University), interview with author, April 10, 2009.

Bloggers are most likely to be writing about a niche, a subject they feel very connected to and are passionate about. They are likely to be very connected and have specialist knowledge and/or experience. And they are most likely to be purists and will jump quickly on issues that have a strong ideological underpinning. This was amply demonstrated by the Motrin front baby carrier ads in 2008 and again in 2010 with the Pampers Dry Max diaper controversy. The Mommy bloggers were central to those stories. They called for boycotts, asked readers to alert the mainstream media, and caused much heartache for Johnson & Johnson and Proctor & Gamble.

The Mommy bloggers are an outspoken lot. Peter Shankman, of HARO (Help A Reporter Out) fame and somewhat of a superstar in the new media space, describes them as one of the most vocal, quickest to blog, "'strongest-to-band-together-and-form-one-opinion-like-the-Borg' collectives out there—The Mommy-Blogging community.'"[*] One Tweeter posted, "note to self … never piss off moms … especially bitter moms … they can be a nasty bunch)."[†]

While moms will be fiercely protective of their young and will fight for their cause (and so would I), so will just about any purist. Shell found that out when a father-and-son blogging team almost brought the company to its knees. A United Kingdom blogger, who is ex-British military, claims that the team's blogging efforts have cost the oil giant $15 billion—yes, $15 billion!

Alfred Donovan, now 90-plus years old, and his son John have been collecting and publishing information online about Shell's activities since 2001. Not only have they been actively campaigning against the company for nearly a decade (they started in 2001), but they own the domain name *www.royaldutchshellplc.com*—Shell's proper name, you guessed it, Royal Dutch Shell.

According to an interview on their blog, the site receives millions of hits per month and many of the people using the site are Shell employees.[‡]

Influential—you bet. The Donovans and their blog are regularly quoted in the mainstream media—no doubt that the father-and-son team is an ongoing headache for Shell.

Face it—blogs are highly emotive. They are also unlikely to offer sourcing of any kind, it's mostly the blogger's opinion. The 2009 Pew

---

[*] Peter Shankman, Help A Reporter Out (HARO), "Moms and Motrin," *The New York Times,* http://parenting.blogs.nytimes.com/2008/11/17/moms-and-motrin/, November 17, 2008.
[†] Ibid.
[‡] Glen Frost, Editor, "Blog Costs Shell US$15 Billion," *The PR Report,* February 14, 2010. (Interview posted on Donovan Father-and-Son Blog, www.royaldutchshellplc.com.)

Project for Excellence in American Journalism State of the Media Report (Annual Report on American Journalism) showed that nearly two-thirds (64 percent) of bloggers had no sources and 22 percent had just one.

One could argue that the influential Huffington Post is one giant blog—certainly an influential news site and one that has the respect of many, including the prominent public relations firm Edelman. Writing on his blog, Richard Edelman, the firm's president and CEO, says that "Edelman considers the Huffington Post a viable first option for clients."*

Craig McGill, Managing Director and creative guy at Contently Managed, digital and social media public relations consultants based in Scotland, offers this advice for dealing with bloggers:

1. You cannot control the message—Not that you really ever did! "You can send a blogger all the stuff you want; if they don't like it, they don't like it. And they will tell the world. What you can do is have a conversation."
2. Never send a press release—Send them a link to your release, if you must. Bloggers like to break stories or (more often) comment on something seen elsewhere, but they will never (or very rarely) just reprint your press release.
3. Take them seriously—Do not treat them like second-class citizens. If you want them to take you seriously, then you take them seriously and extend any courtesy that you would extend to the mainstream media.
4. Make life easy for them. Have copyright-allowed images/audio/video on your site that they can use without asking you.
5. Accept that nothing you say is off the record and that every e-mail you send the blogger may end up public. Ditto with phone calls—ah, we have heard this advice before!
6. Remember the odds are that the blogger will Google the hell out of you before replying, so make sure your online credibility is strong.
7. Most of all, remember that *it is all a conversation. Always introduce yourself.*†

---

* Posted by Richard Edelman, "Huffington Post; Taking the Next Step," 6 A.M. Blog (Edelman Blog), http://www.edelman.com/speak_up/blog/archives/2009/07/huffington_post.html, July 27, 2009.

† Posted by Craig McGill, "15 Tips for PRs Dealing with Bloggers," Contently Managed Blog, http://www.contently-managed.com/blog/2009/08/30/15-tips-for-bloggers-dealing-with-prs/, August 30, 2009.

NEWS CONFERENCES

The news conference, or presser, as they are also known, have long been the staple "diet" for crisis media management. Most often, a news release with a subsequent phone interview will suffice, but rarely if ever in a crisis, as the media demand will be high. Reporters will be swarming everywhere, cell phones will be overloaded and resources stretched. A news conference will be the best option when:

- Media are gathering onsite.
- There are many requests for the same information.
- The news is important enough to interest all mainstream media, plus bloggers and other special interest media (e.g., Fort Hood).
- There is more than one spokesperson needed (e.g., CEO plus technical expert/subject matter expert and/or emergency services representative).

Avoid holding news conferences when:

- Most media are on deadline.
- Information is needed more quickly.
- Few details are known.
- There is limited media interest.
- You are not the principal player in the crisis.
- There is no trained or rehearsed spokesperson.

Even when media are gathered onsite, it is sometimes appropriate to hold an impromptu or "door-stop" conference. That is, bring the spokesperson to the media, allowing him or her to conduct what is known as an "all-in" interview.

A news conference signals that your story (your crisis) is important, that you are putting your face on the story, and that you are making yourself accountable in some way, or at least offering some explanations. There are often very high expectations, so you need to be prepared.

The U.S. Fort Hood shootings in 2009, demanded a news conference. The interest in the story was huge. It had national and international implications, and a news conference was certainly an effective way for the Army to reach a huge number of people simultaneously. CNN and many other networks carried the news conferences live, as many citizen–journalists told their story through tweets and posts to Facebook. So too, with the Gulf of Mexico oil spill, where news conferences became a daily occurrence, as the interest was so high and the impact so huge.

Let's look at how a news conference might work in the digital age.

- Stage One (basic facts are told—what happened stage)
  - Story breaks on Twitter, video posted to YouTube, company named.
  - Citizen–journalists abound—often breaking news. This stage is all about *speed*! And these citizen–journalists may be your staff (e.g., Fort Hood), so be aware and have that policy in place.
- Stage Two (facts are dissected, added to, discussed; the response is highlighted; the unfolding drama stage)
  - Company posts YouTube response.
  - Company tweets to its followers and publishes links to company Web site and other key players like a government authority or emergency relief organization.
  - Mainstream media gather at headquarters or company site for firsthand reporting.
  - Said company holds media conference with key influential bloggers via Twitter and Skype, and in person with mainstream media (TV, radio, national and international newspapers, news agencies, local daily papers, and trade press).
  - Company spokesperson gives one-on-one interviews for key media outlets after the news conference.
  - Company edits and posts interviews to its Web site and to YouTube via a Flip camera, and publishes pictures to Flickr—all properly tagged.

Yes, busy. There are multiple channels to manage and monitor. You'd better have a technically savvy social media player on your crisis communication team.

MANAGING A NEWS CONFERENCE

1. *Designate someone to manage introductions, start and finish*—This person could be the head of corporate communication, public relations, or operations. Their role is to introduce the spokesperson and set the stage for the news conference, explaining the format and time allotted for questions.
2. *Spokesperson starts with a statement*—Hopefully not read and no more than two minutes. Better to deliver your opening remarks

(sound bites in their own right) from memory, particularly the first 20 to 30 seconds.

3. Like any major political news conference, *choose different reporters* from the scrum so you do not allow any one reporter to dominate the conversation.

4. *Keep your body steady*—If you move, move very slowly. A good piece of advice from George Merlis is to imagine that you are underwater: "Visualize how the resistance of the water keeps you from making rapid movements when you are in a lake, a pool or an ocean. That is exactly how you need to be in front of a camera."*

5. *Call for questions and set a time limit*—For example, "We'll take questions for the next 10 minutes." Otherwise you will be there all day!

6. *If questions ramble* or there are multiple questions in one question, just pick the one that works best for you and answer that one.

7. *Work the room*—When making your statement, start at the center, then move to the left and turn your attention to the right. If you get a friendly question, end looking at that reporter. You may get a follow-up question, or you can return to that reporter at another time. If it is more hostile, subtly turn your attention to another part of the room when you have finished. Wrap up the news conference by taking a question from a friendly or at least a neutral reporter. Or you can wrap up by taking a question from someone you know, someone with whom you can predict their line of questioning.

8. *Keep an eye on the clock*—If you have set a time limit, it is a good idea to stick to it, particularly if you have given the reason as wanting to get back to the investigation, clean up, or getting to the bottom of what happened. If it is a very tough situation (e.g., deaths), say that you will take questions for 15 minutes, and at 12 minutes say, "We have time for two more questions."

In addition to posting an edited version or sound bite to your Web site, you may want to provide an audio transcript of the news conference, particularly if the news conference was held via phone. This allows you to reach many audiences at once.

For example, during the anthrax attacks in 2001, the U.S. Centers for Disease Control and Prevention (CDC) often held routine news conferences

---

* George Merlis, *How to Make the Most of Every Media Appearance: Getting Your Message across on the AIR, in PRINT, or ONLINE* (New York: McGraw-Hill), 2004, p. 161.

daily. Vicki S. Freimuth, Ph.D., who was director of communications at the CDC during that time, said that it was rare for the CDC to hold a press conference before that crisis.

> These press conferences began as telephone-only events but evolved into both in-person and phone events. By including phone, we were able to allow many other stakeholders to listen to the conferences live and receive updates at the same time as the media. In addition, we provided transcripts of the press conferences on our Website within a few hours, allowing a much larger audience access to the information.[*]

The veteran U.S. crisis counselor Jim Lukaszewski and others advocate *inviting key stakeholders* to your news conferences so they hear the news firsthand, unfiltered. The 2001 CDC example is testament to this advice.

As with every media encounter, make darn sure your spokesperson is prepped, briefed, trained, and well-rehearsed.

---

[*] Vicki S. Freimuth, "Organizing for Effective Communication during a Crisis," International Association of Business Communicators (IABC), *CW Bulletin*, Vol. 4, No. 2, February 2006.

23

Media Training

If you are prepared, there's no need to sweat.*
      —*Jim Caldwell (Coach of Indianapolis Colts, Super Bowl 2010)*

Professional media training today is a must. There is no winging it anytime you are facing the media and never ever when you are under fire. Media training will help prepare you, "inoculate" you against the pressures and trials of a media interview.

You need a trustworthy, experienced professional who not only understands the media and how it works but understands business, too. You also want to know that they understand and/or have direct experience in dealing with a crisis.

The best media trainers have all those characteristics and more—they are also trained trainers who understand adult learning and how to work effectively with management of all ages and stages of life (see Box 23.1).

Experienced media trainers will teach you more than how to stand in front of a camera and drill you on what to say. They will create a stimulating and "safe" training environment, and they will teach you strategies to help you navigate your way through the media minefield, as well as how to deal with tough questions.

For those of you who are afraid that you will be taught how to spin stories or to be less than genuine, I offer this advice: Media training does not mean learning how to become artificial. As Robin Conn says,

---

* Jim Caldwell (Coach of Indianapolis Colts, Super Bowl 2010), as quoted in the *San Francisco Chronicle*, February 7, 2010.

and I wholeheartedly agree, "Saints preserve us from overtrained executives on television interviews saying 'Dan (smile), I'm glad you asked me that (smile).'"[*]

Media training will help you sort the men from the boys and give you confidence that your organization will more than survive a crisis. It is not a nice-to-do; it is a must-do.

BOX 23.1   CHOOSING THE RIGHT MEDIA TRAINER

While there are many trainers with varying qualifications, it is important to ask these questions.

Does your media trainer:

- Have experience as a journalist? If so, what level, where? They need to be able to walk the talk!
- Demonstrate a strong understanding of strategic communication?
- Have formal training qualifications?
- Teach proven tools and techniques, not just tell stories?
- Explain the theory that underpins what they teach?
- Design workshops that work every time and meet the needs of each participant?
- Understand that no two participants are alike, and can vary their approach with every person and group?
- Offer a detailed analysis of each participant's technique?
- Research your issues before you arrive at the workshop?
- Use a scenario approach to your crisis media training?
- Have crisis experience?
- Work with an experienced journalist and cameraman during training sessions?
- Follow up their training with refreshers, exercises to validate skills?
- Know that it isn't an ego trip for them; it's about getting you the results you want.

Source: Media Skills (Flyer, 2009).

---

[*] Robin Conn, *The PR Crisis Bible: How to Take Charge of the Media When All Hell Breaks Loose*, (New York: St. Martin's Press), 2000, p. 216.

WHO SHOULD BE MEDIA TRAINED?

Many companies I have worked with have a very firm policy that *only* people who have been media trained can do media interviews. This is a wise guiding principle (see Box 23.2).

Now exactly who should that be? I advocate that as much attention, training, and education be given to the front line (security, reception, call center, customer service, operations) as to the senior management and the board of directors.

Clearly, there will be different levels of training—some will be awareness so that everyone understands their role and responsibilities in a crisis—that is so very important. Others, like those at the operational level, who will be at the "scene of the crime," need intensive training, as do the nominated spokespeople and their backups. You want to avoid a single point of failure.

BOX 23.2   SPOKESPERSON STANDARDS

The spokesperson must be:

- Media trained
- Able to perform under pressure
- Highly credible and authoritative
- Espoused to company values
- Informed about the impact of the incident

The following gives an overview and recommendations for who needs to be trained and when, according to the stage when the media report a crisis.

Stage One

A thorough analysis of your organization's risk and vulnerabilities *before* a crisis hits will determine where and when you need spokespeople. In this brave new world where immediacy and speed of response are even more important, there is a need for the front line to be trained—perhaps not to be full-blown spokespeople, but to at least have an awareness of what to do and what to say. At the very least, it is important to have guidelines and

173

a policy for employees on how to handle the media including the social media, particularly Twitter and Facebook.

The U.S. Army discovered firsthand the perils of social media and employee citizen–journalists during the shootings at Fort Hood.

Most employees will want to be seen doing the right thing, but as crisis communication expert Gerard Braud says, we default to gossip, exaggeration, and negativity unless we have been schooled otherwise.

Braud, who is a big advocate of "ambassador" training for crisis preparedness, says you can deescalate the likelihood of negative messages with some basic awareness training. He says to listen to chatter in the grocery line, gather around the water cooler, and you will hear negative gossip.

Take Braud's scenario of a hospital where employees are asked questions about a patient whose hand had been accidentally cut off. The untrained employees are likely to say, "Oh that's not all, not only did we cut off his hand but we did …" *or* "Oh, that's not the first time it's happened …"* That is why most companies feel they need a strict "no speak" policy regarding the media. But media-aware employees will help you, not hinder you, in a crisis.

In an awareness session, key frontline employees will learn to say something like, "That's a very unfortunate situation, and this is how and why we are doing XYZ." Braud says that the conversation is likely to end there—no more gossip, no more negativity.

The U.S. Coast Guard trains all their frontline responders. They firmly believe that the people doing the work should be the ones to talk about what they are doing. Their credo is, *"Maximum disclosure, minimum delay."*

Bottom line:

- Do a vulnerability assessment to help determine spokespeople.
- Train key operational staff at a minimum.
- Develop a media spokesperson policy.
- Develop a social media policy or at least guidelines for employees.
- Develop standby lines for frontline employees.

Stage Two

At this stage, you will know the basics about what happened. You also will have started an investigation. It is time to roll out the key spokesperson, if you have not already done so. This may or may not be the chief executive

---

* Gerard Braud, interview with author, July 9, 2009.

officer (CEO) as we discussed in Chapter 13. Your choice and criteria for choosing a spokesperson will always follow this line of questioning:

- What is the overall impression we want to create?
- Have people died or are lives at risk?
- Are our reputation and values under attack?
- What is the panic and who is best to address that panic?
- How big is the impact and visibility of the crisis—statewide, national, international?

BP had no option but to bring out the "big guns" given the seriousness of the oil spill in the Gulf of Mexico. The "big guns" may also be the heads of government, as we have seen with many of the major crises around the world. Presidents, premiers, and prime ministers get involved when the crisis is of significant magnitude and the company or regulator is seen not to be coping.

During the Fort Hood shootings, the chief spokesperson was Lt. General Robert Cone, who is in charge of the Army base; he was onsite. However, he was not the only official spokesperson, as you would expect for a crisis of this scale. The heavy brass visited and spoke, the president spoke, and the victims spoke. And Colonel John Rossi, the post's Deputy Commander, also spoke, updating and explaining what the Army was doing.

The Army spokespeople performed very well under pressure—as you would expect—and no doubt had been trained and well rehearsed in how to handle the media in a crisis.

The spokespeople also managed the social media well. After the first round of unvetted enthusiasm by a soldier, Tearah Moore, whose Twitter account was quickly suspended, they quickly established a Facebook presence and regularly updated their Web site with comments from Lt. General Cone.

Train and rehearse your key operational people, your crisis management team, and your key crisis spokespeople, and have the frontline involved in crisis media awareness training so they understand their role in Stage Two.

Dealing with an apology is very appropriate training for Stage Two spokespeople. Saying sorry (see Chapter 26) needs to be sincere, and this needs to be tested in the training room. Taking responsibility and showing that you care also need to be tested and validated in the training room.

175

You may also want to review the role of security to determine how exposed your spokespeople are. Where and when will security face the public—your customers, clients, and families of the victims? Many organizations include security contractors in their training sessions. I worked with several security firms and their frontlines doing crisis media awareness sessions in leading up to the 2000 Olympics in Sydney. Remember to include social media in your training sessions, too. Who will be your official tweeter, who will be "speaking" on Facebook, who will blog? What is the role of the frontline in SocialMediaLand?

Stage Two is an important stage. Your reputation will be formed or broken here, so prepare well and choose wisely.

Stage Three

If you are rolling out your spokespeople at this stage, you are likely to be slammed, as Domino's found out. They responded too late, even though we understand they were doing the right thing behind the scenes. They were working in the old-school mode. They presented the company president, Patrick Doyle, some 48 hours after the rogue employees had delivered their foul acts to the Internet via YouTube. Domino's reaction was too late in this instantaneous communication age.

You have no option: You need to train the CEO, the chief spokesperson, the crisis management team (CMT), key operational people, plus experts to cope with the challenging, finger-pointing Stage Three. Think also about any special advisers or third-party endorsers who may add independence and credibility to the efficacy of your response, actions, and messages, remembering that in Stage Three, everyone will have an opinion about you and your response. You need to have a very effective, unflappable spokesperson who can effectively address the "I told you so" syndrome; someone who can deal with blame and is inoculated against biting into the poisonous questions or repeating the negative.

Social media are still important and will in fact keep bubbling along well after the headlines have fizzled out in the traditional legacy media, so you need to ensure that your spokespeople are ready and trained to cope with that frenzy.

Stage Four

Because this stage takes you back to the beginning by providing closure with a funeral, an investigation, a return to work, or product back to the shelves, the consistency of spokespeople, people who have won our trust, is vital.

If you started with an operational spokesperson and stuck to that decision throughout the crisis, then that is the spokesperson who handles this stage.

Train your spokespeople to deal with questions like, "What have you done to make sure that this never happens again? Are there questions of liability? What have you learned?" Ensure you have the appropriate level of compassion balanced with firm resolve, and test this in your training.

Remember that the social media will still buzz with opinions and will need to be monitored and maintained.

Group or Individual Training?

We have discussed who should be trained. Now let's look at whether it should be group training or individual coaching.

Groups are more cost-effective, and participants in small group training learn a lot from watching each other. They may also come up with more effective messaging that can be tested in a safe environment. However, it is rarely effective or productive to have the CEO, boss, or immediate supervisor in the same group as their direct reports. I always recommend to my clients that the most senior spokesperson have his or her training on an individual basis. Personal coaching yields better results for the top executive. And refreshers are most certainly needed, plus rehearsals and coaching when the crisis does hit. Have the phone number of your trusted media coach handy so you can reach him/her when "the proverbial ... hits the fan." You will need them.

HOW OFTEN, HOW MUCH?

Depending on the level of risk in your organization and visibility of your brand, you will need to train at least annually, ideally twice a year. Include media training in your annual risk assessment. And make sure you have top-level support and a decent budget to work with a professional trainer. (A day with a trained, accredited media trainer working with a journalist and camera crew, based on real risks and vulnerabilities in your organization, will be around $6,500 to $10,000. A full training program that includes all your team, including frontline, plus drills and exercises, will range from around $40,000 to $90,000—a tiny fraction of what may be at risk in legal fees and compensation, not to mention the impact on the bottom line.)

177

Media training does not just end with the end of a session. To maximize learning requires practice. It definitely requires your commitment to using the skills outside the training room. Don't wait for, heaven forbid, the next crisis to use the skills. To be good at media interviews, like any skill, needs practice and reinforcement. I always encourage individual study—watch some media interviews, both on the traditional mainstream media like CNN, *ABC News*, or BBC, as well as YouTube. Call a talk-back radio station and practice the tools and techniques with a succinct opinion and/or question. (Better to do this on your own time on a subject that is near and dear to your heart as opposed to sensitive company policy.) It is also a good idea to research how others in your industry have managed a crisis.

The bottom line is that you need to choose your spokespeople according to the values and mission of your organization and train them accordingly. Take a good cross section of your organization and use the media training to test and validate skills and messages *before* a crisis hits.

SECTION IV SUMMARY

How well you fare in an interview with the media in this crazy, acceler-ated world we live and work in will very much depend on the amount of preparation and planning you put into it. Your reputation is on the line, and there are very high expectations of open, honest communication today. Trust of corporations and government is at an all-time low.

Just as everyone can be and is a journalist today, the same can be said for spokespeople. Cisco Systems has a saying, *Everyone's a spokesperson today.*

So, audit your organization to see where your vulnerabilities are, where your strengths are, and plan accordingly. Train your spokespeople, conduct exercises, and in your scenarios be as creative as possible. The more bizarre the scenario, the better. The mere fact that you can think of it means that it can happen.

Use the skills, the advice, and the techniques in this section to good end and with good heart. And remember that every performance is like a piece of theater, except that your life and the lives of others may well depend on how well you perform.

Section V

Communication— Rules and Tools

You can't just say it. You have to get the people to say it to each other.[*]
—*James Farley, (Chief Marketing Officer, Ford Motor Company)*

OVERVIEW

The best message in a crisis is a fast one!

Best practice has decreed it so. But in today's lightning-fast, accelerated age, fast is more minutes than hours, perhaps even seconds. But fast is not your only challenge.

Controlling the message used to be the job of the crisis communicator. You could—more or less—control the message through the traditional mass media. *Control the media, control the message* used to be the mantra. That is virtually impossible today—that's now in the hands of the crowds, the citizen–journalists, anyone who has access to a computer and/or a smartphone.

Messages, too, are short—140 characters or less, 30 words or less, please.

Never has the *keep it simple stupid* (KISS) principle been so relevant, and not just because of the attention deficit disorder (ADD) age we live

---

[*] David Kiley, "Ford Spending 25% of Marketing on Digital and Social Media," *Bloomberg Business Week*, http://www.businessweek.com/autos/autobeat/archives/2009/10/ford_spending_25_of_marketing_on_digital_and_social_media.html, October 16, 2009.

in. Simple, plain English that is pitched at about the age level of an eighth grader is more likely to be understood in a crisis. There was a reason that United Kingdom publisher Lord Northcliffe had this sign—They Are Only Ten—in his Fleet Street offices, reminding reporters of their public's reading age.

Despite the pace, the instantaneous messaging, the lack of control, the advances in communications technology, and the advent of the citizen–journalists, the key principles remain the same. There still is a need for persistent, powerful, and timely communication delivered with transparency and authenticity—humility, too—to the right people, in the right way, with the right tools.

In this section, we will:

- Step back and reexamine some of those golden rules.
- Discuss the role of social media and look at some case studies.
- Examine the role of the apology.
- Look at the best way to construct an effective statement.
- Look at the role of language in a crisis—eighth if not fifth grade!
- Look at why we communicate in a crisis.
- Explore what and where to communicate, including the new tools.
- Look at monitoring so that you have some guidelines for prioritizing your media communication strategies in a crisis.

The new technologies and communication platforms like Twitter and Facebook are examined in some detail, as we know that they play an increasingly important role in crisis media management. We simply cannot ignore them. They are here to stay. As the cover page of the January 2010 Ragan Report screamed, "What's Your Company Waiting for to Introduce Social Media? A 100-Year Flood?"*

---

* "What's Your Company Waiting for to Introduce Social Media? A 100-Year Flood?" (Cover) *The Ragan Report*, Lawrence Ragan Communications, Inc., January 2010.

24

Why Communicate in a Crisis?

Before we get into the nitty gritty of what to say and how to say it, let's be very clear about *why* we even bother to communicate when the stakes are so high, when it may all blow over in a few days, maybe even hours.

For starters the crowds will crucify you if you say nothing. That vacuum will be filled and fast. Rumors and misinformation will abound. Foes and friends, critics and do-gooders alike will grandstand. Every man and his dog, every @tom, @dick, and @harry will have an opinion and the means to express it.

In situations like Virginia Tech, Fort Hood, the Victorian bushfires, and the Haiti earthquake, powerful and rapid communication was a must. There is simply no choice. Lives were at risk. Lives could be saved. People were panicking. If you face a similar situation, get it under control and communicate as quickly as possible. (See Box 24.2 for some tips on using social media during emergencies.)

There is a real urgency to get the word out quickly to a wide range of affected people. This communication may constitute warnings, notifications, alerts, and emergency messages.

Ultimately, the overall goal of crisis communication is to protect "assets," as my dear husband, somewhat of a guru in business continuity circles, advocates. Those assets may be people, but equally property, products, and the brand.

When communicating in a crisis, you need, at all times, to be very aware of the value of your assets—how much you have in the "trust bank." Hard or not, you will have to work to *protect the integrity and reputation* of the organization.

BOX 24.1   TIPS FOR USING SOCIAL MEDIA DURING EMERGENCIES

- Make social media efforts message driven, not channel driven.
- Embrace every possible teaching moment so that your social media networks can grow.
- Tap into all available resources. Do you have a large cadre of volunteers?
- Consider training them as social media ambassadors.
- Keep messages brief and pertinent. People are not really reading; they are scanning.
- Make sure you can receive public input. Remember that social media involves not just you talking to the public but also them talking to you and to each other.
- Use social media to support a unified message. Instead of creating a new message for social media, use social media to support your existing message in a larger communications model.
- Have a Plan B. Suppose phone lines are jammed and/or computers are down—what will you do?
- Forge partnerships for sharing methods and messages. Federal agencies, for example, need to reach out to the private sector, and vice versa.
- Focus on people when formulating your communication plan. Networks of people will get work done, even when there is no electricity.
- Avoid elitism or the belief that people in charge know more and the general public is prone to misbehavior.
- New technologies are not simply new types of media with which to do the same old things. These new media signal a shift in thinking about how we communicate with our audiences.
- Avoid the "shiny new object syndrome" (being quick to adopt every new social media outlet that emerges … as soon as it emerges).

Source: Booz Allen Hamilton, "Goodbye Sources, Messages, Channels and Receivers: Hello Network," White Paper from *American Public Health Association Expert Round Table on Social Media and Risk Communication during Times of Crisis*, www.boozallen.com/consulting-services/services_article/42420696, March 2009. (Reprinted with permission.)

After all, an organization's reputation stands or falls based on how a crisis is handled—how well you demonstrate your core values and how well you communicate. Despite the nanoseconds it takes for someone to believe you or not, just on looks and sound alone, words *do matter.*

Think carefully about the overall impression you want to create and plan accordingly. The court of (Internet) opinion will judge you.

KEY QUESTIONS

To help determine your communication and priorities for communicating in a crisis, go no farther than the five Ws and How (see Box 24.2). They are simply your six best friends when it comes to crisis media management. They provide the six categories of questions that need to be answered at some stage during the crisis to ensure key audiences are fully informed and engaged. They also assist in determining the best methods for reaching your audience.

BOX 24.2

Who: Has been immediately affected? Is involved/on the spot? Should act now? Needs to be reassured? Will be able to get instructions to those who need to act or react in some way? Whose health or well-being is directly at risk?

What: Has happened? Is being done? Should we do now?

When: Did it happen? Will we know the details? Will it be over?

Where: Did it happen? Should we be now?

Why: Did it happen? Have you responded in this way?

How: Did it happen? Is the crisis being managed?

As discussed in Section II, "Stages of a Crisis," the questions most likely to be asked cover the details—the Who, What, When, and Where—of the incident itself. "What happens now?" questions usually follow, before the Why's and the How's start being asked.

185

Essentially, the media's questions—new and old—fall into four broad categories according to the stages:

Stage One—What happened?

Stage Two—How did that happen? This stage involves looking at the possible or probable cause.

Stage Three—Why? (i.e., how was this allowed to happen—the cause has been pretty much established—and who was responsible for letting it happen?) This is the finger-pointing, blame-game stage, which you really want to avoid at all costs. Ask BP.

Stage Four—What have you learned so that this doesn't happen again?

25

What to Communicate?

One of the biggest mistakes you can make in a crisis is to delay your response. "It is a fatal flaw to delay,"* says Gerard Braud, crisis communication expert. Too many companies seem paralyzed by the lack of information. They don't want to say anything until they know everything. This is wrong!

In a vacuum people will make up their own minds, based on previous experiences and/or prevailing perceptions, and generally they assume the worst.

Your organization *must* be prepared to issue a statement *within one hour or less of the onset of the crisis.* This is especially true in the digital age of social media and Web 2.0, where tweets, cell phone images, and videos are shared at the blink of an eye.

That first statement issued might actually be many short continuous bursts of information on Twitter, acknowledging that there is a problem and that you are looking into it, or that you are investigating the issue. Then give updates about what you have found out and are doing. This approach may appear *informal* but that's the way of the future. Whatever tool or channel you use, make it fast and communicate continuously.

The first statement may also be given at a formal news conference. Yes, companies do still have them! Witness Fort Hood, US Airway's miracle landing, Australian bushfires, not to mention the dozens held by various spokespeople for the disastrous oil spill in the Gulf of Mexico. A media conference is essential if the impact is big and lots of people are affected.

---

* Gerard Braud, interview with author, July 9, 2009.

Whether written or spoken, the first statement sets the scene for the rest of the crisis. It should state the basic who, what, when, and where (why and how may come later) of the situation and address the following:

- Outline the nature of the crisis (e.g., state what it is: fire, shooting, recall, embezzlement, explosion, death of key employee; and/or describe it: isolated, tragic, sad).
- Outline steps being taken to rectify the problem (if known)—what you have done or are doing.
- Answer as many of the Five Ws and How as possible and advisable.
- Address the panic.
- State your priorities—both now and in the future.
- Contain a call to action (what is required of others) if necessary.

After the basic facts are given at the media conference (see Box 25.1), the spokesperson should commit to update regularly and state when the next update will be given, ideally within three to six hours.

Post the statement on the Web site and Facebook, e-mail it to key affected people, place it on the bulletin boards where staff can read it, and tweet the basics with a link to the full statement.

BOX 25.1   MEDIA CONFERENCE SAMPLE STATEMENT

Very sadly, I can confirm that five of our workers have been killed and an additional 10 employees were seriously injured in the explosion that happened at 6:00 A.M. today in the plant room at our facility in Westwood. *(Concern, Confirmation)*

The 10 employees have been taken to hospital and are in stable condition. Grief counselors have been called in, and we have identified a team of independent experts from ABC Forensics who will work with us to find out exactly what happened here today. *(Action)*

Our security team, headed by 20-year safety expert Steve Safer, is also working closely with the Westwood Fire Department investigation team, the Westwood Police, and the Coroner's Office to help determine the cause of the explosion. *(Action)*

We are all very shocked that such a tragedy could have happened at our plant, which we thought was as fire and explosion proof as it could be. Clearly that is not the case, and we have a lot of work to do to restore confidence in our safety and testing procedures. *(Context)*

> I can assure you that I will put all the resources that we have in our company to get to the bottom of what happened and why, and if we need to make changes, we will. *(Reassurance)*
>
> The plant will remain closed during the initial investigation and until the authorities have declared it safe to reopen. This means that there may be a shortage of our (product name) in the next few weeks. Please be patient with us while we work to get the factory up and running safely. *(Call to Action)*

The second and ongoing statements will be more detailed, and your spokesperson should be prepared to give more detailed responses. At a Stage Two media conference, when the basic facts are known, the media will question you on your response and what you are doing for the "victims." Remember the key question now, after the basic facts are known, is to get to the bottom of what happened—how did this happen, how could *you* let this happen? The media and everyone else affected wants to know the probable cause in this stage. There will be an *intense focus* on the reasons that the crisis occurred.

You will need a strong opening quote that puts the crisis in context and demonstrates compassion and concern for those affected. The second key element is to state clearly what steps you have taken to get to the bottom of what has happened and then give your perspective. Remember, the focus in this stage is on your response and the victims. The media will be relentless in their questioning of "how could this have happened?"

The Fort Hood statement (Box 25.2) is a real-life example of what needs to be said at the first media conference. Note how Lt. Gen. Robert Cone introduces himself at the beginning. That is important if no one is introducing you. He also immediately describes the shooting—"a terrible tragedy." That too is important—we need a frame for thinking about a tragedy, and the media will take the lead from the official spokespeople, so choose your phrases or adjectives wisely.

In the Queenwood example (Case Study 25.1), the principal states how much the school community is "deeply shocked and saddened." Again, these words are likely to be quoted. They have come from a voice of authority. Notice also how immediately the principal confirms the death of the schoolgirl.

BOX 25.2   FORT HOOD MEDIA STATEMENT

Lt. Gen. Robert Cone: I'm Lieutenant General Bob Cone. I'm the commanding general of III Corps at Fort Hood. We've had a terrible tragedy here at Fort Hood today. The situation is ongoing, although I think we have positive news that we're very close to a resolution. At approximately 1330 hours today, a shooter entered what we call the soldier readiness facility, where soldiers who are preparing to deploy go for last minute medical check-ups and dental treatment, etc. A shooter opened fire. And due to the quick response of the police forces, was—was killed. And at this time, the numbers that we're looking at are 12 dead and 31 wounded. And they're dispersed among the local hospitals here in the Central Texas area. Again, their—their—the extent of injuries varies significantly. And, again, we're—we're getting great cooperation from the Central Texas medical facilities. As I said, the shooter was killed. He was a soldier. We since then have apprehended two additional soldiers that are suspects. And I would go into the point that there were—there were eyewitness accounts that there may have been more than one shooter. They tracked the suspected individuals to an adjacent facility, and they were apprehended. They are soldiers, but, again, they are suspects at this time and we're looking into that. The challenge that we face right now is the installation is locked down. And in many cases, a lot of facilities, a lot of our families, children are locked in facilities. We're making a call right now as to determine whether we think the situation is—is at a conclusion, such that we can release people and get them back to their home.

Source: Transcript supplied by VMS, San Francisco. Statement made to a large group of media on November 5, 2009; which appeared on major TV networks around the globe.

CASE STUDY 25.1
Statement of Queenwood Private School for Girls

In February 2005, an Australian school community woke to tragic news that suddenly thrust their school into the media spotlight. One of the students at Sydney's Queenwood Private School for Girls had died in a freak accident while on a school camping trip.

The news broke on radio at 6:30 A.M. The school had been named. By 8:30 A.M., a media scrum with 30 reporters in attendance had gathered at the school. Buses were unloading the girls from the camp: pictures of distraught parents and students alike. The school, led by the principal, and their communication advisers from the firm, Sefiani, quickly sprang into action.

Robyn Sefiani (Managing Director, Sefiani), an experienced crisis communication consultant, guided the media away from the scene of the grief-stricken parents and daughters to a quieter part of the school; prepared a media statement; and counseled the principal prior to her appearing before the media scrum. The principal quickly checked that her clothing reflected the somber tone of the announcement, delivered her statement, but took no questions.

Sefiani says it was important for the statement (see below) to be delivered in person rather than in written form by the leader of the school, to express the shock and grief the whole school community felt that morning, to convey the school's sympathy to the victim's family, and to reflect the caring culture of the Queenwood School.

STATEMENT FROM KEM BRAY, [THEN] PRINCIPAL, QUEENWOOD SCHOOL FOR GIRLS

I can confirm that one of our year 12 girls was killed in a tragic accident in the early hours of this morning at a campsite near Mittagong.

She was attending one of our regular school camps held every year as part of our student development program.

We are working closely with the authorities to determine exactly what happened, but I can confirm the girl was hit by a tree.

Our school community is deeply shocked and saddened and our heart goes out to her family and school friends.

We have made arrangements to bring all students back from the camp today.

Our primary concern at this stage is supporting students, parents, and staff, and we are providing counseling and support to them.

Thank you.*

---

* Kem Bray ([Then] Principal), Media Statement, Queenwood School for Girls (Sydney, Australia), February 2, 2005. (Reprinted with permission.)

191

STANDBY STATEMENT

Sometimes a standby statement that covers the macro situation will suffice, as we see in this example from Caltrans after a crack appeared in a steel beam of the San Francisco–Oakland Bay Bridge during the retrofit over Labor Day weekend in 2009.

"It's way too early to say what happened," Anziano said. "We have to take a careful look at it."* Tony Anziano is Caltrans's toll bridge program manager.

Certainly, the preparation of these standby statements can be done well in advance and prepared for spokespeople and key frontline staff alike, and then drilled in training sessions.

The key is to be persistent, present, and consistent everywhere. The average person uses eight sources of media each day. That same person needs to hear or see something three to five times from different sources to achieve belief.

Remember, you will be defined by how you manage your crisis. Your character as an organization will be ruthlessly examined. Let your values guide you. May they stand up to the scrutiny and intensity of the media spotlight.

---

* Michael Cabanatuan and Justin Berton, "Bay Bridge Closed after Repair Falls Apart," *San Francisco Chronicle*, p. A1 (front page).

26

To Apologize or Not—The Role of the Apology in a Crisis

Now let's think about the mea culpa—the "I'm sorry," the role of the apology. It seems that everyone who has been in trouble thinks they must apologize—it has become the prerequisite for crisis management, the panacea for every wrong deed. Think Michael Vick, Serena Williams, Tiger Woods, Domino's, Toyota.

Does it work? Is it the best practice? Is there a more effective approach?

At its core, as academics W. Timothy Coombs and Sherry J. Holladay have stated, "An apology is marked by an organization (or individual) accepting responsibility for the crisis and asking for forgiveness."[*]

For many, however, "sorry" does indeed seem to be the hardest word. Lawyers are inevitably against apologizing, claiming it will increase lawsuits and payouts.

But according to veteran crisis management adviser Jim Lukaszewski, "Years of evidence is accumulating that prompt acknowledgment coupled with clear apologies and sensible offers of settlement can eliminate the litigation phase of legal interaction between victim and perpetrator, in favor of an attitude of settlement."[†]

---

[*] W. Timothy Coombs and Sherry J. Holladay, "Comparing Apology to Equivalent Crisis Response Strategies: Clarifying Apology's Role and Value in Crisis Communication," *Public Relations Review*, Vol. 34, 2008, pp. 252–257.

[†] Posted by Jim Lukaszewski, "The Growing Threat to Trial Lawyers: Apology," Crisis Guru Blog, http://crisisgurublog.e911.com/2009_10_01_archive.html, posted 3:36 PM, October 7, 2009.

Owning the problem and not blaming others is the more successful strategy, as Odwalla found out. The natural juice organization was found to have sold batches of apple juice that caused severe illness and, in one tragic outcome, led to the death of a child. Odwalla (highly praised by reporters who I interviewed for this book, for acting swiftly and taking full responsibility) was able to contain the crisis to a three-week period, and importantly, avoid lawsuits.

And the trend is that "sorry" is on the rise, thanks in part, to the "I'm sorry" movement led by The Sorry Works! Coalition based in Illinois. The organization, which started as an advocacy group in 2005, promotes the apology, disclosure, and compensation concept among physicians, insurers, and hospitals, and offers training.

There is also a growing body of apology legislation around the world allowing individuals and institutions to offer an apology as part of their dispute resolution process without fear of legal liability. The provinces of British Columbia, Manitoba, and Saskatchewan have such laws on their books, as do foreign jurisdictions like Australia and 20 states in the United States.

While some lawyers are questioning the value of the legislation saying it may encourage insincere and strategic apologies (Hello! What about Serena and Michael?) and emotional vulnerability in some plaintiffs, others like Coombs and Holladay say that apologizing may not be that effective.

Their study of an industrial accident (importantly, where no cause had been determined) showed that "for non-victims, expressions of sympathy or compensation are just as effective as apology when it comes to post-crisis reputations, anger, account acceptance, and negative word-of-mouth intentions."[*]

But as Coombs and Holladay say, it's a matter of degrees. Yet, if the crisis is lower to middle impact, then they advocate that "crisis managers can confidently offer compensation and/or express sympathy, rather than relying on an apology as the default."[†] Yet, if the crisis has had huge impact and "management knows it is at fault, an apology is advised." It would be unconscionable to do otherwise. Furthermore the media and the community at the Web expect that *mea culpa*. (See Box 26.1 for the key elements of an apology.)

---

[*] W. Timothy Coombs and Sherry J. Holladay, "Comparing Apology to Equivalent Crisis Response Strategies: Clarifying Apology's Role and Value in Crisis Communication," *Public Relations Review*, Vol. 34, 2008, pp. 252–257.

[†] Ibid.

BOX 26.1   FIVE ELEMENTS OF AN APOLOGY

1. *Take responsibility and act fast.* Apologize as soon as possible after the offense.
2. *Describe what you did.* Be specific. Avoid euphemisms that attempt to tidy up your mess. A short, direct statement is best followed by a brief explanation of the circumstances surrounding it to provide context.
3. *Express remorse.* Make your apology as heartfelt as you can without assuming liability. Tone is, as we have already established, *very* important here. The statement must reflect genuine remorse. This is incredibly important in this era of transparency and authenticity.
4. *Shut up.* Afterward, be quiet and listen while people tell you how angry they are. If it's really bad, they'll call for your head. Know that you've done the right thing and time is on your side. Very important for face-to-face interactions and also in the social media world. Take a leaf out of General Motors. Allow and monitor comments on your blog.
5. *Make it right.* In such situations, how you act and what you *do* always trump what you *say*. Therefore, symbolic gestures matter. Your attempts to correct the problem and compensate those who have been wronged are essential. However, be careful not to promise more than you can deliver.

Source: Dan Keeney, APR, "Why Apologies Are a Crisis Communication Staple," DPK Public Relations, www.keeneypr.com, July 26, 2006. (Reprinted with permission.)

There is bound to be resistance among the crisis management team members. However, remember that impressions are everything. What an organization says and does during and after a crisis is a make-or-break time for your reputation, theirs, and that of the organization.

CASE STUDY 26.1
Apology to the Aborigines

The then Prime Minister of Australia, Kevin Rudd, took on that courageous and difficult task when he, on behalf of the nation of Australia, apologized to the Aborigines on February 13, 2008, for the wrongdoings and mistreatment by previous governments, primarily for the "stealing of their children." Rudd referred to "this blemished chapter in our nation's history."

I watched the prime minister give a heartfelt apology with tears streaming down my face (they are streaming again while I write this) as he said "we are sorry" to the stolen generation. He gave his apology from the floor of Parliament House in Canberra, the nation's capital, where many of the stolen generation and their descendants were present for this historic event. And not once but three times he uttered that powerful, five-letter word.

Tony Stephens, columnist with *The Sydney Morning Herald*, wrote, "... when Mr. Rudd said it [sorry] in his formal apology and several times afterwards, it seemed that a seismic shift had shaken the land, liberating the people."[*]

It was an act of radical forgiveness—one that many generations of politicians in Australia had lacked the political will to do. And most importantly, the Aboriginal leaders accepted his apology with comments like, "The nation's Parliament has taken the first step towards the future," "It was very moving to see a prime minister with a bit of heart," and "It was wonderful, just magnificent."[†]

I was especially proud to be an Australian that day, and it is my fervent hope that organizations and nations alike can take a leaf from former Prime Minister Rudd's textbook and apply it to right their wrongs.

---

[*] Tony Stephens, "The Last of the White Blindfolds," *The Sydney Morning Herald*, http://www.smh.com.au/news/national/the-last-of-the-white-blindfolds/2008/02/13/1202760398945.html?page=fullpage#contentSwap1, February 14, 2008, p. 1.
[†] Ibid.

27

Language in a Crisis—Fall in Love with We; No Toxic Language, Please

Apart from keeping language simple, which is the essence of every effective media interview, it is even more critical in a crisis that language be active, positive, and aggression-free.

The other salutary reminder for the key spokesperson and those responsible for preparing statements is that all-inclusive language is important. As I say, "Fall in love with *we*." It is rare that a crisis is contained to just you (your organization). It is your employees and their families, the wider industry, including your competitors, even the country. So include the word *we* in your media statements.

For example, you could say, "This is not just a sad day for our company and everyone who works here; it is a sad day for our suppliers, supermarkets, and indeed the entire industry."

Should you sense that it is taking too long to fix the problem, you could tweet, "We are all frustrated. I am frustrated. The police are frustrated. Anyone who cares about our environment is frustrated that we have yet to find the answer." This is especially important for Twitter, Facebook, and other channels that allow for comment and feedback.

You may find it useful to coach your spokespeople to say *we* in response to journalists' questions when they are pinpointing you. For example:

Q: Aren't you concerned that the cleanup is taking too long?
A: We are all concerned that the cleanup seems to be dragging, but I can assure you that we are all doing everything we can to get to the bottom of what happened here today. I will be here every day until the job is done.

POSITIVE LANGUAGE, PLEASE!

Contrary to popular belief, negative language, stories, and examples that spokespersons use not only verbally, but also in writing, drive negative stories and headlines. Reporters habitually and often intentionally phrase their questions and information requests in negative ways that demand negative responses.

It is critical in any form of communication, and particularly in a crisis, that your effectiveness will increase based on your awareness of *negative questions*. Do whatever you can to *avoid* negative language. Quite simply *negative language is toxic.*

As soon as I say, "That's not the way we think," what are your options as a reporter? You'll ask me why not, why isn't it, and why won't we? These are all negative responses, which drive communication even further off track. Your situation is now sliding into that dark, deep well from which there is little hope of return without harm.

For example, if I ask you to *not* to think of a pink and white striped racing car, or the Statue of Liberty, or the Sydney Harbour Bridge, I'd bet that the picture you have in your head is exactly that: pink racing car, the statue, the bridge.

Better to say what is, rather than what *isn't*.

The critical reality is that if you want to control the conversation and the environment in which communication takes place, then only positive language will give you greater control of your destiny. To be a successful, effective communicator and media spokesperson, particularly in a crisis, *you need to eliminate negative language.*

Tips for staying positive:

1. *Say less.* Make what you say positive, powerful, and therefore more important. As important as it is to show compassion and empathy for "victims," be careful how you express that (concern and empathy). Your words may be interpreted as negative. Make sure your tone is relevant and appropriate, and what you say comes from the heart. Say what is, rather than what isn't. Paint a picture of what you mean in a positive way.

2. *Listen* very carefully to the question and be on the lookout for negative words. For example, "Isn't it true that you are behind schedule with the investigation?" Loaded questions will tempt you into negative language. Another example is, "How can creditors trust you when you won't enter into dialog with the unions over policy? How do you respond to the criticism?" (See more about crisis media interviews in Section IV.)

3. *Rephrase* the negative, loaded question with a positive response to what you do; for example, "At this stage of the investigation, we are typically doing this (give an example)," as opposed to confronting the question at face value.

4. *Take your time* to respond; you have at least two seconds before you need to speak. Use that time to think.

5. *Practice* rephrasing negative language into positive language at least three times a day for 21 days and you will be surprised at how much your communication improves!

28

How to Get Your Message Across

When people are in a crisis, their communication level and emotional maturity really fall off to almost a second- or third-grade level. They're way outside their normal behavior. Having a simple process for crisis management is essential.[*]

—Steve Randich, (Former CIO, NASDAQ)

The challenge in any situation, and particularly in a crisis, is to get your message across succinctly, effectively, and efficiently. While the traditional media have the final say in what is printed or broadcast, you can *influence* the results because public audiences aggregate, share, and tweet what you say and how you say it. The key is to be *quotable and memorable, and to use simple, plain English.*

There are some simple guidelines to follow when formulating your messages. The #1 rule is to keep your language *brief and specific.* You also need to:

- Use simple, everyday, colloquial language and avoid jargon.
- Use visual language. Analogies and metaphors help put the abstract into perspective and help explain complex situations or products quickly and clearly. Even a word or phrase, such as "dropped the ball" or "fire sale," paints a vivid picture and helps cut through the clutter for the journalist and the audience. Colorful words will be exchanged, so choose wisely.

---

[*] Steve Randich, former CIO, NASDAQ, said in the aftermath of 9/11. (Cited in presentation by Norm Meier to the *Crisis Communication Forum*, Sydney, Australia, July 21, 2003.)

- Repeat key words, key themes. For my clients, I advocate repeating a key word three times. For example, "This is a *sad day* for our company, a *sad day* for our customers, and a *sad day* for our industry."
- Use language that an eighth grader understands, and in extreme situations, for example, a 9/11, you will need to bring it down even farther to language of a fifth grader. The simpler the better, as research clearly shows that in a crisis, when under extreme pressure, we default to our native language. If Chinese is your first language, you will most likely start speaking Chinese and could well forget the English words. You need to ensure that your messages can be easily and quickly understood, so simple words, said slowly and with emphasis, are critical in a crisis.

For example, if you want to make a point about the values of your organization (they are on your Web site or articulated on your blog, aren't they?) then tell a story about how your values were acted out in your crisis scenario. It may have been a staff member who went way above the call of duty to rescue a dog or an old lady, or injured workers putting themselves in harm's way. The media love to hear the hero stories, how ordinary people do extraordinary things. And we love to hear about the drama, the courage, and the bravery. It's the stuff of Hollywood movies and reality TV, and it provides the prerequisite human interest angle for TV news.

That anecdote from the chief executive officer, mayor, or emergency worker does more to show you care than you just saying the facts with no color. Do not be afraid to tell a story—all great speakers do, as we saw with U.S. President Obama at the memorial service at Fort Hood. Many have hailed that powerful speech as one of the best so far of his presidency.

Take advantage of Twitter, Facebook, YouTube, and other social media tools like blogging and Flickr, because that's where your audiences gather to get and share information.

Above all, you need to be true to yourself and to your values. Think with your head and speak with your heart.

29

Where? New Media Tools

The possibilities are endless.[*]

—*Kris Olson (Innovis Health, 2010)*

OVERVIEW

The unprecedented shift in media consumption habits and the exponential growth of social media have put pressure on communicators to reach their audiences in new yet cost-effective ways.

And in a crisis, you need to be where your audiences and key influencers are. Increasingly, they are online, and that is where people congregate in a crisis. Studies show that Internet usage increases in the aftermath of a crisis. You cannot ignore the big, sometimes downright scary World Wide Web or the myriad of new communication platforms. Facebook and Twitter simply connect very large clusters of people like never before.

Domino's found out the hard way when they ignored the new media space for the best part of two days. They were operating in the so-called dark ages—doing lots of things right, but not telling anyone in the Social-MediaLand. As a result, they were forced to confront a social media maelstrom after two employees posted some embarrassing footage. The

---

[*] Kris Olson (Vice President of Marketing, Quality, and Physicians, Innovis Health, Fargo, North Dakota), interview with author, March 12, 2010.

YouTube video went viral with more than a million hits before it was pulled.

In an interview with Amy Jacques for the *Public Relations Strategist*, Tim McIntyre, vice president of communications at Domino's Pizza, admitted that their Web response could have been faster. He likened what happened to them to needing a hose: "We've learned that you might not need the fire hose to put out the candle, but in the social media realm, you might want to have a garden hose handy."*

McIntyre advises you to do as much as you can as fast as you can to quickly address the multiple sides of an issue.

While some have been left standing, there is no doubt that social media are useful in a crisis. Take the April 2010 Icelandic volcano eruption. Without social media, the airlines would have floundered completely after the eruption that forced the shutdown of airports across Europe and the United Kingdom, stranding hundreds of thousands of passengers trying to get to and from those destinations. Call centers could not handle the volume, and more and more airlines turned to social media as their primary crisis communication tool.

Treat social media as your friend. Respect its power. It is the place for dialogue and for conversations, not for one-way directives. Use it strategically and wisely and consider how you can engage the power of the people in helping you manage your crisis. Clearly, social media has a big role to play in issues management, but it will be necessary to at least monitor if not engage in Stage Two.

And most importantly, think about how you can get social media up and running, used regularly, and tested *before* a crisis hits. You want to be certain that everything works to expectations, and that you have an established presence with an established audience! You need to establish *trust* and transparency before the crisis hits, just as you need to with the old media.

In this chapter, we will look at the main social media tools (Table 29.1), plus the language and culture you need to adopt, and finally, how to get started so you are well equipped to manage the media in a crisis.

---

* Amy Jacques, "Domino's Delivers during Crisis: The Company's Step-by-Step Response after a Vulgar Video Goes Viral," *Public Relations Strategist*, www.prsa.org, August 17, 2009.

Table 29.1   Social Media Tools

Blogs	Short for Web log, a type of Web site that is updated frequently; written in a conversational tone and contains regular entries of commentary, descriptions of events, or other material
Podcasts	Web-based audio and/or video content made available on the Internet for downloading to a personal audio player
Social Networking Sites (Facebook, MySpace)	Online communities that allow users to connect, interact, and exchange information with those who share interests and/or activities
Microblogs (Twitter, Plurk)	Form of blogging that allows users to write brief text updates (usually 140 characters), and to publish them so that their network can view and comment on them
Mobile Text Messaging	Short text messages exchanged between mobile devices
Wikis	Collaborative Web page or collection of Web pages that allow all users to contribute or modify content
Widgets	Piece of self-contained code (a small application) that can be embedded into a Web site or program to perform a specific function
Social Bookmarking (Delicious, Digg, etc.)	Sites in which a virtual community exchanges links to content and stores links for future use
RSS Feeds	Short for Real Simple Syndication; a file that contains frequently updated information (such as news headlines or blog posts) that can be subscribed to using programs called feed readers or aggregators
Image/Video Sharing Sites (Flickr, YouTube, etc.)	User-generated sites that allow people to upload pictures or videos, and then view and comment on the uploaded content of others
Virtual Worlds (Second Life, Whyville, etc.)	A computer-based, simulated environment in which users interact with each other via avatars, virtual representations of themselves
Internet Forums	Also called message boards; online discussion sites in which users can discuss issues, exchange information, and share views
Mobile Web Sites	Web sites geared for mobile devices

Source: Booz Allen Hamilton, "Goodbye Sources, Messages, Channels and Receivers: Hello Network," White Paper from *American Public Health Association Expert Round Table on Social Media and Risk Communication during Times of Crisis*, www.boozallen.com/consulting-services/services_article/42420696, March 2009. (Reprinted with permission.)

205

WEB MESSAGES: CONTENT BRUTAL AND TO THE POINT

It is vital to get the first couple of words right in the wired world. Gerry McGovern, founder and chief executive officer (CEO) of Customer Carewords and New Thinking, said the following on his blog, citing a study by Jakob Neilsen: "The first two words have a huge impact on whether or not people will click on a link."*

Neilsen's study, which tested links from Web sites of companies like AT&T, Intel, Dell, and UK Directgov, confirms the findings of a 2004 eye-tracking study from the Poynter Institute that most people only read on if they are "grabbed" by the first couple of words. Sounds like good newspaper headline writing to me.

Here is their advice:

- Use plain English.
- Use specific, clear words.
- Use common, compelling words.
- Start with the point; state the conclusion up front.
- Use action-oriented words.
- Lead with the need.
- Focus on what your customers care about.[†]

And be careful with your language—tone as well as the actual words. You cannot take it back. Trying to get something out of SocialMediaLand is, to quote Kris Olson, "a little like trying to get pee out of a swimming pool."[‡] Virtually impossible.

Links and headings should be no more than eight words.

Apply the *so what, who cares* rule. Be brutal and have someone with little or no knowledge of your organization read the copy before you post it, share it, and say it.

TWITTER

Twitter is a microblog, something akin to a breaking news service, even if that news is sometimes way too personal.

---

* Posted by Gerry McGovern, "Writing Killer Web Headings and Links," New Thinking Blog, http://www.gerrymcgovern.com/nt/2009/nt-2009-04-13-web-headings-links.htm, April 13, 2009.

† Jakob Nielsen, "First 2 Words: A Signal for the Scanning Eye," Nielsen Gorman Group (Fremont, California), 2009.

‡ Kris Olson (Vice President of Marketing, Quality, and Physicians, Innovis Health, Fargo, North Dakota), interview with author, March 12, 2010.

Here is one way of thinking about Twitter: It is a bit like a street party—There are people who are only interested in hanging out with their own group as opposed to the whole street party. You need to attend the party and listen to see what conversations are worth joining.

According to Distinguished Professor S. Shyam Sundar,* founder and codirector of Pennsylvania State University's Media Effects Research Laboratory, where he studies the psychology of communication technology, Twitter is predominantly a push mechanism. Using Twitter, you push out information, push links, and push to other, more detailed information like your Web site, emergency services, your blog, or your YouTube TV Channel.

The other big advantage to using Twitter in a crisis is that you can make almost instantaneous updates to dispel rumors, correct misinformation, and reach people very quickly with timely, potentially life-saving information.

Like other media, there are rules of engagement. Here are some basic ones:

- *Be sincere*—Transparency is vital, be as human as you can be.
- *Empathize*—Remember, no one can hear the tone of your voice or see your body language, so your words are your weapon.
- *Be culturally sensitive*—Be aware of the cultural norms of the communities you are dealing with and remember that Twitter is global.
- *Never argue*—If someone has a gripe, let them have a gripe. Seriously, who wants to engage with a company if they perceive you are only interested in arguing? If you argue publicly there are really only two outcomes:
  - You look like a fool.
  - They look like a fool (that will only make the situation worse for you), so take the conversation offline.
- *Provide links to more information*—Push people to more detailed information.
- *Provide context*—Remember that most people can't see what you are responding to.
- *Use proper grammar*—Use proper capitalization. Typing in lower case does not save characters, it is just lazy. If you cannot say it in 140 or 120 characters, reevaluate whether you should be posting it on Twitter in the first place. Use numerals, not words, for all numbers.

---

* S. Shyam Sundar (Codirector, Media Effects Research Laboratory, Penn State University), interview with author, April 13, 2009.

- *Update early and often*—Just like with the old media there is a need to update regularly on Twitter and this medium is absolutely ideal for that. With Twitter, you can update almost immediately. Link for more detail.

For the record, there were *27.3 million* tweets on Twitter per day in November 2009, and *57 percent* of Twitter's user base is located in the United States. In Australia, Twitter's audience levels grew by more than 400 percent in 2009 and nearly one quarter of online Australians (23 percent) read tweets.

If for no other reason, you can use Twitter for more effective media relations.

Media Relations

You can use Twitter to determine who and how to respond to the traditional media in a crisis. For Innovis Health in Fargo, North Dakota, Twitter was a godsend during the 2009 floods. They used Twitter and the more traditional blogs to get out vital information to the community. They were operational; unlike their competitor, they had not shut their doors. The traditional media were isolated and could not get to Innovis, so Innovis became the media. They got the messages and images out there, and within minutes 1,500 media outlets around America were following them, and most importantly, getting the message out that Innovis was open for business.

Similarly, the Federal Emergency Management Agency (FEMA) uses the microblog to direct its followers (more than 12,000 at the time of writing) to specific information in a timely manner in emergencies and disasters. The agency sees Twitter like an instant messaging service and uses it to support efforts of local and state emergency responders.

Once you know who is following you and, more importantly, what is being said about you, you can make an informed decision about what resources to put where. You can customize a more specific, targeted response to address individual concerns. You can address where the most heat is coming from or you can reach out personally to a specific journalist or media outlet.

In a crisis, remember keywords and # hash tags, for example, #Haiti. You need to think and agree in advance of what is the one word you are going to use in a crisis, and make sure that this is agreed by the Crisis Management Team and anyone tweeting within your stakeholder group. Hash tags are important because they improve searchability. You can track and monitor comments and the levels of engagement more effectively.

For example, Innovis Health agreed in advance with everyone in their emergency community what the # would be when preparing for floods in March 2010. Excellent planning.

Protect Your Brand

A word of warning—protect your brand. Just like in the early days of the Internet, there are squatters on Twitter who take over big brand names. They register the names on Twitter, for example, and sit there or, worse, make comments. Coca Cola and CNN found out the hard way. Even if you do not have a Twitter feed, check if your company's name is available on Twitter. If available, grab it. The last thing you want is for someone to hijack your company's name and send erroneous updates to it. Then you will have a crisis.

BP faced this challenge during the oil spill disaster. An imposter launched @bpglobalpr which even used BP's green and yellow logo, defaced with blackened oil. At the time of writing BP had not asked Twitter to take the site down, and Twitter apparently will not do that unless it is asked. The situation is a timely reminder for companies, particularly the big brand names and even more so for those who have very active detractors, of what might occur with their own names in a Twitter context. The lesson? Think about what to do to preserve your corporate identities intact—in good times and bad. And have this in your policy guidelines, particularly for the social media team monitoring the use of the company logo.

Hash Tags (#)

Another important tool for you to use in a crisis, to maximize your message, *or* to search for content that is abusive or fouling your brand in some way is the hash tag (#).

A hash tag is a way to categorize content in your tweets to better find information. To set one up you simply type the # sign followed by pertinent words, a phrase, or an abbreviation. For example, #RedCross, #Haiti, #Icelandic.

During the Nestlé "Kat Fight with Greenpeace" there were several hash tag references on Twitter, including #kitkat, #nestle, #Orangutan, and #greenpeace, mostly negative comments about Nestle. Needless to say there were a bevy of #tags when news surfaced of Tiger Woods' sordid affairs: #tiger woods #joslyn james #email #celeb #golf #affair #cheat.

Hash tags are very valuable for coordinating efforts to raise money for disaster victims, as well as an effective way to help coordinate response and rescue in a natural disaster, or regularly and quickly update information. For example, #tags were used to good effect during the 2009 Atlanta flash floods—#atlflood—with updates on flash floods, road closures, and power outages.

They may never have taken off if it were not for Nate Ritter, self-proclaimed Web chef, consultant, and knowledge broker living in San Diego, tweeting during the San Diego forest fire in 2007. His efforts, according to Chris Messina, written in his FactoryCity Blog, were the first dedicated use of a hash tag to help coordinate a response to a natural disaster.

Be careful not to overdo the #tag communication. To be effective they need to be simple and memorable. As Messina says, "Successful structures should aim for minimum cognitive burden."* Consider your audience and their familiarity with the issue being tweeted about if you want your #tag understood and, most importantly for rescue efforts, to be retweeted.

FACEBOOK

If Twitter is like a street party, then Facebook is more like a barbeque, a family reunion, or a Christmas get-together. You see the same people as you circle the room or go back and forth to the buffet, and they represent all ages and stages of life—just like Facebook.

These people are your friends, your family; you have *chosen* to connect with them and involve them in your life. And you do not pull out the Amway catalog the minute they walk in the door, if ever! Your real friends, those you have engaged will want to know what has happened to you in a crisis. The same applies if you are a *big* brand and have a public scrap, like Nestlé did with Greenpeace. Fans, both pro and con, will galvanize. Opinions will be expressed.

Make no mistake, Facebook is powerful. It has morphed from the "Internet's phone book"† to the go-to place for information, if not breaking news. Within minutes, if not seconds, after a crisis event, you will find thousands of posts on Facebook.

Virginia Tech, Fort Hood, US Airways flight 1549, the Victorian bushfires, the earthquake in Haiti, and the Icelandic volcano eruption all have one thing in common. Each event spurred dozens if not hundreds of Facebook groups often within hours, if not minutes, of the actual event occurring. For example, followers set up Facebook groups during the

---

* Posted by Chris Messina, "Designing Hashtags for Emergency Response," FactoryCity Blog, http://factoryjoe.com/blog/2010/01/18/designing-hashtags-for-emergency-response/, January 18, 2010.
† Posted by Matthew Kaskavitch, "Facebook Use in Crisis Management, Techization Blog, http://techization.com/facebook-use-in-crisis-management/, October 26, 2009.

Virginia Tech tragedy within 15 minutes of the news breaking. A Fort Hood group, "Remember Those from the Fort Hood Mass Shooting," was still very active with more than 46,000 fans at the time of writing.

KLM published a video message from the CEO and president and added a Q & A tab to their Facebook page to reach their stranded passengers during the Icelandic volcano eruption that grounded hundreds of flights and thousands of people in April 2010.

What makes Facebook work is the open platform that enables its massive user base—500 million and counting at an average age of 38 and a whopping 67 percent of all social media users*—to share and exchange information at light speed. Facebook is the world's dominant social network, and it is the top search term at Google, Bing, and Yahoo. Time will tell whether the protests about and inquiries into its privacy issues will topple the giant, though I strongly doubt it.

And in a crisis, Facebook is where people gather to share thoughts, feelings, and emotions. They post pictures and videos, and stream their collective consciousness of the crisis, forming a powerful, virtual news channel.

Distinguished Professor Sundar (Penn State University) says that Facebook is a pull mechanism (information designed to pull you into buying or doing something).† And it is certainly proving its pull strength in a crisis.

Using Facebook on a regular basis will allow it to be used during a crisis to:

- Dispel rumors.
- Post pictures and videos.
- Speak to your "fans"—your staff, your customers.
- Mobilize your "friends" into action.
- Create a "safe" place for people to share feelings, thoughts, and emotions.

As a social media expert, commentator, and blogger, Shel Holtz says that before you launch into Facebook, you need to have a solid strategy.‡ And

---

* The Nielsen Company, "Led by Facebook, Twitter, Global Time Spent on Social Media Sites up 82% Year over Year," Nielsen Wire Blog, http://blog.nielsen.com/nielsenwire, January 22, 2010.
† S. Shyam Sundar (Codirector, Media Effects Research Laboratory, Penn State University), interview with author, April 13, 2009.
‡ Posted by Shel Holtz, "Six Questions to Ask before Launching a Facebook Fan Page," A Shel of My Former Self Blog, http://blog.holtz.com/index.php/weblog/comments/six_questions_to_ask_before_launching_a_facebook_fan_page/, March 23, 2010.

even if you already have a Facebook presence, you would be well advised to take on this advice:

- What are your goals and who exactly are you trying to reach?
- What will you do if critics see your page as an opportunity to express even more hostile feelings?
- Who will manage your page? As Holtz says, you need to keep the page updated. If you leave an open space unattended for a while, what happens? Weeds grow, it is vandalized, or squatters take over.* The same happens in SocialMediaLand.
- Who will monitor the page? Companies look clueless when nothing is posted, or no one responds to fans' questions and comments. It is a must in a crisis and needs to be done with sensitivity and, hopefully, experience.
- How quickly will you respond when a crisis strikes? Exactly who will respond? For example, General Motors enlisted their environmental chief when they were "attacked" by environmental activists.

Facebook Dark Groups

With *New Scientist* research showing that social networking sites like Facebook spread warnings and information more efficiently than traditional communication channels, organizations are looking to use Facebook in their crisis management plans.

University of Wisconsin–Stout, is one such organization. With the assistance of Information and Communication Technologies student Matthew Kaskavitch, the university is using Facebook to create dark groups.

Like dark Web sites, dark groups are visible only to the creator and a handful of people responsible for the crisis planning efforts. They are preloaded with crisis plans and messages. Once the crisis occurs, you simply go live. Kaskavitch says to invite the first 10 to 15 people to follow, become a fan. The group, he says, "will grow exponentially"† with little administration.

Kaskavitch, who is also the university's Student Life Services Web Programmer and New Media consultant, says that in crisis management, you need to consider a few things before using Facebook as a platform:

---

* Posted by Shel Holtz, "Six Questions to Ask before Launching a Facebook Fan Page," A Shel of My Former Self Blog, http://blog.holtz.com/index.php/weblog/comments/six_questions_to_ask_before_launching_a_facebook_fan_page/, March 23, 2010.
† Matthew Kaskovitch (University of Wisconsin–Stout, Student Life Services Web Programmer and New Media Consultant), interview with author, February 24, 2010.

- Will you include photos and videos in the group? If so, will only administrators be allowed to upload media or will everyone be allowed to contribute?
- Do you want to enable the "wall" to allow open conversation?
- Do you want the discussion board enabled?
- Who will manage it in the event of a crisis?*

Another key consideration is whether you lock down a group in a crisis. Is that wise? What impression will that create?

Kaskavitch says no! "Locking down the group and making it a billboard inside a walled garden is not effective."†

Kaskavitch, who has consulted and researched widely on Facebook and general social media crisis strategies within the university system, says you have to be willing to open up and let information flow across the channel in an unfiltered manner. "The speed at which it can go back and forth across this medium could be incredibly useful during an emergency. You want your message to get out, and you should want feedback from your receiving audience as well."‡

Creating dark groups will not, of course, stop other groups from forming, but having an official channel allows you to:

- Direct message all members of your group instantly.
- Control the message and information presented within the group.
- Censor information (only if absolutely necessary).

Like with everything else in crisis planning, you need to think ahead of time how you will use the channel. As Kaskavitch points out, there is a constraint with creating groups ahead of time. You need to name the dark group when you set it up, and you cannot change it later on. Also, you will not be able to put actual situation-specific information in the group name.

I am a big fan of dark sites in general and the concept of a dark group is sound. Kaskavitch suggests, and I agree, that setting up your communication in a Word document is more practical. You may lose precious time—up to 20 minutes—in setup time. But you will have a situation-specific name that can be easily identified by your key audiences. That is important.

---

* Matthew Kaskovitch (University of Wisconsin–Stout, Student Life Services Web Programmer and New Media Consultant), interview with author, February 24, 2010.
† Ibid.
‡ Ibid.

Facebook: The Future

Is there no end to the Facebook capability in a crisis? Perhaps not. Futurist Brian Solis certainly sees the social media darling as a key focus for communicators.[*]

Solis, globally recognized as one of most prominent thought leaders and published authors in new media, says Facebook—with twice as many registered users as Twitter—will be the main way to communicate with audiences.

There is also talk that it will become the #1 spot for people to get their news. It has a massive user base. Stalwarts of news like *The Wall Street Journal* are already publishing content to the popular networking site, and Facebook itself is actively encouraging users to set up news lists. *They want to be your news source.*

If this is not enough to convince you, Facebook is the most used network for professional purposes; the social media powerhouse is the number one choice for research for mainstream media. According to a survey of 1,400 journalists, nearly 40% use Facebook once a week or more frequently to research stories. Facebook is also the social network that journalists join—an overwhelming 90% surveyed reporting membership.[†] They will find you. Why Facebook? All the information is conveniently in one place.

Huffington Post, *USA Today*, *The Washington Post*, not to mention countless blogs, are but some outlets linking content to Facebook.

Web strategists say that Facebook fan page brand-jacking is the new form of tree hugging. Expect more of this in the future, not less.

Is Facebook part of your crisis media strategy? If not, then hop to it. You are missing out on a vital news channel. At the very least, make sure you have your company name registered, or someone will take it and deface it!

Univision: An Alternative to Facebook—Useful for the U.S. Army

Sometimes the culture and goals of the organization, in addition to the type of crisis, determine different choices. For example, the U.S. Army undertook an initiative in 2007 to reach the Hispanic community. They

---

[*] Brian Solis, *Ragan Third Annual Social Media for Communicators Conference*, Coca-Cola Company World HQ, (Atlanta, Georgia), February 23, 2010.

[†] "2010 Journalist Survey on Media Relations Practices," *Bulldog Reporter*, TEKGROUP International, October 2010.

used Univision, a Spanish-language television network in the United States and Puerto Rico, rather than the ever-popular Facebook. This choice was driven partly because of the language capability and partly because Univision offers a moderating service that checks user updates for appropriateness before posting them to its site.

Video and YouTube

The growing use of video-sharing sites means that video communication must play an integral part of an organization's crisis communication plan.

Video is hot! Internet users continue to watch more and more videos online. Year to year figures (March 2009 to March 2010) show that video views jumped a whopping 80 percent! The average online viewer watched a staggering 173.3 videos in that month (March) alone. And by 2014, Cisco Systems predicts that a staggering 91% of Internet networking consumer traffic will be online video.[*]

YouTube leads the way. The total number of videos served on YouTube in one day is a staggering 1 billion.[†] Twenty hours of video is uploaded EVERY minute.[‡] and more than 12 billion videos are viewed each month in the United States.[§]

With these numbers, you can safely become your own broadcaster and take control of your message. Anyone can post content. Toyota did during its massive global recall in 2010. Domino's did. JetBlue did.

United Airlines felt the power of YouTube when Canadian singer–songwriter Dave Carroll posted a "United Breaks Guitars" music video to the site.[¶] The song quickly became a page of Internet history. The video went viral and has been viewed more than 5.5 million times and has prompted more than 22,000 comments, many from people telling their own horror stories about airport baggage handling in general and United Airlines in particular.

To be successful and effective with Internet video, you need to be timely and relevant—just like traditional TV news. But unlike TV news and current affairs, you do not need to be as slick nor as professional. It is often more about speed than glamour.

---

[*] Cisco Systems, "Cisco Predicts Online Video to Be 91% of Global Consumer Traffic by 2014," Press Release, http://www.hardware.com/news/voip/cisco-predicts-online-video-to-be-91-of-global-consumer-traffic-by-2014/, August 2010.

[†] "Internet in Numbers," Royal Pingdom, http://royal.pingdom.com, January 22, 2010.

[‡] "YouTube Fact Sheet," YouTube, www.youtube.com/t/fact_sheet, December 15, 2010.

[§] "Internet in Numbers," Royal Pingdom, http://royal.pingdom.com, January 22, 2010.

[¶] Dave Carroll, Dave Carroll Music, http://www.davecarrollmusic.com/ubg/story/, July 6, 2009.

Kaskavitch explains. His video of the student against the infamous Westboro Baptist Church counterprotest in April 2008, taken with a simple six-megapixel Canon camera, was a hit on YouTube with nearly 50,000 views within hours of posting.[*] Why? Timeliness and relevance.

With the eye of a TV news journalist, he made sure he got all the right angles to tell the story. Kaskavitch "put the lens where it needed to go,"[†] capturing newsworthy and compelling shots such as undercover cops arresting students. He edited the footage and aired it within 35 minutes of the protest being shut down. While it may not have been of the highest quality, it did the job and (at the time of writing) had more than 100,000 views.

Video offers a real-time human response that you can control. You can show the "whites of your eyes," which is so very important in a crisis to achieve credibility. You can demonstrate empathy and compassion, which is hard to achieve in formal, written statements.

You do need to have a credible video response and an established promotion channel as part of your response plan. But just like every other communication channel, particularly in the social media world, you need to have an established presence *before* a crisis hits to be viable.

According to Douglas Simon, president and CEO of DS Simon Productions, a broadcast public relations (PR) firm, organizations need to already have "an established video channel that *informs—or entertains—* your key audiences so that you have built an audience and goodwill before a crisis hits."[‡] He says that "having an online Web presence will increase the speed of distribution and reach of your crisis response."[§]

Simon says there are three key components to successful online videos:

1. *Content creation*—You need a spokesperson who is comfortable in front of a camera. Be professional but not overdone. Authenticity is key.
2. *Promotion plan*—Syndicate to YouTube and other key sites, make sure that the content can be easily shared and posted to sites like

---

[*] Matthew Kaskovitch (University of Wisconsin–Stout, Student Life Services Web Programmer and New Media Consultant), interview with author, February 24, 2010.

[†] Ibid.

[‡] Douglas Simon (Simon Productions), "Fast Forward: Using Web Video to Respond in a Crisis," *Public Relations Tactics*, http://www.prsa.org/intelligence/tactics/articles/view/8149/101/fast_forward_using_web_video_to_respond_in_a_crisi?utm_campaign=PRSASearch&utm_source=PRSAWebsite&utm_medium=SSearch&utm_term=Douglas%20Simon%20July%207%2C%202009, July 7, 2009.

[§] Ibid.

Facebook and Twitter, and aim for coverage on sites like Digg and StumbleUpon. As Simon says, you need your allies in a crisis, so remember to make the content available to trusted business-to-friend (B2F) networks.

3. *Measurement*—You can measure the hits to your video on your Web site, on YouTube, or through a Google search. However, if the crisis is very big, you will need a more detailed measurement to see the impact on the brand.*

I would add the following:

1. Take a leaf out of TV news—Go for the angles that will be relevant to the audience.
2. Keep it short—Nothing over four minutes, ideally TV news length, around one-and-a-half minutes.
3. Include a "talking head."
4. Make sure you are telling the human side of the story with compelling visuals.
5. Link the content and make sure you have the right tags.

Video is not the panacea to solving your crisis, but it is a tremendously useful tool in helping to disseminate a powerful visual message. Many people prefer to learn from watching footage rather than from reading something.

A simple video recorded on a Flip camera may be all that it takes to put the issue into perspective. I recommend that every communication department, indeed everyone who is in business today, needs to have a Flip camera. They are a very valuable crisis management tool—right up there with the mobile phone.

Always use the mantra "What is the overall impression I want to create given situation X." This will help you decide exactly how you will create your content, the look and the feel, and who will be your talking head.

Determining the appropriate person for different situations and determining the shooting location will be very important. And it might not be the corporate video studio.

---

* Douglas Simon (Simon Productions), "Fast Forward: Using Web Video to Respond in a Crisis," *Public Relations Tactics*, http://www.prsa.org/intelligence/tactics/articles/view/8149/101/ fast_forward_using_web_video_to_respond_in_a_crisi?utm_campaign=PRSASearch&utm_ source=PRSAWebsite&utm_medium=SSearch&utm_term=Douglas%20Simon%20July%20 7%2C%202009, July 7, 2009.

CASE STUDY 29.1
YouTube—Macquarie Bank, a Model, and Internet Fame

Australia's Macquarie Bank found itself at the center of unwanted global media attention in February 2010 when David Kiely, a midlevel client adviser, was inadvertently captured on live TV ogling seminude photos of Australian supermodel Miranda Kerr during a live cross to the bank trading room (Figure 29.1). Kiely, who had been opening up the photos of the scantily clad Kerr on his work PC, and Macquarie Bank quickly became Internet sensations.

The episode, which zoomed around the world in hours, is again an example of how quickly a company can face a media crisis when material goes viral in the social media age. As soon as the video was uploaded to YouTube, the footage was seen by millions within days; and as with the Domino's rogue employees' case, the effect was rapidly multiplied by the impact of sharing via Facebook and Twitter.

Not only was the video quickly picked up by the traditional media around the globe, but the e-mail address for the bank's media team was shared across the world when a London-based Web effort was launched to save Kiely's job.

A London-based Web site for financial markets, Here Is the City News, called on its readers to e-mail Macquarie Group headquarters

FIGURE 29.1   Screen capture of Macquarie Bank worker David Kiely, in the background, left, was the subject of a global viral campaign after he was seen viewing pictures of a seminaked supermodel. (The video went viral February 2, 2010, on YouTube with millions of hits. See YouTube: http://www.youtube.com/watch?v=vfX0yHTztNg. Retrieved December 15, 2010.)

in Sydney with the words "Don't fire David Kiely" as the subject title.* Needless to say, their Web site attracted more than its fair share of commentary, too. Here are some of the comments published on their Web site:

- Macquarie will be making a PR mistake if David Kiely is sacked.
- Hopefully management at Mac Bank will see this for what it is-trivial. And think about all that free publicity!
- I used to work with Dave, and he is definitely a good bloke. The pics were harmless, and Mac Bank should stand by him.
- This country is becoming more like the Bible Belt in America. For God's sake, give the guy a break.
- I'm not a banker, but I have joined the campaign regardless. The guy doesn't deserve to be dismissed!†

Not surprisingly, Facebook support groups also sprang up, calling on the bank not to sack Kiely. His voyeurism also made it to Digg,‡ the social media platform that enables you to post your articles, where others can vote on whether or not they like your story. More fuel was added to the media frenzy when Miranda Kerr offered to sign the petition to save Kiely's job. The supermodel was quoted in the *Herald Sun* as saying, "I am told there is a petition to save his job and of course I would sign it."§

The bank launched a forensic internal investigation; Kiely got to keep his job. Whether it was the groundswell of very public support for the banker, a prank gone wrong, or Macquarie Bank showing its heart, we may never really know.

What we do know is that if you are going to be on TV, please look at what is behind you! That is the number one golden rule. Second, have a policy or two in place that guides behavior of your employees, particularly as it relates to social media; and third, expect compelling content to make its way on to the Net very, very quickly.¶

One final point—content is king, just like on successful TV shows. It is the drama, the clever, and the comedy that go viral. Crisis is the stuff of

---

* "Help Save Macquarie Banker's Job—Join Our Campaign," Here Is the City News (London), http://news.hereisthecity.com/news/business_news/9902.cntns, February 4, 2010.

† Ibid.

‡ Digg, http://digg.com/news.

§ Fiona Byrne, "Supermodel Miranda Kerr Speaks Out in Support of Embarrassed Bank Broker David Kiely," *Herald Sun*, www.heraldsun.com.au/entertainment/confidential/supermodel-miranda-kerr-speaks-out-in-support-of-embarrassed-bank-broker-david-kiely/story-e6frf96o-1225826947714, February 5, 2010.

¶ With thanks to Neil McMahon, journalist with The Media Skills Network for his initial report and research. McMahon is a Sydney-based freelance journalist.

human drama: Compelling content *will be shared*. "Hey you've got to see this" is the prevailing mantra in YouTubeLand.

BLOGGING

Blogging is another very effective tool in a crisis, if for no other reason than the technologies that enable blogs, including the Internet and text messaging, tend to be more resilient. For example, during 9/11, the text-messaging capability of the BlackBerry proved to be one of the most effective sources of information exchange between individuals.

According to research on the use of blogs during Hurricane Katrina by the University of Georgia, BlackBerries are effective because uploading and downloading of Web content can occur wirelessly. During prolonged power outages, the BlackBerry can run 24 hours a day for up to a week off a single charge, making blogging a very viable tool in a crisis or emergency.[*]

Blogs are one of the established social media and have evolved from online diaries, where people would keep a running account of their daily lives. We have seen that they have huge influence, and they number in the millions! More than 130 million blogs have been indexed by Technorati since 2004.[†]

Blogs are useful to:

- Share ideas and solutions.
- Get information out quickly.
- Send messages.
- Share news.
- Post news releases and other direct-to-consumer information.
- Push out pertinent information.
- Dispel rumors; correct information.
- Give a voice and access to "average" people, and provide an outlet for expressing public emotion about tragic events.
- Anchor your social communication efforts (see Innovis case study).

---

[*] Wendy Macias, Karen Hilyard, and Vicki Freimuth, "Blog Functions as Risk and Communication during Hurricane Katrina," *Journal of Computer-Mediated Communication*, Vol. 15, No. 1, http://onlinelibrary.wiley.com/doi/10.1111/j.1083-6101.2009.01490.x/abstract, October 2009.

[†] Leslie Gandy, "Majority of Internet Users Still Don't Share," Technorati, http://technorati.com/state-of-the-blogosphere/#ixzz18D8GFTdS, December 28, 2001.

Blogging is most acceptable and commonly used in the United States, but may be less common in other countries. For example, forums are more popular in Australia, according to the Conference Report from the 2nd Annual Crisis Communication and Social Media Summit.*

Following are some tips to help you navigate your way through a crisis in the blogosphere:

Plan—Preparation and detailed planning are crucial to developing a corporate blog that successfully carries you through the good times and the bad. Plan to start your blog *before* a crisis occurs. This gives you ample time to develop relationships and build trust with your key audiences, who will be more likely to believe what you say when a crisis crops up.

Blogs should be part of any communicator's distribution list for press releases and other announcements, taking their place next to journalists, partner organizations, and stakeholders in receiving communication messages.

Who—Appointing the appropriate person to be the official blogger is a critical decision. Anyone can blog, but it takes more than just words. What is important is that the person genuinely wants to connect with others, understands that time is of the essence during a crisis, and has been trained on what to say and what not to say during a crisis.

It does not necessarily have to be the CEO or the official spokesperson. It could be another senior executive; a midlevel manager; or someone in PR, corporate communication, or customer service.

The person does not even need to be a prolific writer. CEO Bill Marriott dictates his posts into a digital recorder, which is transcribed word-for-word by someone on his staff. At Hewlett-Packard, a senior executive calls his posts into a voice mailbox. The posts are then transcribed by staff for posting (see Section III, "Spokespeople—Speed Matters and Perception Is Everything").

What—During a crisis, your official blogger needs to communicate the who, what, why, when, and where as quickly as the information is

---

* Craig Pearce, Conference Report from the *Second Annual Crisis Communication and Social Media Summit* (Frocomm), Sydney, Australia, http://craigpearce.info/wp-content/uploads/2009/11/Crisis-Comm-and-Social-Media-09_Conference-Report_FINAL4.pdf, August 12–13, 2009.

known. If the facts are not known at the beginning of Stage One, some kind of statement such as, "We know an incident occurred today. We do not know any details yet, but we are doing everything we can to get to the bottom of the situation." That can also be posted on Twitter. It is only 28 words, or 137 characters, within the 140-character limitation. Mind you, on your blog you can say more!

As the facts unfold, your blogger should continually communicate updates to prevent misinformation from spreading, avoid possible panic, and protect the company's image.

When writing your blog, it is worth keeping in mind that your headline is key. It is the first and perhaps only impression you make. Keep it short and sweet. Tell the story in five to seven words. And remember search engine optimization. You need to think about how you want "Lord" Google people to find you in a crisis. And remember, what appears on the Internet stays on the Internet—forever.

Feedback—Your blogger needs to be ready to interact and receive good and bad feedback. Blogging is a two-way street. It is not the corporate brochure, although there may be times when you can communicate the company perspective *after* you have built enough credibility. You have to be prepared for and ready to deal with the good, the bad, and the downright ugly.

During a crisis, people will post eyewitness accounts, potentially false, and ask questions. It is important to be monitoring your blog during this time, so you can quickly communicate accurate information and demonstrate relevant concern and compassion. You need to be able to post fast updates.

Regulations—Your blogger should be mindful about the Securities & Exchange Commission (SEC) and regulations to avoid trouble with the authorities, which could cause yet another crisis. There are certain topics that are simply off limits.

Sun Microsystems CEO Jonathan Schwartz does blog about Sun's business, but he is savvy enough about SEC regulations and avoids writing anything that would cause trouble. A *Wall Street Journal* article sums it up nicely: "Blogs and tweets can run afoul of SEC regulations on corporate communications. But sanitizing such posts risks hurting credibility with online audiences."[*]

---

[*] Cari Tuna, "Corporate Blogs and 'Tweets' Must Keep SEC in Mind," *The Wall Street Journal*, http://online.wsj.com/article/SB124078135070257099.html, April 27, 2009.

Statistics—Eighty-one percent of Fortune 500 companies sponsor public blogs, including Walmart Stores Inc., Chevron Corp., and General Motors Corp., according to the Society for New Communications Research.

Monitoring—You should regularly monitor your blogs during a crisis, not only in the traditional mode of PR surveillance but also to aid rescue and recovery efforts through an important alternative communication channel. And put the influential blogs in your industry very high on the radar scale during a crisis. The blogosphere will be smoking.

Blogs are the anchor for your social media efforts. Treat them as your hub where you can direct and drive your communication efforts. Not only that, but they can easily and quickly become the official news channel, particularly in emergencies when other more traditional channels are thwarted for whatever reason. In March 2009, blogs (and Twitter) became a lifeline for Innovis Health (and, to a great extent, the community of Fargo, North Dakota) during the record-setting floods in March 2009. As Kris Olson, VP of Marketing, Quality, and Physician Services, says, "We became the media."[*]

Blogs Are a Must Have in Your Crisis Media Toolkit
CASE STUDY 29.2
Innovis Health—"We Became the Media" (March 2009)

Wet, floods, roads closed. The other main hospital evacuated. A state of emergency. Panic for many.

Innovis Health was fully operational, but few knew. The media were not mentioning their name. The media were isolated, too, and could not get to Innovis.

So, Kris Olson, VP of Marketing, Quality, and Physician Services, jumped into action and onto the social media bandwagon, blogging and tweeting. They had to get their story out—and fast. Lives were at risk.

"We needed to be the media,"[†] says Olson. The mainstream media, which Innovis had relied on in the past to get critical news out, were overwhelmed, understaffed, and not mobile.

---

[*] Kris Olson (Vice President of Marketing, Quality, and Physicians, Innovis Health, Fargo, North Dakota), interview with author, March 12, 2010.
[†] Ibid.

The advertising agency came to the rescue. They turned Olson's "brain-dump, a stream of consciousness"[*] of what was happening at the hospital into a newsworthy, fact-finding blog.

"At 5:15 P.M., the blog went live, and by 5:30 P.M., 1,500 media outlets were monitoring us,"[†] says Olson. In 15 minutes, Innovis had become an important member of the citizen–journalism force.

"The scope blew me away,"[‡] says Olson. Not only did the blog inform key media and stakeholders around their affected community and the country, but it allowed the staff to get on with their critical jobs, too.

Olson explains how the Director of Nursing, with a son in Brazil, a sister in New York City, and another son in San Francisco, was able to point her concerned family to the company blog for information. The director went back to her job with peace of mind that her family knew the facts and what was happening.

The ad agency worked around the clock for 10 days, and not once did Olson make a phone call. Everything was done via e-mail.

This, she says, highlights how incredibly important it is to have a very high level of trust with your service providers. They need to understand your mission, goals, and strategic objectives.

The blog was a very powerful tool that really worked for Innovis and helped other members of the community who didn't have the capacity, including the local shopping malls. Even the competition was getting information from their blog and Twitter account. Innovis used Twitter to push out key information and link to their blog.

Wearing a news director hat, Olson and her team thought carefully about what would be of interest that would also tell the story of what Innovis was doing to help the community. There was also the inevitable "reality TV" moment when they had to build a special landing pad in the hospital parking lot for the Blackhawk helicopters to land. That was a definite photo opportunity, as was the first landing of the helicopter after the rescue of a four-year-old girl and her cat.

Olson's goal throughout the ordeal was to be as transparent as possible and to get the message out that Innovis Health was fully operational and could handle whatever and whoever came in. There were real-time dialog and continuous updates.

It was a 10-day, 24/7 commitment by Olson and her team, and one that not only the Fargo community appreciated, but the wider news media and concerned family and friends of the hospital staff appreciated, too.

---

[*] Kris Olson (Vice President of Marketing, Quality, and Physicians, Innovis Health, Fargo, North Dakota), interview with author, March 12, 2010.
[†] Ibid.
[‡] Ibid.

Eventually, the floodwaters receded, but not the social media efforts. Training for employees has been implemented so that everyone understands their roles and responsibilities, and a formal monitoring system is in place to track media mentions of Innovis Health, both good and bad. Social media are also playing a large role in hospital operational management.

Doctors in the emergency room have Flip cameras, and they record what happens over a busy weekend. They edit and send an update to the local TV stations every week. Needless to say, the media love the footage.

But it's the strategy behind the news gathering that's impressive; Innovis can use the information for the benefit of public health. For instance, if there is a spike in the number of people with flu-like symptoms, Innovis can alert patients to go to the clinic. That information is vital as it helps alleviate the overcrowding in emergency rooms. Great community service and an important communication strategy for Innovis Health.

As Olson says, the opportunities for social media—crisis or not—are endless.

LINKEDIN

LinkedIn,[*] you ask? Do I need to think about that as yet another tool in a crisis? Yes!

Remember, LinkedIn is where the professional and business people hang out. "Facebook for business" is one way to describe the fast growing, business-only social networking site. LinkedIn matters in a crisis as it is highly likely that your (potential) reputation-killer crisis will end up being discussed at length in the various news groups, for example, eMarketing Association (over 231,000 members), Marketing & PR Innovators (over 92,000 members), or PR Wise (over 5,000 members), Crisis Communication (over 1,000 members). These groups have influence.

You can also build up a very large network on LinkedIn that will enable you to communicate directly with people who matter to you and your company in the event of a crisis.

"Lord" Google has also recognized the impact of LinkedIn, as LinkedIn is now searchable by keywords in a Google search.

So, put LinkedIn on your watch list, or at least monitor the news groups for active discussion of your brand.

---

[*] LinkedIn, http://www.linkedin.com/. (Retrieved December 15, 2010.)

DIGG

More than YouTube, Digg is another place where your crisis—news, videos, images—could be bookmarked and seen by millions! At Digg, content, which comes from just about anywhere, is voted on. As it says on its Web site, Digg surfaces the "best stuff" as voted on by its users. You will not find editors at Digg—it's simply a platform where people can collectively determine the value of content.

Once something is submitted, other people see it and Digg what they like best. "If your submission rocks and receives enough Diggs, it is promoted to the front page for the millions of our visitors to see."[*]

Many blogs, and even the traditional media, provide links to Digg, which has more traffic than *The New York Times*, with more than 23 million unique visits per month and more than 4.5 million page views (Technorati). (In comparison, about 25 million people visit Disneyland *every year*; more than 23 million people visit China *every year*. We are talking *per month* for Digg!)

Put Digg on your watch list.

FLICKR

Not the first with online picture sharing, but probably now the dominant force, Flickr has more than 4 billion images on its site.

As they say on their Web site, "Share your photos, watch the world; we want to help people make their content available to the people who matter to them."[†] And they do. The image-sharing Web site, which has only been around since 2004, has played a major role in various crises. Harrowing and sometimes graphic images are shared. These images often tell the real story of what is happening, as they did in the deadly Victorian bushfires.

Flickr is like a giant message board or memorial wall with people's feelings expressed through images, defined by Wikipedia as "an image hosting and video hosting Web site, web services suite, and online community."[‡] It is widely used by bloggers to host images they embed in their blogs and other social media.

Flickr enables you to "get photos and video into and out of the system"[§] in as many ways as you can—from just about anywhere, including mobile

---

[*] Digg, http://about.digg.com/about. (Retrieved December 15, 2010.)
[†] Flickr, http://www.flickr.com/about. (Retrieved December 15, 2010.)
[‡] Wikipedia, "Flickr," http://en.wikipedia.org/wiki/Flickr. (Retrieved December 15, 2010.)
[§] Flickr, http://www.flickr.com/about. (Retrieved December 15, 2010.)

devices and home computers, and from almost any software you are using to manage your content. Flickr in return will push out your images by many methods including the Flickr Web site, RSS feeds, and e-mail, posting to outside blogs.

Know that it will be used in a crisis. Have someone monitor it, as that is where the victims' stories will be told, and that is where the media will look, too. You can also post relevant images there and embed them in your blog.

WIKIPEDIA

If you are not looking at Wikipedia, then you need to! That is the opinion of Marcia Watson DiStaso (Pennsylvania State University) and Marcus Messner (Virginia Commonwealth University), who have been studying the impact of the socially generated encyclopedia on corporate reputation since 2006.

Wikipedia is important, if for no other reason than its influence over search engine results. The free encyclopedia that anyone can edit has gained search engine prominence, essentially dominating Yahoo!, MSN, and Google searches. According to KDPaine's PR Measurement Blog,[*] in one year, an average of 780,053 people viewed articles about 10 of America's most visible companies: Walmart, Exxon, General Motors (GM), Ford, General Electric, Chevron, ConocoPhillips, Citigroup, AIG, and IBM.

Wikipedia is worth watching because if you are in the headlines, the degree of edits and users will increase—significantly. GM and AIG, for example, had a significantly higher number of edits and GM had more than 1.6 million views (as of March 2010).

On the other hand, companies that have embraced social media and engaged in conversations in the marketplace, such as Ford and Walmart, have seen a decline in both the number of edits and the number of users. (At the time of writing, Walmart was facing a massive antidiscrimination lawsuit, so the edits and visits may jump dramatically.)

Some question the reliability and accuracy of Wikipedia. It appears that it is self-editing and has a higher degree of accuracy than one may think. The Web-based encyclopedia quickly became the go-to news source after the tragic shootings at Virginia Tech.

---

[*] "Wondering about Wikipedia? You Should Be," KDPaine PR Measurement Blog, http://kdpaine.blogs.com/kdpaines_pr_m/2010/03/wondering-about-wikipedia-you-should-be.html, March 24, 2010.

SOCIAL MEDIA RELEASE

We have come a long way since Ivy Lee, considered the father of modern PR, wrote the first press release for Pennsylvania Railroad after a crash that killed 50 people. The afternoon of October 8, 1906, changed the media landscape.

One could argue that May 23, 2006, almost 100 years later, changed the landscape again when Todd Defren introduced a template for the social media release (SMR).

If you are playing in SocialMediaLand, then you will need to consider using an SMR to disseminate information in a crisis. As Ane Howard from the United Kingdom–based Rush PR says, "SMRs are not just pretty conversational announcements, they have a real mission."[*]

SMRs can quickly help you disseminate critical content that can be easily shared and bookmarked. Another key advantage is that you can embed links (e.g., a YouTube video, Flickr, Facebook) to a variety of media outlets, both your own and other key audiences, such as your all important allies and friends.

MediaShift defines an SMR "as a single page of Web content designed to enable the content to be removed and used on blogs, wikis, and other social channels."[†]

SMRs typically feature multiple embedded links and blocks of text similar to those found in traditional news releases (e.g., quotes and contact information). (See sample SMR in Appendix C.)

Social Media Newsroom

The social media newsroom is yet another tool at your disposal in helping to effectively manage communication in a crisis.

Ian Capstick, a Canadian media consultant, writing in a MediaShift blog,[‡] says that social media newsrooms are more comprehensive than the SMR. "They allow an organization to host all of their social media releases, contact information, and links to social channels in one place."

Social media newsrooms also allow for that all important search engine optimization (SEO). You must be able to track news coverage,

---

[*] Ane Howard, "Debunking the Social Media Release," Rush PR News Blog, http://www.rushprnews.com/2009/11/03/debunking-the-social-media-release-smr, November 3, 2009.

[†] Ian Capstick, "Social Media Releases Must Evolve to Replace Press Releases," MediaShift Blog, http://www.pbs.org/mediashift/2010/04/social-media-release-must-evolve-to-replace-press-release113.html, April 23, 2010.

[‡] Ibid.

regardless of where it is, in a crisis; and keyword searches help you do that.

As Robyn Sefiani, managing director of the Australian-based Sefiani Communications Group and respected PR and crisis consultant, says:

> Today, a newsroom isn't simply about posting press releases on the company website. Organizations need to incorporate functionality to support SEO, multimedia content, and the option to share content through social media platforms such as Twitter and Facebook.[*]

Social Media War Room

Every major crisis has a war room. You have seen the vision of the BP (oil spill) war room with videos, whiteboards, computers, and a virtual Army of people, literally working around the clock—in shifts—to fix the problem.

Now you need a *social media war room*—one that is set up before you need it. It does not have to be in an underground bunker, but it is best to be in a specified room—a room that you have tested before the crisis hits— tested with well thought out and creative scenarios. Your team needs to know the drill.

I advise my clients to run annual exercises, at a minimum. If you are in a high-risk industry, like an oil refinery, the airline industry, or public transportation, you will need to be validating your training and planning at least every six months.

In the digital age, as Ari Newman says, "You need to activate personnel and procedures with a single tweet."[†]

Newman's questions will help guide you in establishing a social media war room:

- Who will "live" in the war room?
- Whose job is it to engage with social media on a daily basis, and who is empowered to respond to emerging situations?
- Which other stakeholders will be pulled into the war room in the event of a crisis? Every man and his dog will want to get involved in the drama—it is exciting for many people. As Ari says, that is a "sure path to chaos."
- Who will sign off on your response?

---

[*] Robyn Sefiani, Sefiani Communications Group, personal e-mail with author, March 5, 2010.

[†] Ari Newman, "Social Media War Rooms [and Why You Need One], iMedia Connection Blog, http://www.imediaconnection.com/content/26607.asp, April 28, 2010.

- What is the plan? What is the first thing that happens when a crisis is detected, and what steps follow as you rally the team and form your plan? What are the rules of engagement? Which social media critics will you respond to, and how?
- Who has access to the social media monitoring and messaging systems that power the war room, and what are they allowed to do with them? (You do need to decide exactly who is authorized to tweet and post on the company's behalf, and this needs to be well understood *before* a crisis hits.)[*]

WHAT TOOL TO CHOOSE *WHEN*?

So we know social media tools have their place in crisis media management. How do you decide which one to use when?

First things first! Like any good, professional communicator, you need to establish goals for your social media outreach. You need to know who is out there. What are the social media habits of your key audiences, and how do they connect with you *and* the traditional media in a crisis.

Matthew Kaskavitch, new media consultant, says you need to understand what tool is going to give you the most value. Understand the likely return on investment. Just because there is another application on the iPhone does not mean you have to use it! Beware the shiny new object syndrome.

Make sure your social media efforts are "message driven not channel driven … focus on people when formulating your social media crisis plan"[†] is the advice from the American Public Health Association Expert Round Table on Social Media and Risk Communication during Times of Crisis.

And make sure, too, that your goals are focused on building a strong, active community and authentic two-way relationships based on trust. Creating Facebook and Twitter accounts is just the first step. It is easy to get started in social media, but you need to stay engaged to get the solid return on your investment. The right engagement, no matter how challenging, pays off in a crisis.

Table 29.2 gives a brief overview of what tools might work and when, according to the stage methodology.

---

[*] Ari Newman, "Social Media War Rooms [and Why You Need One], iMedia Connection Blog, http://www.imediaconnection.com/content/26607.asp, April 28, 2010.

[†] Booz Allen Hamilton, "Goodbye Sources, Messages, Channels and Receivers: Hello Network," White Paper from *American Public Health Association Expert Round Table on Social Media and Risk Communication during Times of Crisis*, www.boozallen.com/consulting-services/services_article/42420696, March 2009, p. 3.

Table 29.2 Tips for Using Social Media during Emergencies

Stage One	Stage Two	Stage Three	Stage Four
Twitter covers breaking news.	Publish tweets with links to your Web site for more details (remember to incorporate # tags).	Post updates on Facebook to show what you are doing to fix the problem and to ensure it doesn't happen again.	Tweet updates on Twitter.
Video posted to YouTube.	Establish Facebook presence.	Publish video updates on YouTube if needed.	On Facebook, post updates about stories learned, pictures of team meetings, pictures of the memorial service, pictures of the products back on the shelves.
Antifan Club established on Facebook.	Publish messages on Facebook for more personal contact.	Tweet updates and links to more information.	Flickr, too, for the all important human interest and to show your people in action.
	Manage rumors; provide updates, reports, and context on key social media sites.		
	Post relevant pictures, videos, and footage on Facebook and YouTube, showing the human side of the story.		
	Respond to criticism, demonstrating the action you are taking; tweet and blog.		
	Publish links to interviews with talking heads and apologies on Web site, Facebook.		

(continued)

231

Table 29.2 Tips for Using Social Media during Emergencies (Continued)

Stage One	Stage Two	Stage Three	Stage Four
	Consider publishing a statement on LinkedIn in any groups in which your company or employees are active.		
	Showcase heroes on YouTube, Flickr, Facebook.		
	On Flickr, post relevant pictures that show your actions.		
	Demonstrate care and concern and show employees working. (Flip cameras are an invaluable tool.)		

INTEGRATE SOCIAL MEDIA INTO PLANNING

Now, how to integrate the Web and social media into the crisis planning, particularly if you have a tiny staff or there is just one of you:

1. Find a partner to collaborate with you. Or have an intern—working to strict guidelines and criteria—from one of the many communication schools work with you to help build your online presence.
2. Partner with an outside agency with excellent Web credentials and have them be part of your crisis drill. It is critical that you have complete trust in them, as Kris Olson of Innovis Health advocates. She did not even speak once with her agency during their 10-day flood emergency in Fargo, North Dakota, in March 2009. They communicated by e-mail the entire time, so the team could get on with their jobs. Olson says they understood the values of the organization and were able to clearly interpret her e-mail "brain-dump."[*] That type of service is invaluable in a crisis.

---

[*] Kris Olson (Vice President of Marketing, Quality, and Physicians, Innovis Health, Fargo, North Dakota), interview with author, March 12, 2010.

3. Integrate the Web team and social media team into your drills and planning so you know your media relations efforts will run smoothly when the proverbial … hits the fan.

One thing is for sure: You not only need a technically savvy person but a social media–savvy person working in sync with you in a crisis. You do not want to be figuring this out when the spotlight is on you and you have only hours if not minutes to respond.

30

Monitoring: Your Best Defense in a Crisis

You've got to have the ability to stop it in its tracks before those tracks turn out to be a big honking tank bearing right down on you.[*]

Gerald Baron, Crisisblogger

Speed, dare I say it again, is an essential ingredient of effective digital-age crisis media management.

That lightning-fast speed is a double-edged sword. While the real-time nature of digital communication does present challenges in a crisis, it also provides solutions, particularly to mitigate and manage hot issues. When organizations actively monitor the online space, they can often nip crises in the bud or even prevent them altogether.

There is no doubt that listening and monitoring is critical in managing a media crisis in the digital age. As Brian Solis, principle of FutureWorks, says, rumor management is becoming the biggest and most important job in crisis communication.

There are literally billions of conversations happening about you, your organization, and your products on blogs and forums galore. And if there's an issue brewing, the purists, as we have seen, will jump into action—and fast; and before you can blink, you have a viral campaign running against you. A smoldering fire, as we have seen, can quickly ignite and become a wildfire within hours, if not minutes.

---

[*] Gerald Baron, "Searching and Monitoring—More Important and More Powerful Than Ever," Crisisblogger Blog, http://crisisblogger.wordpress.com, posted 4:35 PM, November 10, 2009.

The first place those directly affected are most likely to go to voice their concern is Twitter—often before traditional news outlets even have a chance to pick up the story.

So, you need a strong listening and monitoring strategy and system in place, not only to monitor issues but to help you avert a full-blown crisis. And when you have hit that triggering moment in time and you are rushing—whether you want to or not—into the unfolding drama of Stage Two, it will need to be all-systems-go.

Listening and monitoring is really a means for discovering just who your fans and your foes are and what they are really saying. What are the key words; what is their trigger word? You will be listening and tuning in to their "party lines."

A good monitoring system first listens to the conversations to learn how people perceive your organization. You'll learn their language and what you need to address. But don't rush in to join the conversation. Listen before you leap. "If you don't know the rules, you'll walk into a bear trap,"* says Dan Spiers of Mediascape. Research the issues, take a look at the trends, respond free of emotion and bias. Think carefully before you engage. Your words will be recorded for all to see for a very long time. As we have heard a few times in this book, the damage is done—you can't take that sin back.

When companies set up a process for listening and monitoring, it usually involves an employee or two reading blog posts and tweets, and reviewing videos and images. They then decide whether or not the posts and comments deserve a response, or a more formal monitoring system needs to be in place. In the middle of the crisis, you have no choice; you must have a robust system in place.

Just a few years ago, it was almost enough to have a media monitoring service dedicated to your crisis, giving updates as they happened. Many times I have had monitors on the other end of the phone or even in the war room providing that all important real-time analysis.

Now, I advise clients to have at least two streams running in a full-blown crisis—one for social media and one for the mainstream media (MSM).

Overwhelmed? Not knowing where to start or what and how to use social media monitoring? So many conversations, so many channels. So, where do you start? Dan Spiers recommends starting with the blogs germane to your area. He also recommends human analysis because you can read between the lines and understand the tone and emotion behind the words better than technology can.

---

* Dan Spiers (Mediascape, United Kingdom), interview with author, November 27, 2009.

At the very least, set up a Google alert. Erik Deckers, 14-year marketing and public relations consultant, recommends, "If nothing else, put some Google Analytics on your blog. It's lightweight and updates every 24 hours, but it's free."* His company uses Yahoo! Analytics because it has real-time updates.

To most effectively identify looming crises via Twitter, consider investing in a comprehensive social media monitoring tool such as Techrigy, Radian6, or ScoutLabs. For a monthly fee, these services make it easy to track all conversations related to particular topics of interest, whether they be direct mentions of your brand, discussions of particular pain points, or references to growing problems in your industry.

These services will help you identify and track spikes in conversation, causes for increased conversation, tones of dialog, and links shared to other online sources. These services also help manage workflow to ensure any necessary follow-up takes place.

Orange8 Interactive, a Swiss agency for online marketing and part of the international Goldbach Media Group, tested a series of social media monitoring tools. Their comprehensive test covered a wide array of requirements including:

- Localization of countries and languages.
- Widespread use of data.
- Lists of posts with information reach and user profiles.
- E-mail alerts on delicate topics.
- Workflows.
- Mood analysis.[†]

It also included practical things like costs, interface, and the main competency of analyzing and reporting.

The interface is very important, says Mike Schwede of Orange8. Your monitoring tool needs a modern application interface because "a great variety of people have to work with it on a daily basis."[‡]

Needless to say there were "winners and losers," but as Schwede says, "there are tools matching our point of view and other great tools a bit less."[§] One to be watched included the Australian-focused Dialogix.

---

[*] Posted by Erik Deckers, "Five Essential Tools Any Crisis Communication Pro Needs," Problog Service, http://problogservice.com/category/posts/public-health/, January 4, 2010.

[†] Mike Schwede, Orange8 Interactive (Switzerland), http://www.orange8.com/, received by author via e-mail, May 28, 2010.

[‡] Ibid.

[§] Ibid.

The big winners were Sysomos and Radian6. Following is how Schwede rates the tools:

- Sysomos is a great, easy-to-use tool for monitoring with some possibilities of workflows and engagement. The perfect tool for companies starting a social media strategy or for companies with small social media teams.
- Radian6 is the most flexible tool with the widest range of functions. This tool is for advanced users, for companies with bigger social media teams where you define and roll out complete individual dashboards, manage engagement workflows deeply, and have comprehensive possibilities of (e-mail) reporting. The new Radian6 Engagement Console is a perfect addition for community managers who like to work with tools like TweetDeck.*

Here are some other tools you can use:

The Twitter Times—A personalized newspaper based on Twitter content. It tracks what the people you follow talk about and the tweets of the friends of the people you follow.

RSS Feeds—All blogs produce a unique RSS feed, including text, images, links, audio, and video. When a blogger publishes a new post, the associated RSS feed is automatically updated and passed along to its subscribers.

Klout—Analyzes content from millions of people on Twitter to identify the top influencers on any given topic.

TweetDeck—The popular Adobe Air desktop application for social networks, TweetDeck is your personal browser for staying in touch with what's happening now, connecting to your contacts across Twitter, Facebook, MySpace, and LinkedIn.

Jeff Bullas, an Australian-based digital and technology personality whose years of experience in several industries make his posts worth every minute they take to read, has this sound advice for what's worth monitoring on your social media channels. His list is reproduced below:

Blog
    Unique visitors per month to your blog
    Total posts read
    Subscribers to your RSS feed

---

* Mike Schwede, Orange8 Interactive (Switzerland), http://www.orange8.com/, received by author via e-mail, May 28, 2010.

Total e-mail subscribers
Independent credibility ratings by external authorities such as
    Klout, Adage, Compete.com, or Hubspot (with its Web site
    and blog gradings)
Number of comments
Who is commenting (small players or major players)
Links
Time on site
Facebook
    Number of fans
    Types of fans (ordinary or high value)
    Comments

Twitter
    Number of followers
    How many lists you are on
    How many ReTweets you are generating
    Number of Direct Messages
    Klout rating
YouTube
    Number of views
    Number of subscribers
Quantity of comments[*]

Erik Deckers, vice president of operations and creative services for
Pro Blog Service and former risk communication director for the Indiana
Department of Health, also has a valuable list of useful applications for
crisis communication.

NearbyTweets—Web site search application to find Twitter users in
    your city or state.
bit.ly—URL shortener. Use it on TweetDeck, and then track it with
    Twitalyzer or Bit.ly's click tracker.
StatCounter—Measures Web site or blog traffic from minute to
    minute.[†]

---

[*] Jeff Bullus, "20 Social Media Ratings You Should be Monitoring" Jeff Bullus Blog, http://
www.jeffbullas.com/2010/04/18/20-social-media-ratings-you-should-be-monitoring,
April 18, 2010. (Reprinted with permission.)

[†] Erik Deckers, *Crisis Communication and Social Media for Government Crisis Communicators*
(E-book: http://problogservice.com/crisis_communication_ebook/Social%20Media%20
and%20Crisis%20Communication%20for%20Government%20Communicators.pdf), 2010,
pp. 9, 12. (Reprinted with permission.)

Once you identify who is driving conversations and what the important issues are, you are ready to shape your strategies and engage in the conversation.

Here are a few important tips to keep in mind:

1. Pick your battles.
2. Tap into people's need for comfort.
3. Be prepared for negative feedback.
4. Start before a crisis occurs.
5. Listening and monitoring should be a constant, ongoing effort.

From blogs to message boards to Facebook, Twitter, and whistle-blowing sites like WikiLeaks (see Chapter 15), people are having conversations about their experiences and your organization. Embrace a listening and monitoring strategy to find and participate in the social media conversation—that will help you keep those smoldering issues under control.

Most of all you will need a comprehensive monitoring system in place and tested before a crisis hits. Otherwise you will waste precious time and money if you haven't already got one up and running.

SECTION V SUMMARY

Are you fully prepared for creating and sending the right message, to the right people, at the right time, in the right format, using the right tools?

The bottom line—sloppy thinking, negative language, and poor communication techniques are not the ticket in a universe where there is so much information and so many ideas to choose from.

In a crisis, you have to choose your words carefully and focus on the audience *most affected*. Where's the concern? What about some compassion?

Do what you can to eradicate any crippling fear of the new media or public reaction that will prevent you and your organization from connecting to the people who matter, the people who have the power to withdraw their permission for you to operate. They are increasingly in cyberspace, where distance is nullified and where people can join in from all parts of the globe—and they do.

Social media mirrors life, and that gives a false facade, making us feel that it is vastly different. It's actually not. It's full of real people with real expectations. They want to engage, and they have the tools to do so.

And that's the power shift. In SocialMediaLand you do not "own" the brand; you share that ownership with your community, an active, engaged group of people who thrive on authenticity and trust. Old-school authoritarianism just doesn't belong, as Nestlé found out:

> It's not okay for people to use altered versions of your logos, but it's okay for you to alter the face of Indonesian rainforests? How?[*]

> This is the best example of how a big corporation can screw up, and has no one to blame but themselves, what about emotional intelligence? The manual says, that you should not insult your customers, or fans … and so it goes on.[†]

> Wow what a hypocrite nestle is! Where were your sensitivities when your involvement was destroying rain forests? We will continue using altered version of your logos. You can keep deleting them.[‡]

---

[*] Posted by: Jugular Bean, Nestlé's *Facebook* page, http://www.facebook.com/?ref=mb&sk=-messages#!/Nestle/posts/107128462646736, March 19, 2010.
[†] Posted by: Diego Cast, Nestlé's *Facebook* page, March 24, 2010.
[‡] Posted by: Vikram Sharmato, Nestlé's *Facebook* page, April 2, 2010.

Learning while doing is painful. Hint: Having a light touch changes everything in social situations, real world or virtual. Oh, and starting a status update with, "To repeat ..." is like waving a red flag at a bull.*

Watch your tone, be compassionate, and engage with your stakeholders. In a crisis, this has always been the rule. Take a look at Case Study 30.1 regarding Nestlé for some reinforcement of the rules.

Monitor early and monitor often. Before the crisis you will need to have mapped the key influencers and detractors of the brand. During the crisis you, obviously, will need to be monitoring those detractors, and engaging your "friends." And remember to deploy key words across major search engines so you can more easily track what's being said where.

CASE STUDY 30.1
Facebook Face-Off: Greenpeace and Nestlé in a Kat Fight

There are lessons to be learned from the Nestlé Facebook debacle over its use of unsustainable palm oil sourced from rain forests.

While Facebook has proved to be a very important tool for the 1.5 million local businesses that are on it, things can get sticky and do not always run according to the plan, as Nestlé found out.

The situation began when Greenpeace, known for their unorthodox methods of gaining attention, created a video parody on YouTube of Nestlé's Kit Kat. The video parody suggests that the production of a key ingredient in the product, palm oil, leads to the destruction of the rain forests, which in turn threatens the endangered species, such as the orangutan, living in it.

Nestlé demanded that YouTube take down the video, citing copyright infringement. Instead the video went viral.

Of course, Nestlé had the right to defend its intellectual property, and indeed many applauded the food giant for tackling Greenpeace, but that's not the point here.

What is important is the manner in which Nestlé managed the incident, which, needless to say, attracted mainstream media attention with the inevitable headlines: "Greenpeace and Nestlé in a Kat Fight."†

It was as much about the tone as it was about Nestlé's and Greenpeace's behavior. Nestlé did itself no favors when the individual

---

* Posted by: Tom Guarriello, Nestlé's *Facebook* page, March 19, 2010.
† Robin Shreeves, "Greenpeace and Nestlé in a Kat Fight," Forbes.com, http://www.forbes.com/2010/03/18/kitkat-greenpeace-palm-oil-technology-ecotech-nestle.html, posted 12:00 PM EDT, March 19, 2010.

tasked with responding to messages on their Facebook page behaved rather rudely (for which he or she later apologized). Consider these responses:

Thanks for the lesson in manners. Consider yourself embraced. But it's our page, we set the rules, it was ever thus.*

Here, there are some rules we set. As in almost every forum. It's to keep things clear.†

Not surprisingly, this agitated rant back from Nestlé only drew more attention to the online protest. Next post:

This [deletion] was one in a series of mistakes for which I would like to apologize. And for being rude. We've stopped deleting posts, and I have stopped being rude.‡

What matters in cyberspace matters in real life: Manners do matter. Organizations that decide to play in SocialMediaLand need to understand that social media mirror real life.

Distance disappears; anyone, anywhere, anytime can join in; so be very aware of any skeletons in the closet. They will come out to bite you again, as they did with Nestlé—many posts on Facebook compared the palm oil situation to the milk scandal in Southeast Asia:

Like others I have only joined this group in order to comment on this thread. I have avoided Nestlé products for years after they shipped tonnes of baby formula to Africa after it was banned in the West. The formula was given away "free" and …§

So, the following are some truisms:

- Expect a fight at some stage—poor publicity is inevitable. At some stage you will do something that will upset someone somewhere in the world.
- The train has left the station—even if you're not using social media, lots are, and chances are that they will find a way to express themselves and let it be known that they are disappointed, upset, confused. The word will spread. Be prepared.

---

* Posted by: Nestlé's, Nestlé's *Facebook* page, http://www.facebook.com/?ref=mb&sk=messages#!/Nestle/posts/107128462646736, March 19, 2010.
† Posted by: Nestlé's, Nestlé's *Facebook* page, March 19, 2010.
‡ Posted by: Nestlé's, Nestlé's *Facebook* page, March 19, 2010.
§ Posted by: Rick Hennessy, Nestlé's *Facebook* page, http://www.facebook.com/?ref=mb&sk=messages#!/Nestle/posts/107128462646736, March 30, 2010.

- Expect your crisis to go viral and expect coordinated attacks *if* you behave badly or are perceived to have behaved badly.
- Poor tone begets poor tone—if you are rude then expect rudeness back.
- Social media is time-consuming and challenging if you want to make it work and to remain engaged.
- Live for the best, but plan for the worst.

And above all, remember that SocialMediaLand is the mirror of life. If you commit a sin, fess up, apologize, and treat your customers and fans with respect. They are people. Treat them that way. Humility goes a long way in life; same in the online world.

While there is no doubt that the Nestlé fiasco with Greenpeace may have dented its reputation, caused a huge headache for its social media team, and given fodder galore for bloggers, tweeters, and activists around the world, the reality is that sales of the popular Kit Kat bar only took a small hit. Same is the story for Domino's. Time will tell what the real story will be for sales of Toyota or for BP's bottom line.

So, crisis media management really hasn't changed that much, but then again it has. A crisis is still a reputation-defining moment. Behaviors and expectations have not changed, *but* there is no doubt that we are in a new dawn of crisis communication, and it will be here for a long time.

Find what works for you; match it to your organizational goals; be strategic; beware the "shiny new object" syndrome; and be open, transparent, and human. That is the only defense you have when you are defending your reputation, whether in the kingdom of "Lord" Google, "King" Rupert, or "Dame" Arianna.

APPENDIX A: GUIDELINES FOR BRIEFING SPOKESPEOPLE

Once a spokesperson is selected for a particular crisis and/or a particular audience, it is important to provide a thorough briefing, especially if fronting a media conference.

- Provide date, time, and location of interview/news conference.
- Provide background on journalist(s) and nature of media outlet (including audience).
- Fill in background on previous company's relationship with particular media and reporter.
- Outline the issues likely to be raised.
- Detail who else has spoken on the issue and what they have said.
- Alert to possible "minefields."
- Provide 5 Ws and How.
- Update all information.
- Provide a selection of facts and figures (only those with impact).
- Identify opportunities for inserting the corporate message.
- Provide "human interest" angles, where appropriate.
- Provide specific examples of the impact of the crisis.
- Coach, if necessary, on relevant legislation.
- Provide latest information from the Command Center.
- Provide prognosis where advisable.
- Outline action that has been taken.
- Provide relevant background and context (e.g., precedents, previous crises, and comparable incidents).

APPENDIX B: SAMPLE MEDIA CONTACT INFORMATION LOG

(Use this log to capture information when calls come in. This is particularly helpful for frontline employees.)

Reporter's name:_____ **Time of call:**_____

Media: TV Print Radio Cable Social _____
(name of news organization; e.g., CNN, Fox, XYZ Blog)

Reporter's contact details: _____

Deadline: _____

Information requested:
(Be careful to note key phrases, questions.)
_____
_____
_____
_____

What we told the reporter:
_____
_____
_____

Your name: _____ **Dept:** _____

Contact details:
_____

Follow-up:_____

Thank you for your cooperation.

APPENDIX C: SAMPLE NEWS RELEASE

In Section IV are statements, samples, and actual examples, including Lt. General Robert Cone's statement. Following is an example of what a crisis news release might look like and what you need to consider when preparing one. It is a very good idea to have these templated so that you will not be wasting time when a crisis happens.

What you need to consider:

1. Describe the incident—*what* happened.
2. Confirm *who* is involved—how many employees, how many members of the public, what emergency services and how many of them, what equipment was involved (e.g., numbers of fire units or personnel and other known facts).
3. *When*—give the exact timing of events, the beginning, significant elements, duration or likely duration of incident.
4. Exactly *where* did it happen and what areas/locations were involved/affected by the incident.

Other information:

1. *Why* and *how* did it happen—Note: Be careful to avoid speculation of cause; instead, say that's what the investigation is for. Explain the process for the investigation and who will be involved, and make a commitment to finding out why and how it all happened. Do include *background information on the size and scale* of the company.
2. Do include *spokesperson contact details* and/or Web site/blog for additional information.
3. If a police investigation is also involved, refer the media to the police spokespeople for specific facts dealing with their investigation.

SAMPLE MEDIA RELEASE

EXPLOSION AT [*NAME OF BANK/COMPANY*] BRANCH

[*Place, e.g., New York*] [*Date*] An explosion occurred at approximately 4:25 P.M. today in the banking chamber of the [*name of bank/company*] branch at [*name of location*]. The explosion is believed to have been deliberately caused by a bomb placed in the bank's premises.

The explosion resulted in the deaths of 12 people, including 10 employees of [*name of bank/company*] and two emergency services personnel. An additional 50 people were injured in the explosion and are receiving specialized care at [*name or names of hospital/s*].

[*A spokesperson and/or title*] for [*name of bank/company*], [*Mr./Ms. 1st Name, 2nd Name*], said, "We are shocked and saddened by this tragic event, and we extend our very deepest sympathy to families of the victims and to those people who were injured by the explosion, as well as to our employees who shared this tragic event.

"The bank is working with emergency services and the relevant authorities to conduct a full investigation into the incident. We are increasing our already stringent security measures in all other branches to ensure the safety of our customers and employees," said [*Mr./Ms. 1st Name, 2nd Name*].

At 3:45 P.M. today the bank received an anonymous telephone call advising that a bomb had been placed in the banking chamber at [*Branch locale*]. The branch is one of [*no.*] branches serving the metropolitan area.

The premises and surrounding businesses were immediately evacuated and the [*city name*] Fire Department established a security cordon around the building in the area bounded by [*include specific streets*]. At 4:05 P.M. members of the [*city name*] Fire Department began to search for possible devices. The explosion occurred shortly afterward.

At this stage there is no information as to who placed the device or why the bank was targeted. Together with emergency services and the relevant authorities, the bank is conducting a full investigation into the incident.

"We are appealing to anyone who has any information about this incident, or who may have seen anything suspicious in or around the [*Branch locale*] branch today, to call the investigation team at [*1-800-XXX-XXXX*]," said [*Mr./Ms. 1st Name, 2nd Name*].

[*Mr./Ms. 1st Name, 2nd Name*] assured customers that deposits and bank records were completely safe and not affected by the tragic events. "[*Name of bank/company*] is continuing to provide full banking services to all customers. Customers requiring assistance, information about their accounts, or alternative branch locations should call the customer service center at [*1-800-XXX-XXXX*]," he/she said.

For further information please contact: [*1st Name, 2nd Name, cell and landline for company contact*] or visit [*Web site*]. For specific details on the device and police activity, please contact [*1st Name, 2nd Name of police spokesperson*].

APPENDIX D: NINE STEPS TO A CRISIS COMMUNICATION PLAN*

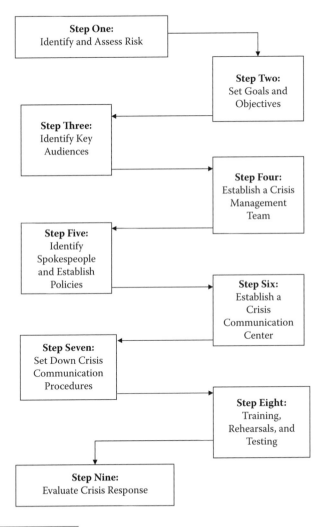

Step One:
Identify and Assess Risk

Step Two:
Set Goals and Objectives

Step Three:
Identify Key Audiences

Step Four:
Establish a Crisis Management Team

Step Five:
Identify Spokespeople and Establish Policies

Step Six:
Establish a Crisis Communication Center

Step Seven:
Set Down Crisis Communication Procedures

Step Eight:
Training, Rehearsals, and Testing

Step Nine:
Evaluate Crisis Response

---

* "Media Skills Methodology," Media Skills, (Crows Nest, NSW, Australia), 2002.

APPENDIX E: USEFUL RESOURCES

In addition to the references from Erik Deckers (see Social Media Resources for Crisis Communicators in Appendix G) there is a wealth of material on the Web. Here are some resources that I have found useful and reliable. The list is a mix of Web sites, white papers, blogs, and people.

CRISIS COMMUNICATION

- *www.e911.com*—Web site where you will find dozens of excellent articles and reference material from the veteran communication consultant Jim Lukaszewski, known to some as "Yoda." Read his blog: http://crisisgurublog.e911.com.
- *Dr. Robert C. Chandler*—Director of the Nicholson School of Communication, University of Central Florida. Dr. Chandler often gives webinars for Everbridge, and they are well worth listening to. Always a nugget or two or a dozen! See: http://everbridge.com.
- *View from the Bridge Blog*—http://www.signalbridge.com/blog.htm, from Bill Salvin. Always a good read; good practical information and case studies.

PUBLIC RELATIONS/COMMUNICATION

- *Richard Edelman*—Chief executive officer and president of Edelman Public Relations, a heavyweight in the public relations (PR) world. His blog is always on the mark, and he has the ear of some of the world's most powerful: http://www.edelman.com/speak_up/blog/.
- *James Grunig*—Professor emeritus, Department of Communication, University of Maryland. For me, Dr. Grunig is the guru. Read anything that he has published. Weighty, academic, but excellent: http://www.comm.umd.edu/faculty/jgrunig.html.

255

- *Shel Holtz*—Principal of Holtz Communication and Technology. Author and coauthor of six books on communication, including *Public Relations on the Net, Corporate Conversations, Blogging for Business,* and *Tactical Transparency.* Cohost of the twice-weekly PR-focused podcast "For Immediate Release" with Neville Hobson. A heavyweight in communication, social media, and crisis. Check out his blog: http://shelholtz.com.
- *Mindjumpers*—Danish-based social media agency. Creative, smart. Good blog: www.mindjumpers.com. Follow Jonas Nielsen on Twitter: http://twitter.com/Mindjumpers.
- *Craig Pearce*—Australian PR consultant, his blog is always good value. He has authored some very good research reports: http://craigpearce.info/.

SOCIAL MEDIA

- *Jeff Bullas*—Australian with an international audience. Very good analysis. Interesting statistics. Very easy to read. Cuts through all the noise that is becoming more widespread on social networks by consistently writing content that is engaging and insightful: http://jeffbullas.com/.
- *Mashable*—The social media guide. Has a following of nearly 3 million. The social media bible, well at least for me it has been! At the time of writing, they had just published 90+ Essential Media Resources: http://mashable.com/.
- *Laurel Papworth*—Australian blogger. Influential, irreverent, and outspoken. Good value. She has been creating and managing virtual communities for 20 years and also has social media courseware. Her blog is entertaining to read: http://laurelpapworth.com.
- *Brian Solis*—Digital analyst, sociologist, and futurist. He has published a couple of interesting books—*Putting the Public Back in Public Relations* and *Engage*—and is the creator of *The Conversation Prism.* His 2.0 blog is always good value, high level, high brow, and on top of the trends. One of the heavy hitters in the Web 2.0 scene: http://www.briansolis.com.

RESEARCH/WHITE PAPERS

- Erik Deckers, *Crisis Communication and Social Media for Government Crisis Communicators* (E-book: http://problogservice.com/crisis_ communication_ebook/Social%20Media%20and%20Crisis%20 Communication%20for%20Government%20Communicators. pdf), 2010.
- Booz Allen Hamilton, "Goodbye Sources, Messages, Channels and Receivers: Hello Network," White Paper from *American Public Health Association Expert Round Table on Social Media and Risk Communication during Times of Crisis*, www.boozallen.com/ consulting-services/services_article/42420696, March 2009.
- Frocomm—Australian-based, Frocomm, is an independent conference producer that "is dedicated to providing world-class, value-for-money conferences." Worth checking out if only for past conference papers. They also produce *The PR Report*: www. frocomm.com.au.
- Holmes Report—Published by the British-based Holmes Group. Founded in 2000 by Paul Holmes, editor and publisher, they publish weekly e-newsletters and Annual Report Cards on the public relations industry: http://www.holmesreport.com.
- Mediascape—Australian-based, Mediascape monitors, analyzes, and provides strategic support for communication campaigns. They provided major support for the Victorian Government during and after the deadly Victorian bushfires. See: http://www. mediascape.com.au.
- Ragan Communications—Publisher of *Ragan's Daily Headlines* with great case studies, tips, and techniques. They also produce conferences: www.ragan.com.
- Pew Research Center—Excellent and free research, mostly American. As they say on their Web site: Numbers, Facts, and Trends (Shaping Your World). Publisher of the annual survey "State of the News Media." Their research was invaluable for this book, and I highly recommend it: www.pewresearch.org.
- "Not Shaken but Stirred: Ten Commandments for Leaders in Tough Times"—a report by Martin Newman for The Company Agency Leadership Council, London, November 2008: http://www. thecompanyagency.com/pdfs/TCA-LeadershipInToughTimes. pdf.

APPENDIX F: SOCIAL MEDIA POLICY RESOURCES

1. *http://socialmedia.policytool.net/welcome/wizard*—This is a free 12-question quiz that writes your policy as you answer the questions. It is a template predetermined by whether you answer yes or no. It will get you started. Has some good reference material for each question. See Iqbal Mohammed's sample reproduced from their questions. ("Sample Policy" below.)

2. *http://socialmedia.defense.gov/*—U.S. Department of Defense policy on new/social media, released early in 2010.

3. *http://socialmediagovernance.com/policies.php*—Comprehensive database of social media policies and guidelines from governments and corporations alike including Australia, the United Kingdom, and the United States. The list, which is U.S. centric, includes American Red Cross, the BBC, Coca-Cola, Dell, Harvard Law School, Hewlett Packard, IBM, Microsoft, National Public Radio, Telstra, and the U.K. Government.

4. *www.af.mil/shared/media/document/AFD-090406-036.pdf*—This is an excellent resource that is fast becoming the base document for corporations and academic study alike.

TOOLKIT

A toolkit is available for around $149 from: www.toolkitcafe.com. According to their Web site, the Social Media Policies Toolkit provides a "straightforward set of documents that you can put to use immediately at your organization." The kit contains two PowerPoint presentations that can be customized and 16 policy templates, plus a directory of resources. The tools in this kit are in HTML, Microsoft Word, and Microsoft PowerPoint formats.

SAMPLE POLICY

Iqbal Mohammed, a creative planner and brand and global social media consultant based in India, put together a mock policy for his company. Posted originally on his MisEntropy Blog (http://www.misentropy.com, "How to Put Together a Social Media Policy in 5 Minutes," March 10, 2010), the policy is easy to read and full of good ideas. Iqbal is a regular panelist and speaker on brands and social media, and his "scribbles" are definitely worth a read. I am most grateful to Iqbal for his kind permission to reproduce the policy. He says that the following is what a policy for his own company "(if and when I start one)" would look like. The MisEntropy policy is based on his answers to the 12-question quiz noted in the list above "(and relative lack of paranoia)."

MisEntropy Social Media Policy

This policy governs the publication of and commentary on social media by employees of MisEntropy and its related companies ("MisEntropy"). For the purposes of this policy, *social media* means any facility for online publication and commentary, including without limitation, blogs; wikis; and social networking sites such as Facebook, LinkedIn, Twitter, Flickr, and YouTube. This policy is in addition to and complements any existing or future policies regarding the use of technology, computers, e-mail, and the Internet.

MisEntropy employees are free to publish or comment via social media in accordance with this policy. MisEntropy employees are subject to this policy to the extent they identify themselves as a MisEntropy employee (other than as an incidental mention of place of employment in a personal blog on topics unrelated to MisEntropy).

Publication and commentary on social media carries similar obligations to any other kind of publication or commentary.

All uses of social media must follow the same ethical standards that MisEntropy employees must otherwise follow.

Do Not Tell Secrets
It is perfectly acceptable to talk about your work and have a dialog with the community, but it's not okay to publish confidential information. Confidential information includes things such as unpublished details about our software, details of current projects, future product ship dates, financial information, research, and trade secrets. We must respect the

wishes of our corporate customers regarding the confidentiality of current projects. We must also be mindful of the competitiveness of our industry.

Protect Your Own Privacy

Privacy settings on social media platforms should be set to allow anyone to see profile information similar to what would be on the MisEntropy Web site. Other privacy settings that might allow others to post information or see information that is personal should be set to limit access. Be mindful of posting information that you would not want the public to see.

Be Honest

Do not blog anonymously, using pseudonyms or false screen names. We believe in transparency and honesty. Use your real name, be clear who you are, and identify that you work for MisEntropy. Nothing gains you notice in social media more than honesty—or dishonesty. Do not say anything that is dishonest, untrue, or misleading. If you have a vested interest in something you are discussing, point it out. But also be smart about protecting yourself and your privacy. What you publish will be around for a long time, so consider the content carefully and also be cautious about disclosing personal details.

Respect Copyright Laws

It is critical that you show proper respect for the laws governing copyright and fair use or fair dealing of copyrighted material owned by others, including MisEntropy's own copyrights and brands. You should never quote more than short excerpts of someone else's work, and always attribute such work to the original author/source. It is good general practice to link to others' work rather than reproduce it.

Respect Your Audience, MisEntropy, and Your Coworkers

The public in general, and MisEntropy's employees and customers, reflect a diverse set of customs, values, and points of view. Don't say anything contradictory or in conflict with the MisEntropy Web site. Don't be afraid to be yourself, but do so respectfully. This includes not only the obvious (no ethnic slurs, offensive comments, defamatory comments, personal insults, obscenity, etc.) but also proper consideration of privacy and of topics that may be considered objectionable or inflammatory—such as politics and religion. Use your best judgment and be sure to make it clear that the views and opinions expressed are yours alone and do not represent the official views of MisEntropy.

Protect MisEntropy Customers, Business Partners, and Suppliers
Customers, partners, or suppliers should not be cited or obviously referenced without their approval. Never identify a customer, partner, or supplier by name without permission, and never discuss confidential details of a customer engagement. It is acceptable to discuss general details about kinds of projects and to use nonidentifying pseudonyms for a customer (e.g., Customer 123) so long as the information provided does not violate any nondisclosure agreements that may be in place with the customer or make it easy for someone to identify the customer. Your blog is not the place to "conduct business" with a customer.

Controversial Issues
If you see misrepresentations made about MisEntropy in the media, you may point that out. Always do so with respect and with the facts. If you speak about others, make sure what you say is factual and that it does not disparage that party. Avoid arguments. Brawls may earn traffic, but nobody wins in the end. Don't try to settle scores or goad competitors or others into inflammatory debates. Make sure what you are saying is factually correct.

Be the First to Respond to Your Own Mistakes
If you make an error, be up front about your mistake and correct it quickly. If you choose to modify an earlier post, make it clear that you have done so. If someone accuses you of posting something improper (such as their copyrighted material or a defamatory comment about them), deal with it quickly—better to remove it immediately to lessen the possibility of a legal action.

Think about Consequences
For example, consider what might happen if a MisEntropy employee is in a meeting with a customer or prospect, and someone on the customer's side pulls out a printout of your blog and says, "This person at MisEntropy says that product sucks."

Saying "Product X needs to have an easier learning curve for the first-time user" is fine; saying "Product X sucks" is risky, unsubtle, and amateurish.

Once again, it's all about judgment: Using your blog to trash or embarrass MisEntropy, our customers, or your coworkers is dangerous and ill-advised.

Disclaimers
Many social media users include a prominent disclaimer saying whom they work for, but that they're not speaking officially. This is good practice

and is encouraged, but don't count on it to avoid trouble—it may not have much legal effect.

Wherever practical, you must use a disclaimer saying that while you work for MisEntropy, anything you publish is your personal opinion and not necessarily the opinions of MisEntropy.

Don't Forget Your Day Job

Make sure that blogging does not interfere with your job or commitments to customers.

Social Media Tips

The following tips are not mandatory but will contribute to successful use of social media. The best way to be interesting, stay out of trouble, and have fun is to write about what you know. There is a good chance of being embarrassed by a real expert, or of being boring if you write about topics you are not knowledgeable about.

Quality matters. Use a spelling checker. If you're not design oriented, ask someone who is whether your blog looks decent, and take their advice on how to improve it.

The speed of being able to publish your thoughts is both a great feature and a great downfall of social media. The time to edit or reflect must be self-imposed. If in doubt over a post, or if something does not feel right, either let it sit and look at it again before publishing it, or ask someone else to look at it first.

Enforcement

Policy violations will be subject to disciplinary action, up to and including termination for cause.

APPENDIX G: SOCIAL MEDIA RESOURCES FOR CRISIS COMMUNICATORS*

BLOG POSTS, PDFS, AND POWERPOINT SLIDE DECKS

What Can Swine Flu Teach Us about Crisis Communication through Social Media
www.problogservice.com/swine-flu-teach-social-media/

Responding to Crisis Using Social Media (downloadable PDF)
www.google.com/url?sa=t&source=web&ct=res&cd=25&url=htt
p%3A%2F%2Fwww.marketsentinel.com%2Ffiles%2FCrisisres
ponseusingsocialmedia.pdf&ei=QID6Sa31LInyMpnshMAE&
usg=AFQjCNG2-h3F3UMMQQrbiQz8UYQMHdrhSw

Social Media and Impact on Crisis Communication, CrisisBlogger (a blog about crisis communication)
crisisblogger.wordpress.com/2007/10/21/social-media-and-impact-on-crisis-communication/

Crisis Communications for the Social Web (PowerPoint slide deck)
www.slideshare.net/geoliv/crisis-communications-on-the-social-web-presentation

Crisis Communications for the Social Web
www.livingstonbuzz.com/2008/11/03/crisis-communications-for-the-social-web/

---

* Eric Deckers (Vice President of Operations and Creative Services), Professional Blog Service, http://problogservice.com. (Reprinted with permission.)

Crisis Communications and Social Media, Advergirl Blog
leighhouse.typepad.com/advergirl/2008/04/crisis-communic.
html

Reinventing Crisis Communications for Social Media, BrianSolis.com
www.briansolis.com/2008/11/reinventing-crisis-communica-
tions-for.html

Using Social Media for Crisis Communications, Conversationblog
www.conversationblog.com/journal/2008/2/7/using-social-
media-for-crisis-communications.html

Social Media and Crisis Communications: My Talk Is Cheap
Presentation, DaveFleet.com
davefleet.com/2007/11/social-media-and-crisis-communications/
comment-page-1/

Social Media Reading for Traditional Communicators, DaveFleet.com
davefleet.com/2009/01/social-media-reading-for-traditional-
communicators/

Crisis Communications and Social Media, ActiveMetrics Blog
activemetrics.wordpress.com/2008/10/01/crisis-communications-
and-social-media/

The New Disaster Media, In Case of Emergency Blog, BreakGlass.net
breakglass.wordpress.com/2007/10/22/the-new-disaster-media/

APPENDIX H: 30 THINGS YOU SHOULD NOT SHARE ON SOCIAL MEDIA

This is an amusing but good reminder of what not to post on social media sites.*

So, to protect your reputation, personal brand, your bank account, and your privacy, you need to be very careful what you write and post on social media channels.

1. What chook you are plucking or cow you are milking on Farmville on Facebook
2. How many you have killed on Mafia Wars or where they are buried ... again on Facebook
3. Party photos showing you inebriated or a hand placed where it shouldn't be
4. That you are having a party ... you might get more guests than you counted on
5. Photos revealing you flirting with the boss's wife at the annual work Christmas party
6. That you are having an affair
7. That you are thinking of having an affair
8. Complaints about your boss
9. That you hate your job and want to leave ... you might get your wish ... involuntarily
10. Don't share photos or an event that reveals that you were not sick that day at work
11. That are you are planning to take a sickie (unauthorized sick leave)
12. Drama with your friends
13. Issues with your parents

---

* I am grateful to Australian blogger Jeff Bullas for this sage advice. Check out the full posting on Jeff Bullas Blog, http://jeffbullas.com/, March 21, 2010. His blogs are very worthwhile. (Reprinted with permission.)

14. Passwords … unless you have more money than brains
15. Hints about passwords like dogs' names
16. Images and videos of your children
17. Updates on Facebook after you have escaped from jail and are on the run (don't laugh, it has happened)
18. Revealing your thoughts about a court case … when on jury duty
19. Don't link personal sites to professional business sites like LinkedIn … don't mix business with pleasure
20. Financial information such as how much money you do or don't have in your bank account
21. Personal information
22. How to get more friends or followers … it already sounds like a scam
23. You are leaving on a holiday
24. The dates you are away on your holiday
25. Your daily schedule … burglars have been known to use these little hints to their advantage
26. Showing you doing something stupid … not good for personal branding
27. Your bodily functions
28. Revealing extreme views on race, religion, or politics
29. What you had for breakfast
30. Finally, if you are not comfortable about it … don't share it

What would be on your list?

APPENDIX I: WORDPRESS STATEMENT

Case Study: Wordpress Statement

WORDPRESS.COM STATEMENT

In February 2010, Wordpress.com, the most popular blog software used by millions of bloggers today, went down.

Wordpress, which is used by more than 2 percent of the 10,000 biggest Web sites, was out for nearly two hours and affected more than 10 million blogs, including big guns like TechCrunch.

To communicate what happened, Wordpress used Twitter and they blogged. That tactic worked for them as their audience—predominantly bloggers—tends to be involved in the social media channels.

They first tweeted "WordPress is down, we're working on restoring service now."[*]

About one hour later:

We're investigating the source & most expedient fix. I hope to have everyone's blogs back & running as soon as possible.—Matt Mullenweg

To confirm, Akismet is not affected by this outage. (Akismet, Antispam Technology Service Supporting the Blogosphere)

We're back running at full capacity now. Closely monitoring for any aftershocks.—Matt Mullenweg.[†]

The Wordpress statement and updates are a very good example of what to do.

WP.COM DOWNTIME SUMMARY

From Matt Mullenweg (Wordpress Founding Developer)

What happened: We are still gathering details, but it appears an unscheduled change to a core router by one of our datacenter providers

---

[*] *Twitter* post by: Matt Mullenweg (Founding Developer), WordPress Blog, http://wp.me/pf2B5-ZS, February 19, 2010. (Reprinted with permission.)

[†] Posted by: Matt Mullenweg (Founding Developer), WordPress Blog, http://en.blog.wordpress.com, February 19, 2010. (Reprinted with permission.)

messed up our network in a way we haven't experienced before, and broke the site. It also broke all the mechanisms for failover between our locations in San Antonio and Chicago. All of your data was safe and secure, we just couldn't serve it.

What we're doing: We need to dig deeper and find out exactly what happened, why, and how to recover more gracefully next time and isolate problems like this so they don't affect our other locations.

I will update this post as we find out more, and have a more concrete plan for the future.

I know this sucked for you guys as much as it did for us—the entire team was on pins and needles trying to get your blogs back as soon as possible. I hope it will be much longer than four years before we face a problem like this again.

Update 1: We've gathered more details about what happened. There was a latent misconfiguration; specifically a cable plugged someplace it shouldn't have been, from a few months ago. Something called the spanning tree protocol kicked in and started trying to route all of our private network traffic to a public network over a link that was much too small and slow to handle even 10% of our traffic which caused high packet loss. This "sort of working" state was much worse than if it had just gone down and confused our systems team and our failsafe systems. It is not clear yet why the misconfiguration bit us yesterday and not earlier. Even though the network issue was unfortunate, we responded too slowly in pinpointing the issue and taking steps to resolve it using alternate routes, extending the downtime 3–4x longer than it should have been.[*]

Wordpress acted decisively, quickly, and authentically. Their statement was short, relevant, and to the point. I particularly like their layout with the key information in bold. A good model for online crises.

---

[*] Matt Mullenberg (Founding Developer), "WP.com Downtime Summary," WordPress Blog, http://en.blog.wordpress.com/2010/02/19/wp-com-downtime-summary/, February 19, 2010. (Reproduced with permission.)

APPENDIX J: SOCIAL MEDIA EMBRACING THE OPPORTUNITIES, AVERTING THE RISKS*

Prepared by

August 2009

INTRODUCTION

There is little question that social media is high on the agenda of corporate and nonprofit decision makers across the United States. Love it or hate it, Facebook, Twitter, YouTube, blogs, and more are increasingly common for effectively reaching both internal and external audiences. Yet, while many in management have embraced the idea of delving into social networking waters, many of these same individuals have supported policies that prevent their own employees from using these new communication channels. Why? What are their concerns? And, more importantly, what are they doing to address them?

In July 2009, relevance management specialists Russell Herder and Ethos Business Law embarked on a research study to gain nationally based insight on these important questions. The results were fascinating. More than 8 in 10 executives said they have concerns about social media and its

---

* Carol Russell (CEO, Russell Herder) and David Baer (President, Ethos Business Law), Russell Herder and Ethos Business Law, "Social Media Embracing the Opportunities, Averting the Risks," White Paper, August 2009. (Reprinted with permission.)

271

implications for both corporate security and reputation management. Yet surprisingly, only 1 in 3 said they have implemented social media guidelines, and only 10 percent have undertaken related employee training.

In the following document, you will read a recap of this important study as well as best practices on development of a sound social media policy.

It is our hope that this information will help management, marketing, and human resource professionals engage in the social media conversation—both using these new communication opportunities and addressing any underlying concerns—not as unilateral dictates, but as natural extensions of corporate values and ethics.

Carol Russell
CEO
Russell Herder

David Baer
President
Ethos Business Law

THE RESEARCH: KEY FINDINGS

Social media has become a fixture on communication agendas across the country, fueled by the fact that Americans spent 73 percent[1] more time on social networking sites in the past year alone. But social media use is also generating its share of corporate heartburn.

According to new research findings, confidence exists in social networking as viable communication outreach, but so do worries about the potential liabilities. Concerns regarding social media use were acknowledged by some 8 in 10 businesses participating in a recent national study undertaken by Russell Herder and Ethos Business Law (see Figure J.1).

Fifty-one percent of senior management, marketing, and human resources executives fear social media could be detrimental to employee productivity, while almost half (49%) assert that using social media could damage company reputation.

Despite these apprehensions, social networking is being accepted as a key communications strategy. According to survey results, 8 in 10 believe social media can enhance relationships with customers/clients (81%) and build brand reputation (81%). Almost 70 percent feel such networking can be valuable in recruitment (69%) and as a customer service tool (64%)

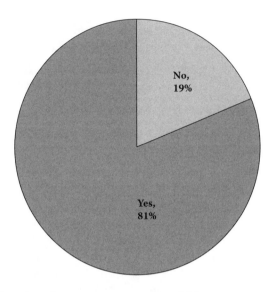

FIGURE J.1   Social media: a corporate security risk?

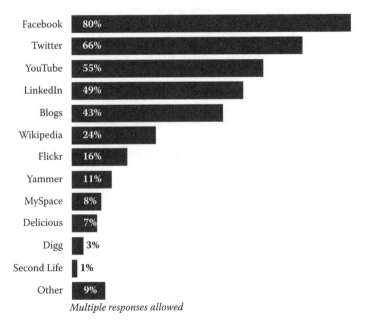

Multiple responses allowed

FIGURE J.2   Social media vehicles being used.

FIGURE J.3   Perceived value of social media.

and can be used to enhance employee morale (46%). The most popular vehicles being used include Facebook (80%), Twitter (66%), YouTube (55%), LinkedIn (49%), and blogs (43%) (see Figures J.2 and J.3).

Particularly as millennials compose a greater share of corporate ranks, social networks are likely to become more popular as communication channels with customers, colleagues, and partners (see Figure J.4).

Much of senior management's direct experience with social media appears to be reactive versus proactive, an interesting fact given the confidence they express in these new media. The majority (72%) of executives say that they, personally, visit social media sites at least weekly to read what customers may be saying about their company (52%) and to routinely monitor a competitor's use of social networking (47%). One in three search social

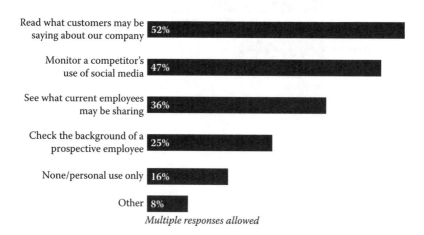

FIGURE J.4   Reasons management use social media.

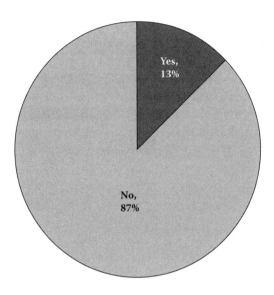

FIGURE J.5 Social media's inclusion in crisis communications plans.

media sites to see what their employees are sharing (36%) or check the background of a prospective employee (25%).

Even though social media communication is growing, only 1 in 10 executives say they have staff who spend more than 50 percent of their time on such efforts—perhaps somewhat surprising given that half of the organizations surveyed employ more than 1,000 people. And *only 13 percent have included social media in their organizations' crisis communications plans* (see Figure J.5).

As well recognized as the benefits of social media appear to be, executives believe social media can potentially be detrimental to employee effectiveness and company reputation. In fact, those surveyed who are not using social media on a corporate basis say nonimplementation is primarily due to concern about confidentiality or security issues (40%), employee productivity (37%), or simply not knowing enough about it (51%) (see Figure J.6).

This may be why many organizations continue to prohibit workplace access to social networking sites. The recently completed Russell Herder/ Ethos study found that 40 percent of companies technically block their employees from accessing social media while at work. At the same time, 26 percent of companies use social media to further corporate objectives

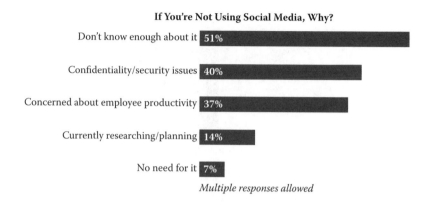

FIGURE J.6   If you're not using social media, why?

(Figure J.7) and just over 7 in 10 said they plan to increase the use of these new opportunities (see Figure J.8).

The most common reasons why these entities are using social media are for brand-building (82%), networking (60%), customer service (32%), and sharing work-related project information (26%) (see Figure J.9).

Remarkably few efforts are being made to mitigate perceived risks. *Only one in three businesses surveyed has a policy in place to govern social media use,* and only 10 percent said they have conducted relevant employee training. Why? One of the main reasons, according to

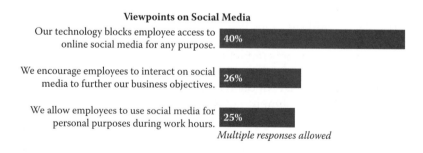

FIGURE J.7   Viewpoints on social media.

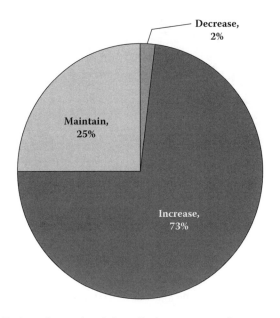

FIGURE J.8 Projected use of social media (over next year).

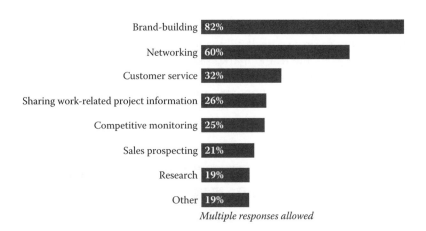

Multiple responses allowed

FIGURE J.9 Reasons for using social media.

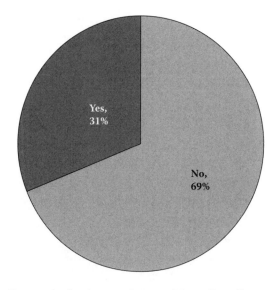

FIGURE J.10 Companies having a written social media policy.

respondents, is uncertainty about what to include in such policies (see Figures J.10 and J.11).

Ignoring the need for responsible guidelines can impede an organization's ability to protect itself, while at the same time hampering efforts to effectively compete in the marketplace. As Forbes.com recently noted about the urgency to establish such policies, "… if you think [social media guidelines] don't apply to you, you are probably already on the endangered species list."[2]

FIGURE J.11 If no policy … why?

BEST PRACTICES: TEN KEY ELEMENTS OF
A GOOD SOCIAL MEDIA PPOLICY

Should employees be encouraged to use social networking to enhance marketing outreach? Or will such activity impede productivity in an already tight economy? And what about reputational risk? These and other questions are clearly on the minds of today's management.

In a 2009 social networking study[3] by Deloitte LLP, 74 percent of employed Americans believe it's easy to damage a brand's reputation via sites such as Facebook and Twitter. More sobering yet, Deloitte reported that nearly one-third of those surveyed say they never consider what management, coworkers, or their clients would think before posting material online.

These behavioral implications are not going unnoticed. In a poll[4] conducted this year by the antivirus firm Sophos, 66 percent of corporate system administrators said they worry that employees who share personal information on social networking sites will put their company's information technology (IT) infrastructure at risk. A quarter of these businesses also reported that they have been the victim of spam, phishing, and malware attacks via sites such as Twitter, Facebook, LinkedIn, and MySpace.

Yet these same security experts observed that *a corporate lock-out isn't the answer*. By denying staff access to social networking sites, Sophos observed that organizations run the risk of driving their employees to find a way around the ban—and thus potentially open up even greater holes in corporate defenses.

The national research conducted by Russell Herder and Ethos Business Law revealed that 8 in 10 businesses have concerns about the potential liabilities of social media. Yet, only a third have a policy in place to govern social media use.

Instead of ignoring the need for responsible guidelines, organizations of all sizes should begin to *define their strategy* regarding social media, and most importantly, the rules for employee engagement. By doing so, management can take advantage of the benefits offered by these new communication channels while mitigating undue risk.

Think you're covered with your current policies? Perhaps not. Social media is a far different animal than traditional technology. A company's current policies on IT matters are usually *not sufficient*.

The truth is, all companies are different. Thus the rules for creating and implementing a social media policy are not universal. They must take the form, substance, philosophy, and culture of the organization to which they apply. However, the following are 10 important elements to include in a good social media policy:

1. *Overall philosophy*—An effective social media policy should define the company's overall philosophy on social media and be consistent with its culture. For example, does the company have a supportive, open philosophy on the use of social media or a stronger, more limited embrace of this technology?

2. *Honesty and respect*—One of the most important aspects of a policy is a requirement that employees be open, honest, respectful, and transparent in their usage of social media—especially in the business context.

3. *Confidential and proprietary information*—Disclosure of confidential or proprietary information through social media can be prevalent. Especially since this type of communication is often viewed as less formal than other, *there is increased risk for inadvertent disclosure.* Guidelines should reinforce the company's confidentiality and proprietary information policies and apply such to the social media environment.

4. *Online identity*—When engaging in online social networking, it is important to differentiate an employee's personal identity from his or her business identity. While regulating employees' usage of their personal identity may be outside of the scope of a company social media policy, defining such is fair game. For example, is it acceptable to have an employee's business name and title be connected to a personal blog post which is critical of a certain political party? Is it acceptable for employees to post their work e-mail addresses on blogs discussing controversial topics? An effective policy must address such issues and define acceptable limits.

5. *Focus on job performance*—There is a lot of discussion on whether social media hurt worker productivity. For example, is it acceptable for an employee to post on a personal blog during his or her lunch break? Or, can an employee tweet on business-related topics during the workday? Remember, *the new work force does not live in an eight-to-five world.* The focus should be on job performance instead of "company time."

6. *Avoid conflicts of interest*—Conflicts of interest come in many forms—especially when engaging in social media. The policy should discuss how to identify potential conflicts of interest, what types of conflicts are prohibited, and whom to talk to when in doubt.

7. *Include a disclaimer*—Employees should make it clear that their views about work-related matters do not represent the views of their employer or any other person. The policy should require a disclaimer, such as the following, when there is the possibility for confusion between business and personal identity: The views expressed on this blog are mine alone and do not represent the views of my employer or any other person.

8. *Monitoring*—The policy should state whether—and to what extent—the company has the right to monitor social media usage and identify any associated disciplinary guidelines.

9. *Universal application*—A social media policy should apply to everyone, not just a subset of employees (e.g., the marketing department).

10. *Other policies*—Other company policies, such as those on workplace environment, discrimination, harassment, ethics, code of conduct, and others, apply even in the cyber-land of social media. An effective policy should remind internal audiences of these obligations and relate them to social media.

While this list is not exhaustive, it serves as a starting point to develop a strategy and policy around social media that can serve to protect corporate interests, yet allow employees to further an organization's overall social media goals.

And while having a good social media policy in place is imperative, it's just as important to educate your team on why compliance is important. *Clearly defined guidelines, alone, will not change how employees behave online.* To truly mitigate the potential risks, a well-defined training plan should reinforce key social media policies while encouraging good decisions based on the company's values and ethics.

An effective training plan should have the following attributes:

- *Engagement*—Social media philosophy and policy should be introduced to employees in a comprehensive, yet engaging, manner, grounded in the company's values and ethics. The focus should be upon educating employees on what social networking is, why it is important to the company, and how employees can—and should—engage with social media.

- *Inclusiveness*—The training plan should cover every employee of the company—from the most senior executive to the most junior intern. It must be clear to employees that social media are accepted and relevant at all levels of the company. While it may be appropriate to vary the training content depending on the audience, no class of employee should be excluded.
- *Training on various topics*—The training should not just be a PowerPoint presentation that summarizes the policy. Such a session should be an interactive, educational opportunity to ground employees in the social media philosophy, motivate employees to participate in such media, and ensure they understand the rules of engagement. This is the company's opportunity to create "social media evangelists" within the employee ranks.
- *Training should be ongoing*—One training session is not enough. Companies should engage in ongoing training that grows as social networking evolves to reinforce guiding principles and ensure employees are best equipped to implement the company's social media strategy.

A well-defined strategy, coupled with clear policies and effective training, will place your company in the best position possible to take full advantage of social media's potential.

METHODOLOGY

The study providing a foundation for the white paper "Social Media: Embracing the Opportunities, Averting the Risks" was conducted by Minneapolis-based Russell Herder and Ethos Business Law in July 2009. A total of 438 randomly selected management, marketing, and human resources executives within companies across the United States completed the online survey, providing a statistical reliability of ±4.8 percent at the 95 percent confidence level.

ABOUT US

Russell Herder and Ethos Business Law provide strategy, counsel, and executive briefings on social media for corporate clients nationwide. Having served clients for more than 26 years, Russell Herder specializes in relevance management—leveraging research, social media, and strategic creative to build meaningful relationships between individuals and organizations. Russell Herder offers clients across the United States deep insights and proven, measurable solutions. Ethos Business Law is a leader and innovator in providing responsive legal services to dynamic, progressive companies through business-centric tools.

To find out more about Russell Herder and Ethos Business Law:

| RUSSELL HERDER | Ethos  BUSINESS LAW |

carol@russellherder.com
612-455-2375
100 S. Fifth St., Suite 2200
Minneapolis, MN 55402
www.russellherder.com

info@ethoslaw.com
612-767-3311
10 S. Fifth St., Suite 700
Minneapolis, MN 55402
www.ethoslaw.com

REFERENCES

1. The Nielsen Company, "The Global Online Media Landscape: Identifying Opportunities in a Challenging Market," The Nielsen Company, http://blog.nielsen.com/nielsenwire/wp-content/uploads/2009/04/nielsen-online-global-lanscapefinal1.pdf, April 2009.
2. Joshua-Michele Ross, "A Corporate Guide for Social Media," O'Reilly Insights on Forbes.com, www.forbes.com/2009/06/30/social-media-guide-lines-intelligent-technology-oreilly.html, June 30, 2009.
3. Deloitte LLP, "Social Networking and Reputational Risk in the Workplace." http://www.corpgov.deloitte.com/binary/com.epicentric.contentmana-gement.servlet.ContentDeliveryServlet/USEng/Documents/Board%20Governance/Ethics%20and%20Compliance/2009%20Ethics%20Workplace%20Survey%20results_Deloitte_052209.pdf, 2009.
4. Sophos, "Two-Thirds of Businesses Fear That Social Networking Endangers Corporate Security, Sophos Research Reveals," www.sophos.com/pressoffice/news/articles/2009/04/social-networking.html, April 28, 2009.

INDEX